CHARLES DICKENS AND HIS HIDDEN FAMILY HISTORY

For Peggie Harrison

CHARLES DICKENS AND HIS HIDDEN FAMILY HISTORY

THERESA MUSGROVE

PEN & SWORD
HISTORY
AN IMPRINT OF PEN & SWORD BOOKS LTD.
YORKSHIRE – PHILADELPHIA

First published in Great Britain in 2026 by
Pen & Sword History
An imprint of
Pen & Sword Books Ltd
Yorkshire - Philadelphia

ISBN 978 1 03619 417 8

A CIP catalogue record for this book is available from the British Library.

Typeset in INDIA by IMPEC eSolutions
Printed and bound in England by CPI Group (UK) Ltd, Croydon, CRO 4YY

The Publisher's authorised representative in the EU for product safety is Authorised Rep Compliance Ltd., Ground Floor, 71 Lower Baggot Street, Dublin D02 P593, Ireland.
www.arccompliance.com

For a complete list of Pen & Sword titles please contact:

PEN & SWORD BOOKS LIMITED
George House, Units 12 & 13, Beevor Street, Off Pontefract Road,
Barnsley, S71 1HN, UK
E-mail: enquiries@pen-and-sword.co.uk
Website: www.pen-and-sword.co.uk

or

PEN AND SWORD BOOKS
1950 Lawrence Rd, Havertown, PA 19083, USA
E-mail: uspen-and-sword@casematepublishers.com
Website: www.penandswordbooks.com

MIX
Paper | Supporting responsible forestry
FSC® C013604
FSC
www.fsc.org

Contents

PART THREE: THE BARROWS

PART FOUR: DIVERS STRAINGERS: THE CASTEELS

Acknowledgements

My grateful thanks to the late Professor Michael Slater, Professor Malcolm Andrews and Mark Dickens for their support and encouragement; Frankie Kubicki, Emma Harper, Cindy Sughrue and the staff of the Charles Dickens Museum; Hugh Petrie, Heritage Officer at the London Borough of Barnet Archives; the staff of the British Library, the London Archives, the National Archives, Bristol Archives and Bristol Museums, the library of the Royal College of Physicians of Edinburgh; Dr Devra Kay, Geoffrey Lancaster, Amy Jordan at Pen & Sword Books, for her eternal patience, Professor Jonathan Barry - apologies to anyone I have forgotten, and for any inadvertent errors. Last, but not least, my thanks to Diane Gholam, for seeing me safely across the road, as usual.

Some of the content of Part Four appeared in The Dickensian, Spring 2020, Issue No 510, and in The Jewish Chronicle, 23 May 2022.

Family Trees

Charles Dickens's Barrow family tree, simplified.
'b' indicates year of baptism, where known.

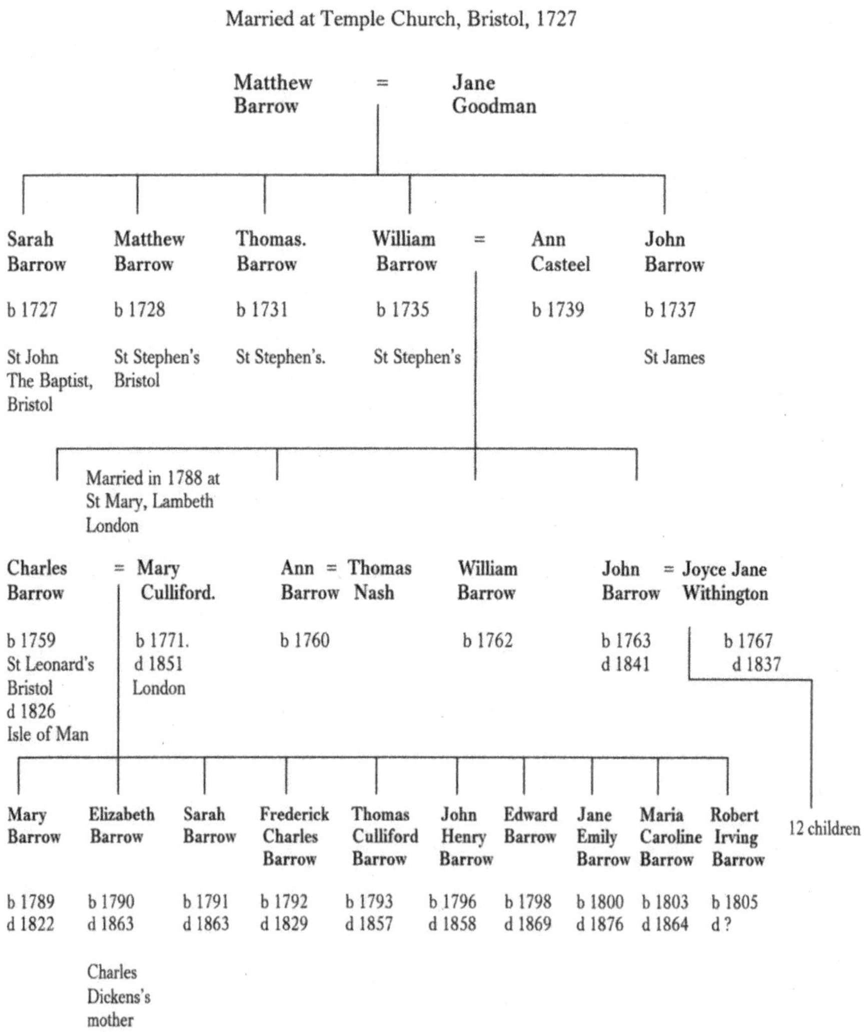

Potential family tree for Charles Dickens's Casteel ancestors.

'b' indicates year of baptism, where known.

Casteel has many variations, here I have standardised the spelling.

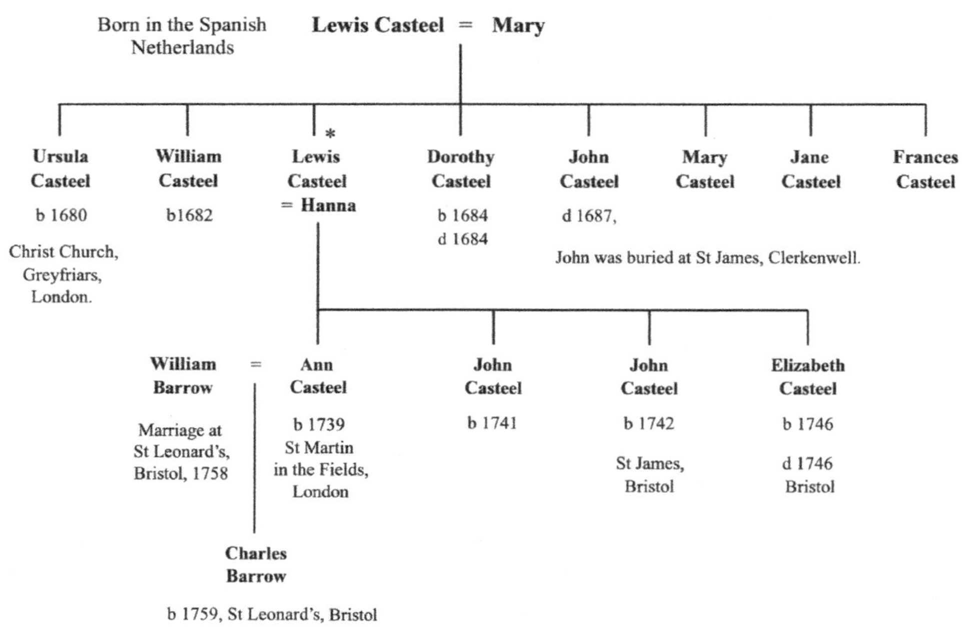

*This would suggest a late or perhaps second marriage – or possibly indicates that the Lewis Casteel who moved to Bristol was a son with the same name, of the one born in 1682. The unusual combination of names and having the same occupation makes it likely that this is the same family, however.

Charles Dickens's paternal family tree.

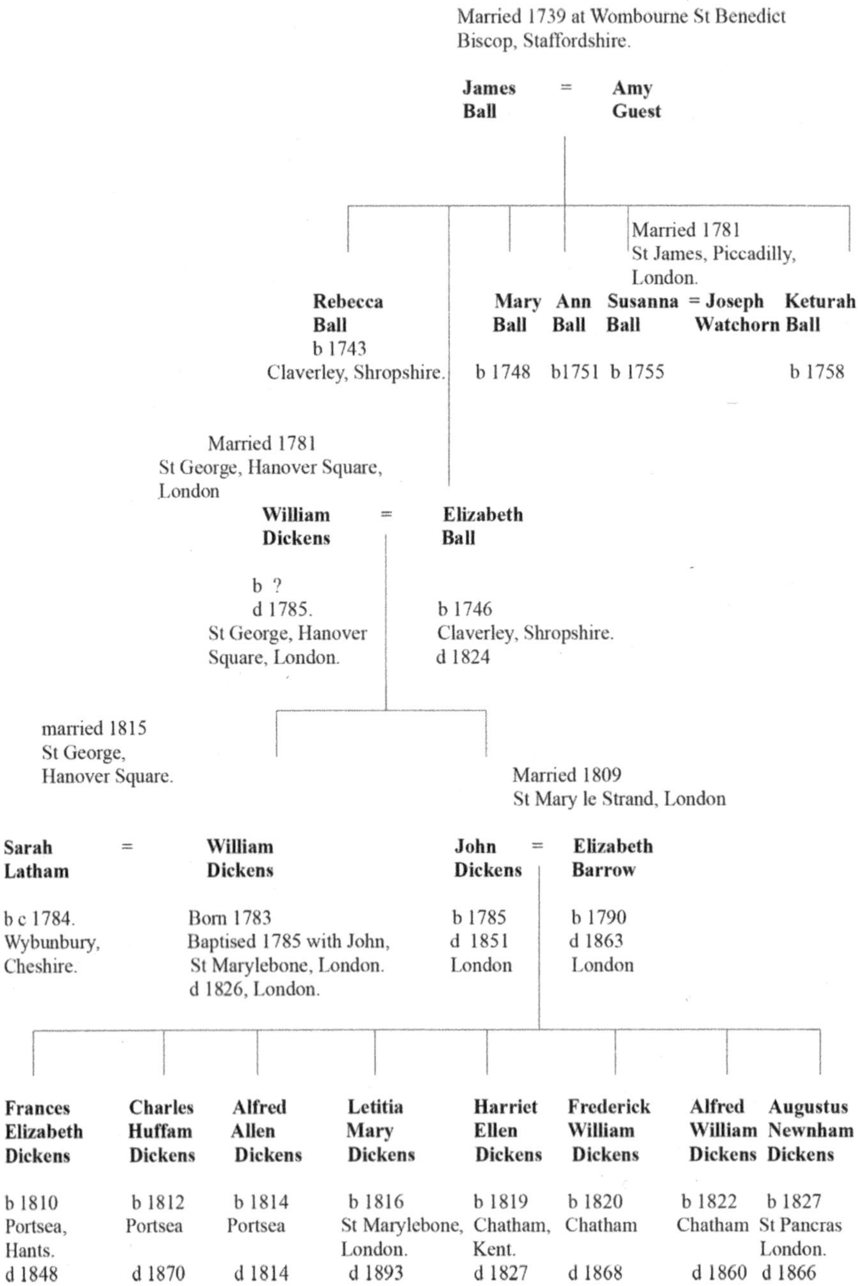

Foreword

I never had anything left to me but relations

Other than a lifetime of responsibility for his family, Charles Dickens's only acknowledged inheritance was the legacy, from his father's mother, of a 'fat old silver watch', a possession which he had by luck retained, when every other article of worth owned by his family had been sold, in the grim period before and during his father's residence in the Marshalsea debtors' prison.

Due to the financial restrictions dictated by John Dickens's eventual release from imprisonment, the value of the family's wearing apparel could be no greater than £20, so on his half-holiday from the misery of work at Warren's blacking manufactory, Charles, then a small, slight child, only eleven years of age and looking much younger, was sent to see the official appraiser, to show that the clothes he wore were of little worth. He recounted this event in later life, in the writing of what would become known as the 'Fragment', an account of his childhood given to his friend John Forster on the understanding that it should be published only after his death: two years after he died, Forster included it in the first volume of his *Life of Charles Dickens*.[1]

> Certainly the hardest creditor would not have been disposed (even if he had been legally entitled) to avail himself of my poor white hat, little jacket, or corduroy trowsers. But I had a fat old silver watch in my pocket, which had been given me by my grandmother before the blacking-days, and I had entertained my doubts as I went along whether that valuable possession might not bring me over the twenty pounds. So I was greatly relieved, and made him a bow of acknowledgment as I went out.

Presumably the watch given to him by Elizabeth Dickens had been a family piece: most likely it had belonged to her husband, his late grandfather William Dickens, butler to John and Frances Anne Crewe, the wealthy and influential couple by whom she had also been employed, as housekeeper. But clearly this object was of great personal significance to Charles, hidden in his pocket in the long hours working in the blacking factory, travelling to and from his solitary lodgings and on his visits to the Marshalsea. A small act of defiance, perhaps, holding on to the watch against all the odds – a talisman of some sort, from a time of better fortune for his family: proof of their former respectability.

Throughout this period of alienation from family, school and friends, the watch remained with him, in those darkest days, its totemic value far beyond the material worth of the watch itself. It had escaped the attention of the appraiser, but more importantly, it had survived the consequences of his father's failure – and so would he.

There was, however, an additional inheritance for Charles Dickens: less tangible than the fat old silver watch, less obvious than the weight of obligation to his relatives, but one he also carried everywhere with him, as a child, as an adult and as a writer, holding its own significance – the legacy of his family history: a hidden history that he was reluctant to acknowledge and which has remained hidden from view, until now.

Dickens would complain, in later life, when struggling with the demands of his ageing mother's dementia, that he had had nothing left to him 'but relations'. For much of his life, from an early stage, the role of responsibility for Dickens had been reversed, the child burdened with the care of his mother and father and even his siblings, organising their lives, providing financial support, patronage or guidance and constantly called upon by a range of relatives beyond his closer family; cousins and dependents with any tenuous connection to him. His lifelong habit of intervening in the lives of his relatives was not, in truth, just a matter of duty, but part of a wider compulsion to edit the story of his family life so that it better suited his purposes. Any content that could not be accommodated to his satisfaction was cut from the text, or rewritten – and this policy was applied not only to his immediate family, but to anything which touched on their past lives, or background, and did not fit with Dickens's preferred version of events, or his position and public profile as a hugely successful writer and household name.

The creation of his own narrative, as fictionalised as any published work, was a continual process for Dickens, driven by a need to protect his career, status and reputation. He was adept at hiding or suppressing anything that might be damaging to the public perception of his character, hiding areas of his personal life – his relationship with Ellen Ternan being the most obvious example – and he would often take action to suppress the emergence of any scandal or embarrassment caused by his relations, as well as due to his own indiscretions.

It has been little understood how far he went, in his lifetime, to ensure that any information that had the potential to compromise his position did not reach the public domain, using his influence – and his wealth – to prevent the exposure of such stories. At times, in fact, as we shall see, Dickens found himself, or feared he might be, at the mercy of what was very close to a process of extortion, or blackmail. This may seem an extraordinary claim to make, but we will examine evidence that may well support such a possibility and present new evidence that will now show the extent to which he appears to have been prepared to go to protect his reputation.

Dickens destroyed many of his letters, ten years or so before his death, in the early years of his affair with Ellen Ternan, basketfuls thrown on to a bonfire at Gad's Hill – but of course this was correspondence received, not sent: he had no control over the thousands of letters he had written and that remained, along with other irretrievable documents, in the possession of others. A collection of his own letters would be published, after his death, but carefully edited by his daughter and sister-in-law, now able to control the presentation of his life's story, of his reputation and legacy, just as he did throughout the years of his success.

He may have expected that his relationship with his young mistress would not escape notice by future biographers less loyal and discreet than Forster: he chose to include her in his will, after all, knowing that the generous bequest he had made would be placing in plain sight the importance of his regard for her. Perhaps the truth was that he cared less about being known, after his death, to have left his wife for a younger woman than the thought of being exposed, in his lifetime, as having been a child labourer whose parents had been resident in a debtors' prison.

It is certainly true that in the 1930s and 1940s, when the first questions began to emerge about some of the previously hidden aspects of Dickens's life, it was his relationship with Nelly that was the subject of curiosity, rather than the details of his unorthodox and dysfunctional family background.

The 'Fragment' that Dickens gave to Forster, detailing his unhappy childhood, was perhaps not so much a voluntary admission of the truth as a calculated response to Forster's questioning of him, having heard rumours that related to his time working for Warren's. It was, if you like, Dickens's way of controlling the revelation of his childhood misery, in his own way, after his death; of claiming the future editorial rights to his own mythology. Even in his own lifetime, however, he was acutely aware of the risk of exposure.

In 1849, Thomas Powell, the writer, forger and embezzler, who had fled to America after stealing money from his employer, published a book – *The Living*

Authors of England[2] – in which the work of his former friend Charles Dickens was mercilessly critiqued, and the man himself presented as being talented only as being 'a sketcher of low life'. Powell's vituperative essay went straight to the heart of Dickens's vulnerability. As someone who knew the Dickens family well, and their history, he chose with perfect deliberation to allude to what he knew about his subject's background and upbringing. As early as the second paragraph he refers to Dickens finishing 'the little education he received' and goes on to suggest that his interest in 'low characters' is a consequence of his family origins, as is his 'absurd deference', once a successful writer, 'to men of rank'.

> Notwithstanding the attention he receives from a few of the nobility … he is unpopular with the fashionable circles, and is merely asked as they would invite Tom Thumb, the Siamese, or any other lusus naturae, merely to increase the dramatic attractions of the evening; but the weakness of feeling flattered by the attentions of rank or wealth, is a common failing with most men, especially when they have sprung from a humble class in society …

Seventeen years after Dickens's death, Powell returned to the subject in an article published in a Sunday magazine,[3] comparing his writing with that of Thackeray, whom Powell considered to be of far superior background, talent and tastes.

> Thackeray's better education, and his family's superior position in life, enabled him to draw higher types of men and women than his great rival could; for all the entourage of the Dickens race was low, and I never saw one of the entire family that has the faintest pretensions to gentility, not even shabby gentility … This is the reason why Charles Dickens never could create a high-bred lady, or a high-bred natural gentleman …

He finishes with a final crushing insult: '… the author of "Pickwick" belonged to a very common family, and had very little education except what he picked up in the streets …'

Dickens took a great deal of effort in 1849 to try to silence Powell, even publishing a private pamphlet as part of his strategy. He is also supposed by some to have based the developing and increasingly unflattering portrayal of Uriah Heep in *David Copperfield* on Thomas Powell, in a form of literary revenge.

Dickens's fear of embarrassment caused by the revelation of his family's activities and circumstances was not restricted to the story of his childhood, or the behaviour of his relatives: it extended beyond the present, to his family's background. His success as a writer, and his membership of the social circles to which he was admitted, necessitated – or so he felt – a large degree of ambiguity about his own origins. He liked to imply a sort of faded gentility somewhere in the past, a circumstance in which he would place so many of his fictional characters. He seemed to feel no problem in annexing a Dickens coat of arms, to which he had no right. Little did he know that his father's family line was likely to have once included the sort of landed gentry background that he had wished for himself – or, just perhaps, as we shall explore, followed an entirely different route, and linked him to a far more privileged association.

George Orwell, in his essay on Charles Dickens,[4] published in 1940, describes his writing as being both radical and subversive, yet accuses Dickens of being somehow still representative of 'the urban bourgeoisie': criticising aspects of society and social injustice, but wanting 'an idealised version of the existing thing'. Orwell repeats a story of Lenin supposedly walking out of a theatrical production of *The Cricket on the Hearth* on the grounds of its intolerable middle-class sentimentality – he claims Dickens retained the prejudices of the 'shabby genteel', holding contempt for the lower ranks of the aristocracy, hating the idea of revolution at the same time as being repelled by such social horrors as slum dwellings, preferring to focus on heroes with 'soft hands', and the depiction of feudal servants, comic servants and faithful family retainers. Perhaps Orwell, the Etonian-educated socialist, did not appreciate the extent to which Dickens, as the grandchild of faithful family retainers and the child of 'soft-handed' parents whose failed attempts to preserve their own shabby genteel lifestyle had left such an impact on his young life, needed to explore – and deconstruct – the tangled threads of class, status and identity.

The trauma of Dickens's early years, and in particular his sense of abandonment and humiliation when taken out of school and put to work for Warren's Blacking, put on display in the window of the manufactory, was, as John Drew observed – in reference to Edmund Wilson's essay in *The Wound and the Bow* – the 'necessary wound' that sustained his creative process.[5, 6]

Some have questioned why Charles Dickens felt quite so deeply affected by his time in the blacking factory: the period of his employment was only a year or so and at the time many children were labouring in far worse conditions, from very young ages. Such criticism misses the point: few children would have experienced such a dramatic change in circumstances as he did, having been brought up by parents who were educated, cultured – respectable people. His father, John Dickens, styled himself as a gentleman and clearly felt entitled to a comfortable standard of living: as the son of favoured senior servants in the household of the Crewe family, he had been used to living on the margins, at least, of a privileged society. Dickens's mother, the former Elizabeth Barrow, had known only the comfortable homes maintained by her father in London, including an apartment in Somerset House when he was a respected senior official in the Navy Pay Office.

Although it would have been reasonable for Dickens, as a small child, to have assumed that his life would be that of every other middle-class boy he knew, protected from the fear of poverty and deprivation, he probably did not realise the extent to which the stability of both his parents' younger lives had been as precarious as his own, particularly that of his mother. It was not only in Dickens's lifetime, or that of his parents, that this cycle of insecurity was apparent, however.

Looking closer for the first time at the previous generations of his family history reveals, behind a veneer of respectability, the same degree of instability, of constant ambiguity of social status, the struggle for financial security: temporary success so often ended by folly, or misfortune. The unexplored family history of both his parents, examined more closely, reveals, one might argue, the pervasive impact of intergenerational trauma, and a burden that he carried with him all his life: a sense of inadequacy, a fear of failure; a fear of breakdown. And here is the fault line that runs through much of Charles Dickens's work, a place on which so many of his characters stand, waiting for the ground to open up beneath them, always no less than one step away from disaster, humiliation and loss.

This is territory familiar to all classes in his work: from Lady Dedlock and the merchant Paul Dombey, who will lose everything; the middle-class Nicklebys, struggling to survive their loss of home and status; David Copperfield losing the security of a loving mother and put to work; and, of course, Oliver Twist in the workhouse, the last refuge of those without any further to fall. Those characters who overcome the challenges Dickens places before them do so by their own merit, as he did, regardless of class or privilege. At the same time, he was very conscious that others would always perceive him to be marked by his family's lack of social standing, and it is unquestionably why he took so much trouble to hide a greater public knowledge of his family life and background.

The ever-loyal Forster, in his *Life of Charles Dickens*, despite offering an abundance of detail regarding his subject's childhood based on the evidence offered by the subject himself, also ensured that reference to his friend's more distant family background was suitably managed – or rather, barely touched upon at all. The extent to which this was the choice of Forster, or the result of inadequate or inaccurate information from Dickens, is unclear. Forster's apparent lack of curiosity, however, set a precedent that was faithfully observed by Dickensian scholars and biographers well into the twentieth century.

The first generations of researchers that followed Forster had little access to primary record sources and largely relied upon the necessarily cursory work of archivists and librarians to make any progress in research into Dickens's ancestry. When it became clear, from initial enquiries, that this pursuit would not, with any ease, deliver a distinguished pedigree, interest seems to have died down and nothing much more was done. This created an opportunity for speculation, false assumptions – and fantasy.

That Forster chose to avoid noting the parents of Dickens's father John, and their positions in service to the Crewe household, can only be seen as a deliberate omission, as Dickens was well aware of their background, knew his grandmother Dickens, who died in London, when he was twelve years old – and he had in later life cultivated the close friendship of Richard Monckton Milnes, whose wife Annabel was the Crewes' granddaughter: she claimed later to remember his grandmother, their housekeeper. It is highly unlikely that Forster did not know this.

The only mention by Forster of any of Dickens's grandparents, in fact, is in the context of a reference to his aunt Mary, his mother's sister who lived with them in Chatham and whose connection with the Lamert family led to Charles's childhood employment with Warren's Blacking. Forster describes Mary as being 'the eldest daughter of Charles Barrow … a lieutenant in the navy'. This is a curious way of describing Dickens's grandfather and the father, quite obviously, of his own mother – a deliberate distancing of the relationship, one might think. There was a very good reason for this.

It is entirely untrue that Charles Barrow was a naval lieutenant. The grandfather after whom Dickens had been named was an ordinary mariner, from Bristol, the course of whose later career – or rather careers – saw him move to London, become a musical tutor, a partner in a musical instrument making business, then gain a position in the Navy Pay Office, where eventually he was revealed as a fraudster who had stolen a large amount of money, was forced to flee the country and spent his last years in exile on the Isle of Man.

Charles Barrow's wealthy and influential brother John, later to become Mayor of Bristol, had refused to cover the repayment of the money he had stolen. In a moment of acutely ironic timing, the period of his great uncle's term of office as Mayor was the same year in which young Charles began work at the blacking factory. While John Barrow had temporarily moved from his Jacobean mansion on a hill looking down on Bristol to take up residence in the Mayoral house, located in the most exclusive square in the city, his niece's son Charles Dickens was labouring in a dismal, rat-infested workplace in London, pasting labels on bottles of blacking, his education abruptly ended, as far as he knew, a child abandoned to the care of strangers, while his family were detained in the Marshalsea.

Charles Barrow died when his grandson was fourteen years old: they may never have met, but the family had remained in communication with him and his widow moved back to England, dying in Islington in 1851, when Dickens was at the height of his success. Ten years earlier he had stated in a letter to a relative: 'I am utterly indifferent to the fact of her existence' – complaining about her sponging money from him once he had become famous.

John Barrow, the great uncle whose life story has never previously been investigated, had been a charity school pupil whose rise to prosperity and position of power had placed him at the highest level of the mercantile and civic elite that dominated and controlled the city of Bristol, then the second most important port in England. His life would end in financial disaster and personal humiliation, however. Just as his great nephew was on his way to huge success as a writer, the former Mayor and Master of the Society of Merchant Venturers was reduced once more to dependence on the charity of the city authorities he had once led – and on the kindness of friends for a home.

John Barrow's forgotten story is a tale that repeats a cycle of rise and fall – often a dual cycle where one falls as the other rises, one that occurs with relentless frequency within the wider and further family history of Charles Dickens, and a pattern that will be shown to have had a profound influence on his work, as well as his personal life. Inequality in fortune, reversals in fortune; the striving for respectability, the fear of failure, the tiny details of circumstance and appearance that tell the story of lives measured in movement up and down the scale of social status: these narratives and their characters are the mark of Dickens's genius, and they were born from his own unique experience of the full range of social distinctions and class definitions of the period in which he lived, a sense of displacement and uncertain social identity, played out against the backdrop of a family background that has hardly been acknowledged, or even looked at in any detail, until now.

There are many questions that emerge from a closer look at areas of his family life and background that have not been investigated and in some cases were not known about at all yet can be shown to have had a direct influence on his work. For example, who were the Barrows, Dickens's maternal line of ancestry? How far can they be traced? We will take the first close look at Dickens's mother's family background in Bristol, including their connection, in the eighteenth century, to the legacy of the notorious slave trader Edward Colston. What traces of his Bristol Barrow family can be found in Dickens's work?

What is the story of Charles Dickens's father John and his uncertain paternity: who really was his grandfather? Was it the Crewes' porter turned butler William Dickens, or, as John may have wanted to believe, Richard Brinsley Sheridan? Or was his connection to the aristocratic Crewe family rather closer than has been understood until now? Looking closer at the family association with his grandparents' employers offers a much deeper and more interesting understanding of *Bleak House.*

Why did Dickens fear the taint of insanity in his mother's family and take part in his aunt's removal to Bedlam? What links this to the creation of Miss Havisham in *Great Expectations*?

What was the full story of Dickens's relationship with Eliza Davis, the Jewish woman who dared to take him to task for his antisemitism: how might it relate to his seventeenth-century migrant ancestors from the Spanish Netherlands and his own probable Sephardi Jewish ancestry?

Why did Dickens's youngest brother, before he fled to the USA with his mistress, go into business with a member of the same family that had employed Charles as a young boy in the blacking factory?

And last, but not least, why did Dickens give a property in Hendon, worth £1,500, to an Irish bootmaker, in an agreement that was signed off in the middle of the chaotic week in which he separated from his wife?

The lives and experiences of earlier generations of his family – not just his parents, grandparents, uncles and aunts, but those who came before them – whose stories he may have known, or partly knew; some not at all: all played a part in forming the person and writer that Dickens became, in a way that has previously been overlooked but will now be explored in some depth, in a way that has proved to have identified much new material.

It might seem extraordinary to claim that there is still anything to discover in regard to Charles Dickens's life – but we shall investigate some of the lesser-known strands of his own story, reveal highly significant new biographical material, and trace the influence of these previously unacknowledged factors upon his work, with an emphasis on some of the family members, in his lifetime and beyond, whose mark can be shown to have informed the creation of his characters and narrative.

PART ONE

The Lord No Zoo

It has been rumoured, and it is needless to say the rumour originated in the same base quarters, that a certain male Chuzzlewit, whose birth must be admitted to be involved in some obscurity, was of very mean and low descent. How stands the proof? When the son of that individual, to whom the secret of his father's birth was supposed to have been communicated by his father in his lifetime, lay upon his deathbed, this question was put to him in a distinct, solemn, and formal way: 'Toby Chuzzlewit, who was your grandfather?' To which he, with his last breath, no less distinctly, solemnly, and formally replied: and his words were taken down at the time, and signed by six witnesses, each with his name and address in full: 'The Lord No Zoo.'

Chapter One

Who was your grandfather?

The first chapter of *The Life and Adventures of Martin Chuzzlewit*, 'concerning the pedigree of the Chuzzlewit family', mocks a tradition of aspirational genealogy that would, in time, be the driving force behind the earliest Dickensian researchers, even though they too were forced to concede that, like the Chuzzlewits, 'the Family do not seem to have been ever greatly distinguished by the possession of landed estate ...' But here, in the first chapter that sits so uneasily with the rest of the book, ('being a model of bad writing', according to Thomas Wright), Charles Dickens seems determined to write, at some length, about ancestry for no good reason other than perhaps it was something he had thought about regarding this own background. And he reminds us, in this prolonged discourse, that it is a wise man who knows his own grandfather – a question that, as we will see, might well have had some personal significance for him.

Dickens's father's family was problematic for the early Dickensian researchers, in presenting grandparents who were servants and a marked absence of any line that might seem worth pursuing for more distinguished forebears. There was, they knew, or at least some of them did, an outside chance of some more notable relations on this side: but in suggestion only, and a possibility tainted by illegitimacy: not something that the early guardians of Dickens's reputation wanted to explore. Dickens's father's family, in fact, was looked on as something of a dead end: of little interest, due in part to the early exit from the family narrative of his grandfather, William Dickens.

John Dickens's tendency to live beyond his means may well have been the consequence of his upbringing as the child of favoured servants, William and Elizabeth Dickens, who were butler and housekeeper in the household of Lord Crewe: older parents who appear to have been very generously treated by their employers, and whose second son, Dickens's father, born only two months before the death of his grandfather William Dickens, is thought by some to have benefited from their support in the sponsorship of his education. It would seem likely that it was their patronage, or the influence of their friends, that led to his securing a position at the Navy Pay Office.

That John Dickens wished to present himself as a gentleman is evident from the first documented references to his son, who was born in Landport, Portsmouth, on 7 February 1812. In at least two Hampshire newspapers, on 10 February, an announcement of his birth was published:

> BIRTHS – *On Friday, at Mile-end Terrace, the Lady of John Dickens, Esq. a son.*

Looking more widely, however, it becomes clear that in at least two London-based papers of the same date – the *Morning Post* and the *Sun* – there were also announcements, albeit somewhat less assertive in tone:

> *On Friday last, at Portsmouth, Mrs Dickens, of a son.*

A curious difference in presentation, probably because John Dickens felt that too many people in London knew he was making a claim to a level of gentility that the son of a servant, however senior, might reasonably not expect to possess. Here is the first instance in the life of Charles Dickens where an ambiguity in status was at the heart of his identity.

Charles was the first son and second child of John Dickens and the former Elizabeth Barrow: Frances Elizabeth Dickens had been born in 1810, and several more children were to follow: Alfred Allen, who was born and died in 1814, Letitia Mary in 1816, Harriet Ellen, who was born in 1819 and died as a young child; Frederick in 1820, Alfred Lamert in 1822, and finally Augustus Newnham Dickens, in 1827. Five surviving siblings, all of whom, in the future, would become dependent, in some way, on their brother, as indeed were his parents; his father, and then his mother having failed in their parental duty and obliging him to take responsibility for the safeguarding of their wellbeing, despite their abandonment, as he saw it, of his own needs in a childhood marked by insecurity and deprivation.

Dickens's paternal ancestry has traditionally been viewed as too difficult to trace: there is so little evidence to start from, for one thing: almost nothing was known about his grandfather William Dickens: no one could be sure even of his age, or place of birth. The record of his burial, in 1785, does not tell us how old he was, and although it is often asserted that he was in his sixties when he married, there is nothing to confirm that this was the case, only the probability that a much younger man would not have been likely to have received a promotion, as he did, from ordinary house servant – a footman, or porter – to butler, around the time of his marriage, four years earlier.

Rumours about John Dickens's paternity appear to have been the focus of speculation from an early point, and there is a genuine case, which must be carefully considered, for doubting that William Dickens was really the father of John Dickens. It has been suggested that his real father may have been either John Crewe, or perhaps the playwright Richard Brinsley Sheridan, who was a close friend of the Crewes, a frequent guest in their household, and for several years the lover of Frances Anne Crewe. On both counts, what may seem at first glance to be an unlikely possibility might, on closer inspection, have some credibility, particularly in the case of Sheridan. It is not hard to see why the idea of Dickens's grandfather being someone other than William Dickens might have attracted attention, bearing in mind the early Dickensian biographers' sense of discomfort that anyone with the mark of literary genius could have sprung from one whose grandfathers were apparently a former sailor turned navy clerk, who was exposed as a fraudster, and an aged butler.

We will explore the question of John Dickens's paternity in some depth, as new evidence suggests there may have been some credibility, after all, to the rumours that cast doubt over his parentage: first, however, we must explore the background of both William Dickens and Elizabeth Ball.

William and Elizabeth were married on 22 November 1781, at St George's church, in Hanover Square. William is generally described as being perhaps about sixty years of age, and his bride as probably thirty-six or seven: his death only four years later might support the idea that he was an older man, but we cannot be sure, and this uncertainty has made it harder for previous researchers to establish his family origins.

Some early sources suggest, without much conviction, that Dickens's ancestry may have been related to the Dickens or Dickins families of Bobbington, in Staffordshire. There has previously appeared to be no firm evidence offered to support this idea – or indeed any connection with the many other less well-placed Dickens or Dickins families in the wider area around Claverley, and Tong. But a closer look at the evidence now available might indicate that there was after all an association with this part of Staffordshire – and perhaps even with Bobbington.

In the past, one or two Dickensian researchers have speculated about a possible link between William Dickens, servant to the Crewes, and a John Dickins, or Dickens, who was butler to the Duke of Cumberland, at his residence in Grosvenor Square. It can now be confirmed that surviving records show there was indeed a John Dickens recorded as butler in the household of the Duke of Cumberland, from 1752 to 1765.[1]

There is a record of a will of a John Dickins of St George, Hanover Square, that was proved in London on 15 June 1765, and a burial record of a John Dickins in the parish registers four months earlier, on 24 February, who may well be the same individual. In the will, John Dickins describes himself as a 'yeoman', and leaves bequests of a gold ring to each of his brothers Edward and Samuel, and, if she was still living, £50 to his sister, Mary, wife of Samuel Bowdler.

At first glance, the description of 'yeoman' may seem confusing, with rural connotations, but this archaic term was also used to describe a servant or official in a noble or royal household. The case for the 'yeoman' John Dickins being the same as the butler to the Duke of Cumberland might therefore be a sound one.

The household of HRH, Prince William Augustus, the Duke of Cumberland, would certainly fit the definition of a household with yeoman staff. Son of George II, and uncle of George III, the Duke was known as 'Butcher Cumberland', after his ruthless suppression of the Jacobite rebellion at Culloden, and he had moved into Old Grosvenor House in Upper Grosvenor Street in 1763, after a less than glorious end to a long military career. He was supported by a large establishment of servants, from Chamberlain to Gentlemen of the Bedchamber, to Grooms of the Bedchamber, Pages of the Back Stairs, and so on. The term 'yeoman' is used in these accounts, regarding 'Yeoman of the Wine Cellar' – a Mr R. Champion held this position, circa 1750.

Cumberland played an important role in establishing the first 'Rockingham Ministry'. The Rockingham Whig faction included many of the well-known political figures of the period, some of them part of the same circle as the employer of Charles Dickens's grandfather, John Crewe, who had succeeded to his father's estates in 1752, and entered Parliament in 1765 as Whig member for Stafford, maintaining a house in Grosvenor Square.

The will of the 'yeoman' John Dickins, who died only months before the Duke, has a clue to his place of origin. He refers to his sister Mary Bowdler, and clearly at the time of writing, which was six years before his death, he did not know if she had died: but he gives full details of where she had lived, which is written as 'the Wood, Church Street, Salop'. Church Street would seem to be a mistranscription of Church Stretton.

The executor of John Dickins's will was a William Dickins, whose relationship to him is unstated, but clearly was a close family member: perhaps a nephew.

William is described as a plasterer, living in Shepherd's Court (now Shepherd's Place), a turning off Upper Brook Street, only a short distance from Upper Grosvenor Street – and Grosvenor Square. There are several entries with the name William Dickins listed in rates records at this address, over a period of many years, from the mid-1740s to the mid-1780s. Perhaps significantly, also in this relatively short street in 1749 lived a William Walkden: someone of this name was a witness at the wedding of Elizabeth Dickens's sister Susanna, in 1781.

Previously to this, there is a John Dickins noted as living in Upper Brook Street, the listed entry immediate to those in Shepherd's Court, which might suggest perhaps that it is in fact the same house, on the corner of both streets: there are records of a coffee house kept by a John Dickins on the corner of Upper Brook Street, apparently in the 1730s – possibly the same individual as the 'yeoman', before entering service in the Duke's household – or another family member.

The John Dickins who lived in Brook Street during this period can be found in the records of the Old Bailey (now online), as the victim of a robbery at his house, in the summer of 1736, in which a silver cup was stolen, while his maidservant was out of the room. From 1746 to 1752, there is no John Dickins listed as resident in Brook Street – but a couple of entries for someone of that name living in Tom's Court, off Duke Street, to the north-east of Grosvenor Square.

A William Dickins who died in 1730, and whose will again points to an origin in the same area of Shropshire, is described as a victualler, of St George's parish, Hanover Square, who seems to have died relatively young, as he left bequests to both his parents, his unmarried sister – to be inherited when she married – and a nephew named William who would come into his inheritance when he was twenty-one. This may or may not be the plasterer, of Shepherd's Court – or it could be William Dickens, Charles's grandfather.

The will states that his parents, John and Margaret Dickins, lived in 'Lybootwoods, Salop'. This is Leebotwood, only 3 or 4 miles from Church Stretton. Also named are a sister, Margaret; a brother, Matthew; and another brother, John Dickins, who is to be his executor. It seems possible that this brother is John Dickins, 'yeoman' – probably the butler to the Duke of Cumberland.

As will be shown later, there are associations with service to royal households that connect William Dickens's friend and best man Joseph Bott, which would appear to add to the evidence that Dickens's grandfather's family are connected in some way with the yeoman John Dickins.

The plasterer William Dickins who lived in Shepherd's Court died in 1790 and his will refers to (yet another) William, his nephew, who is the son of a

Thomas Dickins – and is also a plasterer in London. At this point perhaps we might pause to remember *Little Dorrit*, and the plasterer Mr Plornish, tracked down by Arthur Clennam shortly after his visit to the Barnacle household – in a shabby mews leading off Grosvenor Square. Dickens would seem, in this part of the story, to be trailing around the area known to his own Dickens family, as well as the Dickins plasterers.

Looking at the parish records for Leebotwood – perhaps the same as 'the Wood', referred to in the yeoman John Dickins's will in 1765 – there are many references to Dickins baptisms, marriages and burials, and it is possible to see connections with the family members mentioned in the two wills proved in London. The baptismal records of the children of John and Margaret Dickins match the details of those mentioned in the wills: there is also reference to what appears to be the burial of this John, in 1758, aged eighty-eight, and – a crucial piece of information – his rank is described as 'gentleman'.

In the records of Leebotwood parish is the burial, in 1764, of a Richard Dickins, of Preen: he was a member of the family who owned Preen Manor – the same family who were Lords of the Manor of Bobbington and lived at Leaton Hall.

William J. Carlton had noted in an article in the *Dickensian* in 1961[2] that there was a family of this name who had held the manor of Bobbington from 1429 to 1606. Proof of a connection would have offered the sort of pedigree for Charles Dickens that Carlton and others of this period seemed to have thought ought to be his by right. It now seems likely their interest in this particular line was on the right track, after all.

Looking at the source of Carlton's claim, it is clear that John Noake, in his guide to Worcestershire, published in 1868,[3] was in fact writing about the village of Churchill, 'situated between Kidderminster and Stourbridge', and he observes that, 'The Dickens family, of Bobbington, were lords of this manor from 1432 to 1657, and it is said that from this family Mr. Dickens the novelist, is descended.'

To summarise: the Dickins family who had links with the Grosvenor Square area were from Church Stretton in Shropshire, but their family originated 30 miles or so away in Bobbington, Staffordshire, which was only 3 miles from Claverley, the probable place of origin of Elizabeth Ball. The Dickins family of Bobbington were of the background that Carlton would have dearly loved to link to Charles Dickens: but is that possible?

The new information regarding the 'yeoman' John Dickins, who was butler to the Duke of Cumberland, might appear to support this theory.

There is clear evidence that there were members of a family named Dickins in the same area around Grosvenor Square at the same time as William Dickens, Charles Dickens's grandfather, was employed there: this family had its roots in Shropshire. One member of the Shropshire family was in service, until 1765, as a butler to the Duke of Cumberland, who moved in the same Whig circles as John Crewe. This Dickins family had its origins in the same part of Staffordshire as that sometimes suggested to be the home of an arms-bearing Dickins family from which at least one early source thought Charles Dickens might be descended and was not far from the probable place of origin of Dickens's grandmother. The names William and John are repeated in both families: at least two generations moved to the same area of Mayfair and retained contact with relatives in both Shropshire and London. Dickens's grandfather William, butler to John Crewe, could well have been another nephew or son of one of these family members, who moved to London from Leebotwood, or was born in London to one who had earlier made the same move. Alternatively, he could be from a branch of this Dickens family then still in the Bobbington area.

There is no definitive proof that Dickens's grandfather was a descendant of this family – with so much uncertainty about his age, and a shortage of any other evidence of his life, it is impossible to be sure – but perhaps the weight of probability is on the side of it being most likely.

Chapter Two

Elizabeth Ball

After living in Portsmouth, the Dickens family had returned to London for a brief period, then settled in Chatham, returning to London again in 1822, when Dickens's grandmother Elizabeth was retired from her post as housekeeper, and living in the Oxford Street area. There were two short periods, therefore, one of three years and then another of around two years, in which she may have featured as a person of influence in the life of her young grandson Charles. Clearly her character was of sufficient strength that it left some lasting impression: apart from the portrayal of Mrs Rouncewell, housekeeper at Chesney Wold, in *Bleak House*, there are other elderly women of a certain type in his work that would appear to be informed by the character of his grandmother, including another housekeeper, Mrs Sparsit, in *Hard Times*, whose apparent aristocratic connections, Coriolanian nose and black eyebrows may well have been inspired by the memory of his formidable grandmother. One might wonder if Mrs Sparsit's keen sense of loss of social status reflects Mrs Dickens's nostalgia for her previous position of authority within the Crewe household, and if it helped create Dickens's own acute sensitivity to the nuanced detail of class, fate and fortune.

In an article in *Household Words*, for example, published on 1 January 1859, he recalled his younger self, on another New Year's Day long ago, taken to have a present bought for him, in Soho Square. He describes his companion as 'a grim and unsympathetic old personage of the female gender, flavoured with musty dry lavender, dressed in black crape', with something clinking in her pocket – not the old watch, but presumably some coins. He recalls her taking him down a street diverging from Oxford Street, to give him a shaking, and then wiping his nose 'on the screw principle'. He did not know why she had decided to buy him a present but now concluded 'that she had done something bad in her youth, and that she took me out as an act of expiation'.

In the short story *Holly-Tree Inn*, published in 1855, as the sixth Christmas special edition of *Household Words*, the first section by Dickens, written in the voice of the narrator, Charley, features a childhood memory of a woman fond of telling him, a child still young enough to be in the nursery, stories of the most gruesome nature, the first of which sounds very much like a variation of the tale of Sweeney Todd:

> My first impressions of an Inn dated from the Nursery; consequently I went back to the Nursery for a starting-point, and found myself at the knee of a sallow woman with a fishy eye, an aquiline nose, and a green gown, whose speciality was a dismal narrative of a landlord by the roadside, whose visitors unaccountably disappeared for many years, until it was discovered that the pursuit of his life had been to convert them into pies …

The story-telling continues, identifying '… a brave and lovely servant-maid (whom the aquiline-nosed woman, though not at all answering the description, always mysteriously implied to be herself)'.

The phrase 'brave and lovely servant-maid' is repeated three times, in ironic tribute to the self-styled description given by the woman in question – or Dickens's former servant-maid grandmother, perhaps? Some years later, the fishy-eyed, aquiline-nosed woman marries, and eventually discovers her husband is the very same criminal. He is disposed of, and she is taken to see King George to be complimented on her 'great discretion and valour'. There is more:

> This same narrator, who had a Ghoulish pleasure, I have long been persuaded, in terrifying me to the utmost confines of my reason, had another authentic anecdote within her own experience …

This tale, involving dead parrots, a Newfoundland dog and bloody sheets in a stable, is introduced with an observation that might fit well enough, if the female storyteller really was based on his grandmother:

> She said it happened to her brother-in-law, who was immensely rich, – which my father was not; and immensely tall, – which my father was not. It was always a point with this Ghoul to present my clearest relations and friends to my youthful mind under circumstances of disparaging contrast.

The reference to a 'disparaging contrast' rings true, as we shall see, if the stories that are reported of Elizabeth Dickens referring to her feckless son John are accurate – and certainly in her will she left less money to him, with the reason given that he had already had money from her.

The telling of 'barbarous' tales and references to wealthy relatives may fit well with the identity of the woman in this Christmas story as Dickens's grandmother. The teller of gruesome stories in his infancy is often taken to be the maid who worked for the family in Chatham – but one might suspect, if only from the evidence of the *Holly-Tree Inn* stories, that it is likely that his grandmother, known to be a keen story teller, according to one of the Crewe grandchildren, may also have filled his mind with such ghoulish tales.

Did Dickens visit Crewe Hall, as a child, when Elizabeth was still housekeeper, as some sources claim? It is not impossible, but would have been when he was very young, if during the first period when the family was in London, between 1815 and 1817. Frances Anne Crewe died in 1818, so if he visited before then, she may have seen him – and his older sister, who was named Frances – or indeed they may have been taken to the Crewe townhouse in Grosvenor Street.

Investigating the earlier life of Dickens's grandmother Elizabeth Ball presents difficulties, as has the quest for traces of his grandfather, William Dickens, for the same reasons: uncertainty of their age, and as for many who came to work in London from rural locations before the era of census records, no documentation to suggest place of origin.

Elizabeth did not begin her career in service with the Crewes, but where was she before her marriage to William? We know that she was formerly a servant in the household of a Lady Blandford, her employment there now verified by references in records of her investment of savings in 'consols'. How long she worked there, however, or exactly when, and where she had lived before entering service, is not known, although there are stories that suggest she may have worked at Tong Castle, in Shropshire. This may be significant, as we shall see, in terms of a later association with her grandson: but it is also interesting that Tong is only 8 miles or so from the Crewe family's other estate at Madeley (even though by then the original manor building was in ruins, they appear to have maintained an association with the area and later built a new manor house).

It would seem that the areas likely to have been the place of origin for both of Dickens's paternal grandparents are within the same region of England where there were properties owned by the Crewes, bordering on the adjacent counties of Staffordshire, Shropshire and Cheshire.

The only further useful documented clue to Elizabeth's background is that one of the witnesses to her marriage to William was a Susanna Ball, who was almost certainly her sister.

Searching records for traces of Susanna soon turns up her marriage, a month after Elizabeth's wedding, on 17 December 1781, at St James, Piccadilly, to a Joseph Watchorn. Elizabeth Dickens was one of the two witnesses present. Where they came from is not certain: many have favoured the idea of an origin in Claverley in Shropshire, as the daughters of a James Ball and Amy Guest, and it is fairly likely that this is the correct family.

James and Amy Ball had several daughters: Elizabeth, baptised on 10 January 1746, and Susanna, on 22 April 1755; also possibly Rebecca, baptised in 1743, Mary, in 1748, Ann in 1751, and Keturah, also known as Kate, in 1758. Keturah signed her own name in the marriage register, and clearly the Elizabeth and Susanna Ball in London were also literate. In the 1841 census, members of the Ball family in Claverley include a blacksmith, and two older women of independent means, one of them with a servant, so it is possible that the family were reasonably comfortably placed, some of them perhaps of the tenant farmer class. An Edward Ball is witness to many local marriages, suggesting that he was some sort of church warden – and around 1700 the local minister was a Reverend Guest, the same surname as James Ball's wife.

There is a story, perhaps apocryphal, that at some point before marrying William Dickens, Elizabeth Ball worked at Tong Castle, a dozen or so miles from Claverley (and not much further to Bobbington). Tong was then the residence of the Durant family: George Durant had made a massive fortune out of the slave trade, and invested it in this estate, purchased in 1764.

There seems to be no more than anecdotal evidence for the origins of the story that Elizabeth Ball worked here, and it may be that the idea is derived from, or encouraged by, the notion that Charles Dickens set one of his most famous literary scenes, the death of Little Nell, in the *Old Curiosity Shop*, in this location.

There is reason to believe, however, that there may have been some connection between Dickens's grandmother and Tong, if not between this location and Little Nell, if we are to believe the accounts given by a former vicar of the parish, the Reverend J.E.A. Auden, who arrived in the parish in 1896, and later recorded what he knew of Dickens's association with the area. His thoughts are expressed in a short article for the *Dickensian*, in 1908,[1] and are also within his notes published by the Shropshire Archaeological Society in 1937 under the heading 'Some Erroneous Traditions'.[2]

In summary, Auden, in the course of his recollections, dismisses the idea that Little Nell was anything but a fictional character, but freely admits, apparently exasperated by the volume of visitors determined to find her grave, to encouraging the sexton to take visitors to one that belonged to an eight-year-old child, marked with the letter 'E', rather than that of one Eleanor Lee, who died in January, 1817, aged thirty-nine, and who was sometimes said to have been the subject of stories told to Charles Dickens by his grandmother.

Auden recalled that when newly arrived in Tong he had had a conversation with an elderly woman, 'widow of the late Clerk who had been in office 1872–93', who claimed she had spoken to Dickens when he came to visit the area, 'when he brought over a couple of friends from Wolverhampton or Shrewsbury …' This was a slight variation on the story related in the *Dickensian* article, where the Reverend Auden had claimed it was 'told many years ago by an old inhabitant of Tong, and then written down by a friend who has recently handed them over to me …'

Dickens was dead by the time the elderly woman's husband had held his position, but if she meant that she had met the writer earlier in her life it is not clear exactly when this could have been. Did he ever visit the area? It is not impossible: there is a tradition repeated by several sources that Dickens stayed at the Harp Inn at nearby Albrighton. Dickens, of course, is said to have stayed in many inns, and hotels, but he may well have come very close to Tong in November 1838, when he and illustrator Hablot Browne were travelling through this district, en route to Shrewsbury.

Reference to the Reverend Auden's memories of Tong is made in the article on Dickens's ancestry by W.J. Carlton in the *Dickensian*, in 1961.[3] Carlton is momentarily distracted by the possibility mentioned by Auden of the Dickens family having origins in a village 5 miles from Claverley, and then goes on to tell us that Percy Fitzgerald (who is not the most reliable source) claimed that the Vicar of Tong told him Dickens had mentioned to Archdeacon Lloyd of Shrewsbury that he had been to see Tong, and that the church was the scene of Little Nell's death. However, Lloyd was indeed Vicar of St Mary's Shrewsbury, but from 1854. It is, of course, possible that Dickens met him on his known later visit to Shrewsbury, on a reading tour, in August 1858.

As several commentators have noted, what is of real interest is touched on by Carlton almost in passing: that Dickens's route in 1838 had originally been planned to go via Bridgenorth, near Claverley: and that this plan was his father's idea, evidenced by Dickens's letter on 1 November to his wife from the Lion

Hotel, Shrewsbury. He explains here why his journey had been via Birmingham and Wolverhampton, rather than his intended route: 'We remained at Stratford all night, and found to our unspeakable dismay that father's plan of proceeding by Bridgenorth was impracticable as there were no coaches.'[4]

He was unhappy about the change in his plans, and the resulting journey: '… through miles of cinder-paths and blazing furnaces and roaring steam engines, and such a mass of dirt gloom and misery as I never before witnessed.'

Interesting that it had been 'father's plan' to take the route via Bridgenorth – had John Dickens suggested his son do so, to visit Claverley (or indeed, Bobbington, only a short distance away from the former) because of family connections? A detour of only 4 miles or so from the road to Bridgenorth would have been easy enough. Dickens's father's suggestion at least would appear to indicate some personal knowledge of the area.

Whether or not Elizabeth Ball did work at Tong, we do know that she was a servant in the household of a Lady Blandford, the then elderly widow of William Godolphin, the Marquess of Blandford, who had died in 1731, leaving no direct heir.

This Lady Blandford, who had a distinguished circle of friends, died in 1779, leaving a will in which she is referred to as the Right Honourable Maria Catherina, Marchioness Dowager of Blandford. It had been her first husband, William Godolphin, who was Marquess of Blandford, however. In 1734, Maria married Sir William Wyndham, who died seven years later. Despite her second marriage, Maria retained her previous title as Lady Blandford, presumably because she was determined to maintain a higher status as the widow of a Marquess, rather than that of a mere Baronet.

As well as a town house in Grosvenor Square, number 43, now 48, she also kept a country retreat at East Sheen, sharing her home for some years with her widowed sister, the dowager Countess of Denbighshire.

For Dickens's grandmother, employment in this household meant that there must have been plenty of opportunity to observe at close quarters some of the more interesting and eccentric leading figures of the time. Lady Blandford, as it happens, often features in the correspondence of her friend Horace Walpole, who lived in Gothic splendour not far away at Strawberry Hill, and who describes her in several letters in terms that suggest they were very close.

Clearly Walpole enjoyed the opportunities offered by his friendship with Lady Blandford (and the rest of his 'witches', as he referred to his circle of female confidantes) to make mischief, as he reported in a letter to Lord Montagu in 1765: what the servants made of such larking about, we can only wonder:

'I dined last week at Lady Blandford's with her, the old Denbigh, the old Litchfield, and Methuselah knows who. I had stuck some sweet peas in my hair, was playing at quadrille, and singing to mes sorcières.'

Amongst Walpole's verse there are lines written as an invitation – 'A Card To Lady Blandford' – in which he proposes that she and a group of other ladies attend a gathering at Twickenham – or 'Twitnam'. Elsewhere, in 1774, he describes a disastrous return from Lady Blandford's house, a journey that required taking the ferry across the river during a period of heavy rain, which had left all his meadows under water.

The waspish Walpole seems to have relied heavily upon Lady Blandford and their circle of elderly lady friends as a source of gossip and entertainment. He may have found it difficult to cope without this network: the disappointment he felt in their absence is made clear in a letter to the Earl of Strafford in November 1774, in which he remarks rather forlornly: '… Dowagers are good for propagating news when planted, but have done with sending forth suckers. Lady Blandford's coffee house is removed to town, and the Duchess of Newcastle's is little frequented …'

In October 1779, not so long after her death, Walpole wrote to Lady Ossory: 'Lady Blandford is gone; her antediluvian dowagers dispersed; amongst whom I was still reckoned a lively young creature …' He had earlier written to her of the courage their friend had shown in her last illness. The character we see reflected in the letters of Walpole and others suggest Lady Blandford may well have been an exacting and perhaps capricious employer, but no doubt Elizabeth Ball's time in her service had prepared her well for the larger-scale dramas of the Crewe household, and left her well suited to the service of a household whose family moved in even more exclusive fashionable literary and political circles, whose members were notably unconventional in their private lives, a lifestyle necessarily demanding a certain sort of discretion from the attending staff.

Walpole was acquainted with the Crewe family, members of which lived not far away, at Richmond, and a letter to him from his cousin Henry Conway, in June 1766, asks if he may bring the newly married Mrs Crewe and her friend Mrs Bouverie (and 'four or five men') to breakfast with him at Strawberry Hill. 'They are very desirous of seeing the place …'

It would seem more likely than not that Dickens was well aware of his grandmother's employment with Lady Blandford: the connection was noted by early researchers such as Gladys Storey, who knew his daughter – and Dickens, as we know, was certainly aware of Walpole's letters, and his style of commentary, as we learn from Forster, who reports at least two references to such by him.

Chapter Three

William Dickens, your butler

Around the time of the marriage of William Dickens and Elizabeth Ball, William was promoted to the post of butler. We know this because of an extract from the accounts of the Marquess of Crewe, published in an article on Dickens's ancestry in the *Dickensian* in 1949.[1]

Here we learn that on 23 August 1785, two days after the birth of Dickens's father John, 'William Dickens your Butler' received £40 (minus 3d for a stamp to mark the payment) as wages and board wages. For what period of time this payment was made is unclear. William, of course, died seven weeks later – but this promotion had been a significant one, not least because of the former position in which he had been in service to the household, which was, as new evidence now suggests, in a comparatively menial role.

Board wages are also mentioned in an earlier entry for April 1783, the year of the birth of their first son: William was paid a year's wages, which amounted to £20, plus an extra payment of £13 2s 6d, for thirty-five weeks of 'Board Wages', at a rate of 7/6d a week. This extra payment would have started sometime around the beginning of August 1782: the reason is not certain, but usually these additional allowances were given to servants when a household had moved to one of their other properties: perhaps William had stayed in London, while the family had moved to Crewe Hall, or gone abroad.

The three extracts published in the *Dickensian* article can, of course, only tell a limited story. Why exactly William Dickens moved from being an ordinary servant – earning only £20 a year – to the much higher rank of butler is not clear, except it seems to have occurred during the period in which his sons were born.

There is now evidence, however, confirming the nature of the position held by Dickens's grandfather before his marriage, one that documents an incident in his life that brought him face to face with a moment of human tragedy, albeit an event that was a common enough occurrence in a city that saw so much destitution and human suffering.

Dickensian researchers were given the first new insight into the life of William Dickens when Westminster Coroners' records, now published online,[2] revealed a record of no little interest: an inquest, held on 14 October 1779, into the death of a woman found dead in the Thames by one William Dickens, described as 'Porter to John Crewe of Lower Grosvenor Street'. The title of the inquest document is 'A woman unknown'.

The discovery had been made the previous day, at eight o'clock in the morning, when William Dickens had been out walking along the riverside with a man named Joseph Bott, a friend who would two years later act as witness to the marriage of William and Elizabeth Ball. William Dickens had already left his signature as a witness to the marriage of Joseph to a Mary Allin, or Allen, in 1777, in the register of St George, Hanover Square: the earliest record we have of him.

On the morning in question, William's statement says, he and Bott were 'between the Cuts of the River leading from the Fire Engine to the Wooden Bridge at Chelsea', when he had seen the woman 'whom he did not know', floating in the river, her face downwards, some part of her clothing being above the water. Joseph Bott used a stick to pull her towards the shore, but she immediately sank. William then alerted a Mr Taylor at the Fire Engine, who used a 'hitcher' to pull the dead woman up to the shore. He reported that he had observed 'no Marks of violence' upon the deceased. A local publican's wife gave evidence that the woman had bought beer and gin from her on the night of 12 October, pouring the gin into a bottle and remarking, rather ominously, that it would 'serve her, twice'. It would seem probable, therefore, that the woman had taken her own life, although the verdict made no conclusion as to the cause of death.

Electoral records show that from around 1787, a Joseph Bott was a victualler and stable keeper at premises known as the 'Horse and Dolphin', in St Martin's Street, in an area that is now part of London's Chinatown. There is also evidence, however, from records of the Royal household that shows a Joseph Bott was from 1775 a 'Groom of the Hobby Stable', and from 1777, a Footman, under the Department of the Master of the Horse. Elsewhere undated sources suggest that at one time a Joseph Bott was resident at Engine Court, St James's Palace: presumably the same person, and perhaps attached to the Stables at the palace. Masonic records show that a Joseph Bott, aged forty-four, circa 1790, was a member of 'The Cornerstone Lodge', giving Engine Court as his address.[3]

Joseph Bott's will reveals that he died in Windsor in 1827, leaving property to his son John, who appears to have entered service to the Royal household in

1793 as a 'Page to the Backstairs'. John Bott,[4] or possibly his brother Joseph junior, would seem to be the 'Mr Bott' referred to in the shorthand diaries of one of the royal physicians, Robert Willis, during the crisis of George III's illness in 1810–11: he reports on one occasion that his Majesty had spoken to Mr Bott of his 'usual error' about Lady Pembroke, for whom the King had acquired an infatuation, sometimes suffering from a delusion that they were married.[5]

Some family tree information on the Ancestry website claims that Joseph Bott was born in 1751 – if so, and they were contemporaries, clearly this would mean that William Dickens was not as old as some have assumed. Interesting, however, that Joseph's wife was a Mary Allin: the position of Groom in the household of the Duke of Cumberland was held by a John Allin in 1745: it might be that these two were related, suggesting, if so, that the Duke's butler, the 'yeoman' John Dickins, may indeed have been a member of the same family as Dickens's grandfather William. In which case, it may be relevant that this John Dickins's employer, the Duke of Cumberland, resided for much of the time at Windsor, at what became known as Cumberland Lodge, 3 miles or so from the Castle, where the Bott, Allin and Dickins families may have all worked in service to members of the Royal Family.

Speculation, of course, but worth consideration: the common factors of service, at a senior level, in royal or aristocratic households, between the Bott family, Charles Dickens's grandfather William, and the 'yeoman' John Dickins, quite apart from the Allins, certainly seem to offer some interesting parallels and connections – and may perhaps support the idea of a link both to the London Dickins as well as those in Shropshire.

It is impossible to read Dickens and not be aware of the constant theme, in so much of his work, of death by drowning, or a looming presence of the threat of drowning, and of the recurrence in his work of the river as a metaphor for the flow of life and death, as a place almost of redemption. It is the place where people are drawn at moments of crisis, or a point of significant development in their life's narrative. It is often a place where some are compelled to make their living: in *Our Mutual Friend*, literally providing a living out of the dead for Gaffer Hexham and his daughter, hauling corpses out of the water; for Dickens, it was where he was trapped, as a boy, labouring in a dark, verminous, waterfront manufactory, pasting labels on blacking bottles. It is also the place he travelled to, in almost ritual fashion, across and around, in the course of his 'Night Walks' described in *The Uncommercial Traveller*: a nocturnal journey into the heart of the metropolis, and the centre of his subconscious, where the river is both a boundary, and a route from the past to the future. It is also a place of death, and in particular of suicide:

> But the river had an awful look, the buildings on the banks were muffled in black shrouds, and the reflected lights seemed to originate deep in the water, as if the spectres of suicides were holding them to show where they went down.

In another story published in *The Uncommercial Traveller*, 'Wapping Workhouse', Dickens becomes lost in a maze of streets by the river, and stops to talk to an 'apparition':

> I asked this apparition what it called the place? Unto which, it replied, with a ghastly grin and a sound like gurgling water in its throat:
>
> "Mr. Baker's trap."
>
> As it is a point of great sensitiveness with me on such occasions to be equal to the intellectual pressure of the conversation, I deeply considered the meaning of this speech, while I eyed the apparition – then engaged in hugging and sucking a horizontal iron bar at the top of the locks. Inspiration suggested to me that Mr. Baker was the acting coroner of that neighbourhood.
>
> "A common place for suicide," said I, looking down at the locks.
>
> "Sue?" returned the ghost, with a stare. "Yes! And Poll. Likewise Emily. And Nancy. And Jane;" he sucked the iron between each name; "and all the bileing. Ketches off their bonnets or shorls, takes a run, and headers down here, they doos. Always a headerin' down here, they is …"

The motif of a fallen woman whose end is waiting in the river below a bridge is a commonplace one in nineteenth-century morality tales, and Dickens refers directly to this end in the words of Nancy, the prostitute in *Oliver Twist*:

> Look before you, lady. Look at that dark water. How many times do you read of such as I who spring into the tide, and leave no living thing, to care for, or bewail them. It may be years hence, or it may be only months, but I shall come to that at last.

It seems an interesting coincidence, therefore, that virtually the only sight we have of Dickens's grandfather, as an individual with a life of his own, should be in regard to a drowning in that river, witnessed in the course of a walk: a woman, with an unknown story terrible enough to have driven her to an act of self-destruction.

Was William Dickens's story one that had become a family tale, passed on by his grandmother, or second hand, by John Dickens – perhaps the only event that Charles could associate with his father's father, a figure unknown even to his own son? The telling of such a tale would certainly fit well with what we know, or have good reason to suspect, about the type of terrifying stories told to the young boy by his grandmother.

It might be argued that this experience of William Dickens finds a distinct echo in some parts of the description, in Chapter Nineteen of *The Uncommercial Traveller*, 'Some recollections of Mortality', and the section in which William's grandson describes viewing the body of an unknown woman who has drowned in the canal, hauled out with a 'long pole from a tree', by a passing park keeper and a cab driver, and laid on the towpath. If Dickens's grandmother was as vivid a storyteller as has been claimed, and perhaps the 'ghoulish' fables related in *The Holly-Tree Inn* are examples of the sort of tale she liked to relate, it might be that this lurid story was passed on in some way, either by her son John, or directly to her young grandson. If so, it would have been a rare and memorable insight into the life of his long-dead grandfather and perhaps left the trace of an idea of the link between mortality and the river, the ebb and flow of life and death.

Chapter Four

Praising Amoret: Frances Anne Crewe

Hard is the task to shape that beauty's praise,
Whose judgment scorns the homage flattery pays?
But praising Amoret we cannot err,
No tongue o'ervalues Heaven, or flatters her!

The School for Scandal

Richard Brinsley Sheridan

Perhaps it was through service in the social network that connected the Sheen and Richmond areas, and Grosvenor Square, that Elizabeth Ball became introduced to William Dickens.

Before 1777, both would have been working for most of the time in Grosvenor Square, for their respective employers, when they were in town: William with the Crewes, and Elizabeth with Lady Blandford. These respective households were in the same corner of the Square, in fact, although on adjacent sides. The Crewes later moved to Little Grosvenor Street, just off the Square, at this same corner, so the two households were very close.

The head of the family was John Crewe (1742–1829), a very wealthy landowner from Cheshire, who was MP for the county for many years, although his parliamentary career was less than notable, and he is said to have spoken only rarely in Parliament.

Some interesting details of the Crewe family history were included in a work published in 1856 by a family member, Edward Hinchcliffe, nephew of John Crewe. His polite description of his uncle struggled to find much to say, but concluded 'without brilliancy, he was useful'. Hinchcliffe's expansion on this was: 'He was not a man of great talent and acquirement; but had a clear head and strong common sense …'[1]

Crewe had succeeded to his father's estates as a ten-year-old child, coming of age when abroad on the obligatory Grand Tour in 1763. He had become Sheriff of Cheshire the next year, and then was elected MP for Stafford in 1765, before representing the Cheshire constituency.

According to Hinchcliffe, John Crewe was a progressive agriculturist and model landlord, popular with his tenants, and striving always to make them 'comfortable and happy'.

> At the east end of the church-yard, Barthomley, are buried several of his servants, with the length of their service engraven on their tombs, – forty-three years, fifty years of service, & c, speak very forcibly to his character as a master, as well as to their conduct as servants.

Clearly Dickens's grandparents would have enjoyed a close and valued relationship with their employers.

In the 'Butler's Pantry', Hinchcliffe tells us – presumably a room once used by Dickens's grandfather – there was at one time a portrait of one Joseph Bleamire, formerly coachman at Crewe Hall, who had died in 1756, leaving a generous charitable bequest to provide bread for the local poor. The tradition of long service in the Crewe household continued: we do not know how long Dickens's grandfather worked for the Crewes, but his grandmother Elizabeth certainly seems to have had a connection with them that lasted many decades.

An engraving of an interior scene at Crewe Hall was published in 1809, from a drawing by Charles Parr Burney: he was the grandson of Dr Burney, the close friend and frequent guest of Mrs Crewe; Charles was a nephew of Madame D'Arblay, Fanny Burney. The engraving presents an oddly haunting image, showing the ornately carved Jacobean staircase, featuring rather flamboyant heraldic figures, and we also see the figures of three women, two of them in vaguely classical robes, following what seems like an older female attendant, wearing a type of mob cap, who is indicating a door to the right. Who they are, or what they are doing, is unclear – one might like to imagine this is the housekeeper, Elizabeth Dickens, giving visitors a tour of the building, as was the tradition then – but the enigmatic engraving gives an idea of the distinctive character and brooding presence of the Hall.

There are references in Hinchcliffe's account to not just the longevity of attachment of the Crewes' household staff, but also to the degree of intimacy that they enjoyed with the family they served: at Christmas, for example, we read of festivities in which 'master and servant, visitor and tenant' dined together in the Hall and took part in games – and theatrical performances. These included scenes from Shakespeare, but also musical performances.

The plays were 'ably conducted' by the Crewes' gamekeeper, Thomas Fawcett, and his wife. Hinchliffe tells us that Fawcett was the brother of a celebrated actor of 'genteel comedy', and that some of his children went on the stage. This was John Fawcett, the actor manager, who ran Covent Garden theatre for many years from 1800 and moved in the same circles as Mrs Crewe's intimate friend, and reputed lover, Sheridan. John Fawcett earned praise for his own portrayal of Sir Peter Teazle in *A School for Scandal.*

Thomas Fawcett died in 1817, aged sixty-four, after being in post for twenty-one years – it would therefore be likely that he was employed when Elizabeth Dickens was housekeeper, which means that she would presumably also have taken part in, or at least witnessed, the games and theatrical performances at Crewe Hall, including the Christmas entertainments. It is not impossible that Dickens's father and uncle were also present at some of these performances, and that Charles Dickens heard from his grandmother, father and uncle tales of these events, during which the demarcations of the usual social order were put to one side, for a brief time, while the household enjoyed together the plays, games and festivities organised by the Crewe family.

Dickens would, in his time, take part in many amateur productions, either at his home, or with friends such as the Watsons, who lived at Rockingham Castle: during one stay with them he chose to stage scenes from *A School for Scandal*, as well as from his own work. He played Sir Peter Teazle on one occasion, and for years he wrote to Mary Boyle, the friend and fellow guest who played Lady Teazle, in the role of a 'teasingly' amorous Sir Peter.

We will return in greater detail to the implications of Sheridan's association with the Crewe household, but Rockingham Castle and Crewe Hall, of course, are both reflected in the creation of Chesney Wold, in *Bleak House*, the work that, as we shall see, is so deeply embedded in the story of Dickens's family's history. Visits to Rockingham took place in the period not long before he first began to think about *Bleak House*: it seems probable, therefore, that the place where he played the role of Teazle, as a guest of wealthy landowning friends, is associated to some degree with the process of thought that led to this novel – although it would be a mistake to think that, as some have claimed, Rockingham was the sole source of inspiration for Chesney Wold.

It is particularly interesting, after reading Hinchcliffe's account, to note Forster recording a letter sent by Dickens from Rockingham Castle in November 1849, remarking upon the enjoyment of the staff witnessing their performances:

> To see all the household, headed by an enormously fat housekeeper, occupying the back benches last night, laughing and applauding without any restraint; and to see a blushing sleek-headed footman produce, for the watch-trick, a silver watch of the most portentous dimensions, amidst the rapturous delight of his brethren and sisterhood; was a very pleasant spectacle …

Singling out the housekeeper, the footman – and a silver watch – cannot be other than personally significant: all features of his Dickens family history, but the role reversed – the grandson of the Crewes' housekeeper performing for the servants of his wealthy friends. At Crewe Hall his grandparents attended the needs of their employers and their house party guests – including, for long periods every winter, Sheridan: at Rockingham, their grandson was the honoured guest, waited on by his friends' servants, and revelling in playing one of Sheridan's most famous characters as part of the household's entertainment.

Perhaps the earliest influence of the Christmas traditions so firmly associated with Charles Dickens – and even his love of amateur theatrical productions – might, in some way, be traced back to memories of the Crewe festivities, as recounted by his grandmother, or by his father and uncle: a notion of Christmas as it never really was then, except for a privileged few, and their favoured servants, reclaimed by him for a new era, and a newly emergent middle class, determined to establish their own customs and indulgences.

When it came to the subject of Frances Anne Crewe, Edward Hinchcliffe, one of the extended family members who would be invited to such entertainments at the Hall, finds himself barely able to restrain his enthusiasm:

> But of Frances Anne Lady Crewe, am I to say nothing? If I were to be silent about her the very bricks of Crewe Hall would cry out. She was one of those bright beings formed to fascinate and adorn. High-birth; brilliant wit; a good amount of general reading, with quickness of applying it; beauty of person, of which Madame D'Arblay speaks in her journal: "1779. The elegance of Mrs. Sheridan's beauty is unequalled by any I ever saw, except Mrs. Crewe"; a feminine softness of character, brought to an exquisite polish by manners the most refined, made her the cynosure of neighbouring eyes.

He describes the triumph of Fox's election in 1784, and the vital role played in this success by Mrs Crewe, who attended a celebratory dinner given by the

Prince of Wales at Carlton House and dared to respond to a toast given by the Prince: hardly the wittiest riposte, but bold enough for the conventions of the time, according to which women should not engage in political activism, or any sort of public speaking, and an anecdote that always surfaces in any reference to Frances Anne:

> In the evening of the same day, His Royal Highness and the greater part of the same company met in Grosvenor Street, at the house of Mrs. Crewe, who is described by Wraxall as "one of the most accomplished and charming women of her time," and as having "exerted herself in securing the election of Fox, if not as efficaciously, yet as enthusiastically, as the Duchess of Devonshire." At this party ladies and gentlemen wore the then costume of whiggery, buff and blue. After supper the Prince of Wales gave the following toast: "Buff and blue, And Mrs Crewe …"
>
> Which was answered immediately by the fair lady herself, with the impromptu: "Buff and blue, And all of you" amidst rapturous applause. The quickness, not the cleverness, of the rejoinder from female lips, seldom opened for public speaking, was so sudden and unexpected as to entrap all in a furor of admiration.

Mrs Crewe was the former Frances Anne Greville (1748–1818), the daughter of Fulke Greville, who had served as an MP and then a diplomatic envoy, and the Irish-born poet Frances Macartney, with whom Greville had eloped. Frances Anne and John Crewe married in 1766, and would have two surviving children, John born in 1772, and Elizabeth Emma, in 1780: two others, Frances and Richard, died in early childhood: presumably it was Richard who was the baby born in July 1770 and described in an announcement in the *Northampton Mercury* of 30 July as a 'Son and Heir', delivered at the house in Grosvenor Square. Frances was born some five years later and died when she was about eight years old: she was captured as a sweet little girl, in a hooded cape and long gloves, in a touching portrait by Sir Joshua Reynolds. Her brother John, the new heir, was also portrayed by Reynolds, dressed as young Henry VIII: the boy in regal Tudor court costume, standing legs apart, in a swaggering pose. He was destined, however, for a less than glorious future, dispossessed of his inheritance by his father, and dying in exile, disgraced and estranged from his family.

The Crewes moved between their homes at Crewe Hall, and in London – first at number 3 Grosvenor Square, until 1777, then a short distance away, just around the corner, at number 18, Little Grosvenor Street. From around 1792, Mrs Crewe, if not the entire household, would spend time at a 'cottage', or villa, in the hamlet of North End, Hampstead, very near to Jack Straw's Castle, a well-known inn.

The Crewes' North End retreat, long demolished, was described by their friend Fanny Burney, in a letter to her sister, as 'small but commodious'. Jack Straw's was a hostelry later favoured by Charles Dickens, and this part of Hampstead was probably quite familiar to him from his earlier life, having stayed there, according to some sources, during one of the many short-term residences of his family in the wake of his father's financial difficulties and release from the Marshalsea in 1824, and again possibly in 1832: and we know John Dickens was lodging with a laundress at North End in 1834. As a married man, Charles would also choose to spend time at Wyldes Farm in North End with Catherine, in 1837, both of them struggling to recover from the loss of her sister, Mary.

Mrs Crewe was considered one of the outstanding beauties of her time; she was also vivacious, charming and witty, and like the equally charismatic Georgiana, Duchess of Devonshire, a well-connected and highly influential woman, entertaining and moving within the same social and political network, whose friendships – and extramarital relationships – were to a large extent formed within the same small circle. At all their homes, the Crewes entertained many of the most interesting and important political and literary figures of the time: Charles James Fox, Burke, Sheridan, Reynolds, and George Canning were frequent visitors, as well as Dr and Miss Burney, and Mrs Thrale. Fox, Canning and Sheridan were all reputed to have had affairs with their hostess.

At Crewe, Frances Anne had created a model dairy, where according to Hinchcliffe 'she, with her maid, sometimes retreated for a little quiet, from the whirl of fashionable life', and to entertain 'visitors and neighbours'. For the same purpose she created a 'cottage orné' in the grounds of the Hall, on a hill by the lake. The example of Marie Antoinette, at Versailles, visited by Frances Anne on her trips to Paris, would appear to have left its influence on Mrs Crewe's reinvention of her husband's estate, and perhaps the French queen's toying with her own faux hamlet and model farm provided a solution to Mrs Crewe's own search for seclusion, and privacy: somewhere to receive her more favoured guests …

Edward Hinchcliffe was discreet and naturally spoke nothing of Frances Anne's more intimate friendships, but he was clearly captivated by her – and at the same time wary of her reputation, declaring: 'If ever woman was likely to be spoiled by flattery, Mrs Crewe was …'

According to Dr Burney's memoirs, Mrs Crewe, in the same location as her farm, had opened a similarly romanticised model school for girls at some point in the 1790s (he appears to have seen it on a visit in 1797), based on the idea of a convent. 'Amoret' was the pet name for Mrs Crewe used by Sheridan, and his wife, as well as by her other admirer and reputed lover, Charles James Fox. Fox was not only a close friend of the Crewes, he was supported financially by John Crewe – at considerable cost: according to Horace Walpole, in a letter to Horace Mann, on 13 July 1773, Crewe was giving 'twelve hundred a year for him ... literally for him, being bound for him'. Reward for such efforts would come in 1806 in the form of a peerage for John Crewe.

We may see further reflections of Frances Anne Crewe in several letters and memoirs of the time, particularly in the diaries and letters of Fanny Burney – and we have some of her own writing in a journal she created from a series of letters to an unknown friend, while on her second visit to Paris, in 1786.[2]

More on this later, but in these letters we find reference to a few servants: Dolly, a maid who appears to have been charged with the care of her small daughter Emma (Dolly is also the name of an unseen servant that had been used by Sheridan in *The Rivals*), a male servant named Toby, and an unnamed personal maid: presumably not the recently widowed Elizabeth Dickens, who had a new baby and a two-year-old child to care for. Unless, of course, she had returned to employment with the Crewes and had left her children in the care of others.

Chapter Five

Elizabeth Dickens, servant at your town house

We know that at least by April 1783, before the birth of the couple's first son, William Dickens was still only earning £20 per annum: his promotion from what is now revealed to have been the position of porter to butler took place sometime between then and the birth of their second son, Charles Dickens's father John, in August 1785.

Returning to the same *Dickensian* article of 1949,[1] we see that it includes in the extracts from the Crewe family accounts a later entry referring to Elizabeth Dickens, in 1798, as 'Servant at your town house', showing that her annual wage was eight guineas: almost certainly indicating she was a personal servant, rather than one involved in routine domestic labour. But it is not until later still that she was to become a housekeeper: perhaps once her sons were old enough to support themselves, around the turn of the century.

Looking again at her payment in 1798, however, it is interesting to note that her year's wages were supplemented by a very generous disbursement of £23 4s – for 'Board Wages' and payments made to her. Why was she given four times the amount of her salary as an additional sum? Apart from 'Board Wages', which would probably constitute no more than half the extra sum, at most, for what service or extra costs was the extra money given?

Perhaps the Crewes were particularly generous employers: from the limited details we have, however, taken from the Crewe family papers, it is not easy to explain why it was that the couple were able, as we shall see, to save large amounts of money from relatively moderate servants' salaries, over the course of their employment. Before his promotion to butler, as we now know, William Dickens had been merely a porter: a servant who would have worn livery and waited on visitors arriving at the door of the house in Lower Grosvenor Street, and presumably at Crewe Hall. It was a significant advancement in terms of trust, and delegation of responsibility, by a family of the wealth and status of the Crewes, to promote him from the position of porter to butler, with all the demanding duties and high standard of service that that would have entailed.

Elizabeth Dickens is believed to have remained in employment with the Crewe household after the death of her husband – there is no evidence of this, in fact, but the household accounts show that she certainly was working for them again by 1798. She was on a modest salary, at that stage, despite having two young sons to look after. One might wonder where they all lived, in this period. It would be unusual for a servant to be allowed to live in, if accompanied by two young boys – it may be that they were away at school or looked after by relatives.

When exactly Mrs Dickens attained the post of housekeeper is not clear, although according to the possibly unreliable memories of Lady Annabella Houghton (usually known as Annabel), a granddaughter of the Crewes, born in 1814, Mrs Dickens was the housekeeper at Crewe Hall when Annabel was a small child. Lord Crewe's heir, his only surviving son John, was estranged from the family and lived abroad, and his daughter-in-law died in 1820: the widowed Lord Crewe (Frances Anne died in 1818) took responsibility for his grandchildren, arranged for them to be made wards of court, and kept them under his care at Crewe Hall. Annabel had later claimed that she remembered Elizabeth Dickens as one who enthralled the Crewe grandchildren with her story telling: according to Gladys Storey in *Dickens and Daughter*, published in 1939:[2]

> She possessed strong story-telling powers, which were remarked during the latter period of her long service. These romances – many of them fairy-tales – were entirely the invention of her clever and original brain. They were related for the entertainment of the Crewe grandchildren, whose greatest treat was to be allowed to make their way to the housekeeper's room, and there sit in wrapt attention to "old Mrs. Dickens" while she, in her delight, unfolded yet another story for their enjoyment.
>
> When little Annabella Crewe was grown up and married to Lord Houghton, with children of her own, she would recall the extraordinary story-telling powers of the old housekeeper; emphatic in her conviction that never since had she met anyone who possessed so surprising a gift for extemporising fiction for the pleasure of others.

Storey's account echoes the observations made by Sir Thomas Wemyss Reid, biographer of Lord Houghton, published in the *Daily News*, on 8 October 1887, in which he says he remembers Lady Houghton '… speaking to me with enthusiasm of Mrs Dickens's wonderful powers as a story-teller. It was her delight as a child to listen to the tales which the old lady was able to relate with so much dramatic force and feeling ...'

Dickens and Richard Monckton Milnes, later Lord Houghton, were friends for more than thirty years – a friendship that began well before the marriage to Annabel Crewe: one might wonder at what point it was – if at all – that Dickens confided to his friend that his grandmother had been housekeeper in the Crewe household. He would have known that the wedding, at the end of July 1851, took place at Madeley, one of the Crewe family properties, the ceremony conducted by two relatives, followed by a reception at Crewe Hall, and this would surely have prompted him to allude to the family connection, if not before. Or perhaps he said nothing, and it was only after his death that Lady Houghton discovered the link, and recorded her memories about his grandmother, as implied by the statement by Sir Thomas Wemyss Reid in his letter to the *Daily News*, that 'later in life, Lady Houghton still recognised in the illustrious author of David Copperfield the grandson of the favourite of her childhood'.

It must be of no little significance that within four months of his friend's marriage to a member of the Crewe family, Dickens had begun to write the beginning of *Bleak House*, and to include, as central to the plot, a narrative, and characters, that reflect his personal, if unacknowledged, connection to this family.

Annabel's brother became the third Lord Crewe, and held the title in much of Dickens's lifetime: he was known as Hungerford: a family name, but one that could only conjure up the most unwelcome memories for Charles Dickens, living with the secret knowledge of his time as a boy labouring for Warren's Blacking, at the company's rat-infested warehouse on Hungerford Stairs: its association with the family in whose service his grandparents had worked no doubt serving to remind him, even in the days of his adult life, his worldwide fame and enormous public popularity, of the tenuous nature of his success and acceptance by an establishment that knew nothing of his early background.

Two weeks before the end of his life, as related by Forster, and by Gladys Storey in *Dickens and Daughter*, Charles Dickens had been with Lord and Lady Houghton at a dinner given for the Prince of Wales, and the King of the Belgians: the royal guests kindly allowing Dickens, who was suffering badly from gout, to remain downstairs, where they met him. This was certainly an event that the Crewes' former housekeeper, Dickens's grandmother, could not possibly have foreseen.

According to the article in the *Dickensian* in 1995 by Gilian West on the subject of the influence on Dickens of the Crewe family – particularly in regard to *Bleak House*, 'Until 1800 Mrs Mary Dobbins was housekeeper at (Crewe) Hall, and from 1818 Mrs Ellen Hilditch held the post', therefore it would seem it was between those two dates that Elizabeth had the same post: unless of course her position was only ever at the London property. If she had been housekeeper at Crewe at some time between these dates, it would suggest Lady Houghton would have been perhaps too young to remember Mrs Dickens with any great powers of recollection, but as well as claiming to have enjoyed sitting and listening to her story telling, she also reported that the housekeeper spoke of her son John, Dickens's father, in critical terms: according to Gladys Storey, '... referring to him as "that lazy fellow John, who used to come hanging about the house ..."' adding, 'and many a sound cuff on the ear I've given him'. Again Sir Thomas Wemyss Reid offers a similar version of this reported impatience with her son in his account in the *Daily News* letter: 'Old Mrs. Dickens had one grievance which Lady Houghton still recalled as she told me about her. It was the conduct of her son John – Charles's father – against whose idleness and general incapacity she was never tired of inveighing.'

These reminiscences offered by Lady Houghton, or reported as offered by her, might not be entirely credible, however, as she would have been only six years old when Mrs Dickens left her position as housekeeper, whether at Crewe or elsewhere – although it is possible she then held a position in another family establishment, or perhaps back in Little Grosvenor Street, until she is believed to have retired, in 1820.

Gladys Storey's accounts are always interesting, but she is not very good at attributing sources for her claims: her friendship with Dickens's daughter Kate Perugini, cultivated with great determination over a period of some years, is offered as the stamp of authority. How much is true, and how much Storey's own interpretation – or invention – is hard to tell; or indeed in the case of Lady Houghton's remarks, how much was taken from Wemyss Reid.

Despite earning a modest income, according to another article in the *Dickensian* in 1987, by Michael Allen,[3] Elizabeth Dickens was able to continue to make significant savings.

After her husband's death, substantial amounts of cash continued to be invested by Dickens's grandmother. Michael Allen notes that it was Elizabeth who appeared to be in the habit of acquiring savings in the bank, but also that William Dickens's legacy to her – of £450 – 'was not ... the result of a lifetime's saving, but was gathered over a very short period'. He then observes that William's widow continued to make substantial payments – as well as make some large withdrawals: 'Over the following 27 years she added to her account on eleven different occasions, with sums varying between £25 and £225. In that same period, she made six different withdrawals, each of £100.' The latter payments, he suggests, may reflect a comment made in her later will, in which she explains that her younger son John Dickens would be inheriting less than his brother due to money being given to him during her lifetime.

But how did the Dickens family accumulate such relatively large amounts of money? Allen thought the answer lay in the 'vails' system of tipping staff, but some might disagree: certainly after the death of William Dickens, one might expect that with two small children to support, his widow would not be in such a comfortable position that her income would allow her to make such a level of investment.

It is true that Elizabeth, before marriage, had made sustained efforts to save money. Allen's article mentions investment by her in Bank of England 'consols'. New evidence now suggests that according to lists published by the Bank, held by the British Library, for some years Elizabeth, and in at least one year her husband, were owed dividend money on at least some of these investments. The outdated details in these publications, largely from the 1790s and 1800, refer variously to Elizabeth Ball, spinster, servant to Lady Blandford, Grosvenor Square, and Elizabeth Dickens, of Grosvenor Street, widow – and one list in 1791 to William Dickens, servant to Mrs Crewe, of Grosvenor Street, years after his decease. There is at least one reference, however, to Elizabeth Ball, spinster, in a list published in 1823. Why such careful savers had failed to claim these apparently forgotten dividends is not known.

There is also a reference within these records to an Elizabeth Dickens, servant to a Lady Isham, in 'Spring Gardens' in 1786 – the year after William Dickens died. It might be that this is Dickens's grandmother: in which case it would appear that rather than being employed by the Crewe family immediately after the death of her husband (and the hurried baptism of her two infant sons), she went to work for a brief time for another household: that of the elderly Lady Philippa Isham, widow of Sir Edmund, the sixth Baronet, who died in 1772. Lady Isham died in December 1786, leaving bequests to servants, but only those who had worked for her for two years or more, so disqualifying Elizabeth – if this was indeed the same woman.

Chapter Six

The odd love-child, here and there

The marriage of William and Elizabeth Dickens was to be a short-lived union, as William died only four years after their wedding – supposing of course, as seems probable, that he is the William Dickens noted as having been buried on 18 October 1785, in the parish registers of St George, Hanover Square. His death left Elizabeth with two infant sons: two-year-old William and the newborn John Dickens: Charles Dickens's uncle, and his father.

John was less than two months old when William Dickens died, if the reported date of death of his father in early October is correct – and indeed the stated date of John's birth. It might appear to have been a sudden death, rather than because of long illness, as he was paid weeks earlier for his post as butler, immediately after the birth of his second son, and he would seem to have left no will.

Rather unusually, John Dickens and his older brother were baptised together, only six weeks or so after their father's death: at the point of baptism, John's date of birth is given as 21 August 1785: William's is stated to have been 21 September 1783. This suggests, at the very least, a certain amount of sudden haste by Mrs Dickens, at a time of mourning – and also indicates, somewhat curiously, that the parents had not been earlier concerned, even at a time of high infant mortality, not to mention a sense of religious duty, about leaving their first son unbaptised for more than two years. It also poses the question as to when and where exactly William and John were born, as there is no evidence of where this was – as well as why their widowed mother then hurried to arrange a double christening within weeks of the death of her husband: almost as if to confirm their identity as the sons of a father now deceased – and destined never to play a significant role in their future lives. Another odd detail is the place of baptism: why St Marylebone, rather than their local church of St George, Hanover Square?

At this point it is necessary to consider the rumours about the disputed parentage of John Dickens. Is it really possible that William Dickens was not his father? Hard to reconcile, perhaps, the idea of the formidable, elderly retired housekeeper that Dickens would have known in his childhood with that of a woman who might have had a child as a result of some sort of adulterous liaison: but that is to forget that Elizabeth had once had an independent life of her own, before marriage, about which little is known.

The level of society in which the employers of William Dickens and Elizabeth Ball moved was one bound by rigid conventions, to an outward extent, but at the same time it remained tolerant of a wide range of irregular relationships – if discreetly undertaken. The arranged marriages of eighteenth-century aristocrats were essentially strategic and dictated by material considerations – sealing alliances, controlling the distribution of property and ensuring the continuation of inherited estates or titles: romantic love had little or nothing to do with these unions, and in not a few cases, once duty had been done and an heir secured, such couples quite often engaged in extramarital relationships, inevitably sometimes resulting in the birth of illegitimate children.

To give a full account of the web of entanglement and sexual intrigue that bound together the same group of figures within the Devonshire House set would be an enormous challenge. Suffice it to say that the network of relationships between Georgiana, Duchess of Devonshire, her sister Harriet, Lady Bessborough, and Georgiana's intimate friend – also her husband's mistress – Lady Elizabeth Foster, was highly complex and unorthodox.

Frances Anne Crewe had her own group of intimate friends and admirers, but many of them were part of the same circle of engagement as the Devonshires, including the politician Charles James Fox – and of course the playwright Richard Brinsley Sheridan: the latter relationship lasting for perhaps as long as ten years. Sheridan dedicated *The School for Scandal* to Frances; he and Fox wrote verses to her: as we know, both referred to her by the name of 'Amoret', first coined by Sheridan's remarkably tolerant wife Eliza when her husband's fascination with their new friend first became apparent.

In much later life, in a letter written in October 1814, to his second wife 'Hecca', Sheridan said that when he re-read the verses dedicated to Mrs Crewe: 'Oh! How it reminds me of what an ardent romantic Blockhead nature made me … NB I was not then 25 – by the way …' And he admitted: 'She was in truth the Handsomest of the set.'

Fox, in his offering *To Mrs Crewe* (Horace Walpole's Strawberry Hill Press printed the verse in 1775), asserts that his love for her, despite her beauty and sweetness, is platonic: '… my Wishes, which never were bounded before, Are here bounded by Friendship, and ask for no more …' Whether that was really the case, we do not know.

With Sheridan, on the other hand, it is highly unlikely that their relationship was not one that was sexually intimate, and his public dedication to her of *The School for Scandal* effectively puts this in plain sight, evident beyond the more formal expressions of admiration directed at 'Thee my inspirer, and my MODEL—CREWE!' Frances Anne Crewe's personal charm and her intellect were clearly as great an attraction for him as any opportunity her friendship might offer for his own social and political advancement, although the latter benefit, at least in the beginning, must have been a persuasive factor in his pursuit of her favours – and perhaps this was the line he took with his wife, whose apparent indifference to his philandering must have been tested severely by so public a declaration of devotion.

As for John Crewe, it would seem likely that he too had affairs with other women: and significantly, according to a source referred to in a footnote in Gilian West's article, an unpublished history of Crewe Hall, there were rumours 'that both John Crewe and his wife had illegitimate children'.[1] This has proved to be an idea that was worth exploring further.

John and Frances Anne Crewe's son John, who would become the second Lord Crewe, spent much of his adult life in debt, eventually dying abroad in exile, ultimately to be disinherited of any claim to his father's estates. One of the younger John Crewe's acts of dishonour was to have tricked a young woman into believing she had married him in a bogus service in the chapel at Crewe Hall, performed by a local billiards marker, whom the 'groom' had persuaded to act as the minister. As a result of this fake marriage, a daughter was born. According to the same unpublished history of Crewe, this daughter remained close to the Crewe family, and perhaps entered into marriage with another relative, also born from an extramarital affair:

> Hearsay evidence suggests that this daughter, when she grew up, married to the illegitimate son of John's mother, Lady Frances Crewe. This piece of evidence has been disputed, however, as it is possible that the illegitimate son may have been that of the first Lord John Crewe, rather than that of his wife. The climate of morality in those pre "Victorian" days was not always what we nowadays think it might have been, and it is more likely that in an age when it was common-place for married ladies to have children by men other than their husbands, the odd love-child here and there would have been happily assimilated into a family circle.

It might seem unlikely that an illegitimate daughter of the younger John Crewe would have married an uncle – or half-uncle, that is to say an illegitimate son of the first Lord Crewe, or Lady Crewe. But not impossible, perhaps. It is also possible that this story was confused with a more regular marriage that did occur later in the Crewe family's history: as a Crewe descendent, Cynthia Colville, mentions in her autobiography when discussing Frances Anne Crewe, and the dedication by Sheridan of *The School for Scandal*: '… though, of course, she and Sheridan never married, their descendants did in fact do just this, for my father was Frances Crewe's great-grandson, and my mother … was Sheridan's great-great-great granddaughter.'[2]

If there is a confusion with this later marriage, it is interesting that it relates to Sheridan, who was Frances Anne's intimate friend for so many years – and has been suggested by some to have been the father of John Dickens.

It is certainly true to say that John Crewe was believed by some to have had at least one 'natural' son, and as we know, it is a matter of fact that several of Frances Anne's contemporaries who moved within the Devonshire House set, society women and political hostesses, did have illegitimate children – or rather children born in the course of a marriage, but fathered by other men.

It was apparently rumoured that a man by the name of Robert Hawgood Crewe, who served as Secretary to the Board of Ordnance for many years, was the illegitimate son of John Crewe. Entries in *The Black Book; or Corruption unmasked! Being an Account of Persons, Places, and Sinecures*, first published in 1820, claim that 'R.H. Crewe' (sometimes given as Robert 'Hargood' or even Robert Henry Crewe) was 'a near relation' of Lord John Crewe. Included in the Clarendon Press edition of the letters and journals of Fanny Burney there is a letter to her brother Charles, written in November 1816, which mentions her forwarding correspondence 'under cover' to 'Crewe Esq, Office of Ordnance, Pall Mall', on behalf of a Dr Kaye, Charles's friend and her son's mentor at Cambridge. The editor's note refers to the 'Black Book' and comments that the description 'near relation' is a euphemism for 'natural son'.

There is no further evidence to prove this was the case – but the idea that Robert had been given a post in the Ordnance Office due to Lord Crewe's influence, as a family connection, was not so far away from the notion that John Dickens might have received his place in the Navy Pay Office through some similar act of patronage: either by the Crewes, or perhaps, as has also been suggested, due to the intervention of the Crewes' close friend Sheridan.

Fanny Burney was a long-term family friend of the Crewes, as had been her father, Dr Burney. Fanny's half-sister Sarah would become governess to the granddaughters of Lord Crewe in 1822, continuing the family connections. It is perhaps significant, therefore, that a Burney family member should be trusted with the task of passing on letters for one supposed to be the 'near relation' of Lord Crewe.

There is also some evidence to suggest the existence of other apparent illegitimate Crewe children, including a boy who is likely to have been fathered by disgraced younger son John – if not by his father.

As mentioned in one of the footnotes to an article by Gilian West in the *Dickensian* in 1995,[3] in the Crewe Hall accounts there are payments made on behalf of someone with the name 'Master Haswell' at a Yorkshire boarding school: we know he was there for some years, and at least from 1820 was a favoured 'parlour boarder' at the doubled fee of £40 per annum.

As well as Master Haswell, there is said to have been a daughter by the woman who took part in a bogus ceremony in Crewe chapel, remembered by Cynthia Colville, the great-great granddaughter of John and Frances Anne Crewe, as having been treated 'kindly' by the family.

In addition to these two children, there are one or two families who believe that they are descended from another son of the younger John Crewe, one John Griffiths, who was brought up in Herefordshire, in circumstances that might appear to hold further significance in terms of potential explanation of the paternity and upbringing of John Dickens, as we shall see later.

Further investigation now tells a very interesting story about young Master Haswell, however. The first Lord Crewe died in 1829, and his will, written originally in 1824 and appended with codicils, covers many pages, taking care to divide his estate between members of his family – and, most importantly, to make arrangements that would effectively disinherit his only surviving son, General John Crewe. Within this will there is reference, with no explanation as to his connection to the family, to one Frederick Crewe Haswell, whom the will states to be residing with a Mrs Simpson, at Woden Croft Lodge, near Barnard Castle, and who is given an annual allowance of £52 10s. This is the same person listed in the Crewe accounts, but mentioned here with his full name, which might imply a close, if unspecified, relationship to the family. If Frederick was a nephew, or cousin, this would have been acknowledged in the will, as would have been the case if he were a godchild: he was a responsibility of Lord Crewe, but not one that he cared to explain. The story of Frederick Crewe Haswell also has an association with Charles Dickens that might not immediately seem apparent but might help explain one of the most compelling plotlines in one of his most loved novels: the story of Dotheboys Hall in *Nicholas Nickleby*.

Chapter Seven

Frederick Crewe Haswell and Dotheboys Hall

Woden Croft Lodge was formerly one of the academy schools in the area around Barnard Castle – the 'Yorkshire schools', known in this part of Yorkshire (as it was then, although now in County Durham) as 'London schools', because of the origins of many of the pupils. To these establishments could be sent any boys who were unwanted, inconvenient, disabled; stepchildren, illegitimate children, or as Dickens put it in his preface to *Nicholas Nickleby*, 'neglected or repudiated children'.

Some parents, unable to afford the much higher fees of public schools, may have thought that these academies offered a good standard of education, having been taken in by the promises made in newspaper advertisements, and prospectuses. Any maltreatment of their sons, or failings in standards, may not have come to their attention, as many of these establishments prevented any sort of correspondence that might have alerted families to their child's plight, and some children remained at the schools for years without seeing their families. Some of the parents or guardians may not have wanted any sort of communication, using these establishments as a way of disposing any responsibility for their children, stepchildren, or wards: happy to receive assurances that there would be 'no vacations'. For twenty guineas a year, these boys could be sent far away from home, out of sight – and virtually forgotten.

More recently some have tried to argue that the Yorkshire schools were not as awful as we have been led to think and there are a few accounts by former pupils that appear to present no criticism of their schools. Weighed against the amount of evidence of deplorable conditions, however, it would seem clear that what happened at these establishments was very often abuse of a sort that would not have been considered acceptable in any school other than those which kept families largely estranged from their own children for years at a time, and parents in ignorance of the poor standards of care that their sons were receiving.

It seems highly likely that Frederick Crewe Haswell was an illegitimate son of either John Crewe, the younger, or his father, and had been consigned to one of the Yorkshire schools along with many others in his position. Whether the Crewe family knew about, or cared about, the standards of care at Woden Croft is not clear, but the fact that he was still living at Woden Croft in the year after an infamous court case involving the treatment of boys at another local academy might suggest that there were no concerns regarding his wellbeing.

Within five years of the death of Lord Crewe, Frederick was married and living on the other side of the world, in Sydney, New South Wales. He worked in various clerical and managerial posts and for a few months served as editor of the *Sydney Gazette*, but died in Australia in 1841, in his early thirties.

Here of course, we are obliged to acknowledge the famous fictional representation of those terrible schools in *Nicholas Nickleby*, and Charles Dickens's depiction of Dotheboys Hall and the odious Wackford Squeers. As Dickens tells us in his preface to an edition published in 1848, he had heard about the Yorkshire schools as a child but claimed he could not remember exactly how.

'I cannot call to mind, now, how I came to hear about Yorkshire schools when I was a not very robust child, sitting in bye-places near Rochester Castle ...', so very young. Dickens left Chatham in 1822 – he also mentions a vague association with a story about a boy who had been at one of the schools, suffering from an abscess that a master is supposed to have ripped open with 'an inky pen'.

The fact that his grandparents' employer had an illegitimate son sent to one of these schools, supported regularly financially by the Crewe family, and mentioned in Lord Crewe's will, would probably not have been a secret from long-serving members of the household, such as Elizabeth Dickens. It is possible that John Dickens and his mother knew about the boy and talked about it: perhaps curiosity about the mysterious child packed off to one of these establishments piqued the interest of Charles Dickens.

That Frederick Crewe Haswell was a 'parlour boarder' is worth a moment's reflection: this term was used for more favoured pupils at a boarding school, whose higher fees might mean their accommodation would be with the headmaster's family – or at the very least they had their own room. In *David Copperfield*, Dickens uses this term to describe Steerforth – and indeed it is not impossible that he adapted this character's surname from the place name 'Startforth', which is in the outskirts of Barnard Castle and was the location of some of the Yorkshire schools.

It is certainly true that the extent of Dickens's interest in the subject was such that he determined to travel all the way up to Yorkshire one winter, enduring a long and uncomfortable journey by stagecoach with his illustrator Hablot Knight

Browne, in order to see the schools for himself: a personal interest might explain the motivation for such an arduous expedition.

Dickens could have stayed at home and gained enough information about the Yorkshire schools from newspapers – and he did decide to look at court reports and advertisements in papers from fifteen years earlier, although after he had made his visit, as a note in his journal at the time informs us. He was particularly interested in the schools as they were in the past, rather than as they might have been in his own time – and the period about which he seemed to be curious included the time when Frederick Crewe Haswell was a pupil at Woden Croft Lodge.

There is another possibility that might explain Dickens's interest. This school had been founded by Edward Simpson sometime around 1792 and therefore had been running as an enterprise, along with other establishments in the area, at the time when Dickens's father and uncle were young boys. It is tempting to wonder if the widowed Mrs Dickens, who was working for the Crewes at least by 1798, had packed her sons off to Yorkshire in order to maintain her position with the Crewe household: at that point William would have been fifteen and John thirteen, so both were of an age to be sent to boarding school. Forster described these places as 'the cheap schools' – a suitable place of education, then, for the sons of a widowed housekeeper. A personal connection would certainly explain Dickens's enthusiasm for tackling this subject: for the long, difficult journey north, to see the place for himself.

The expense involved would have been substantial, even at the comparatively low rate charged by these schools – but for a widowed mother with a certain amount of savings looking for a practical education for her sons, it might have seemed a suitable option. Twenty pounds a year for board, tuition, and clothing would perhaps have seemed like good value. The Yorkshire schools offered the sort of education that the aspirational parent with limited means would have thought a route to advancement for their sons: not the purely classically based curriculum that was the norm for public schools and grammar schools. As Robert J. Kirkpatrick observes in his study of the Yorkshire establishments:[1]

> … the schools offered a very middle-class education, with subjects such as Latin, Greek Mathematics, Book-keeping, Surveying, Navigation, Trigonometry, Mensuration and Geography … such a varied curriculum was aimed at boys who were destined for trade, business, commerce clerkships and similar occupations.

A suitably practical education, in short, for boys who would be expected to work for their living.

It has been suggested by some sources that the Crewes helped with the education of John Dickens: Michael Slater, for example, has noted that Dickens's father 'had apparently received a good education, probably thanks to Crewe …'[2] It would seem at least possible that a relatively inexpensive arrangement could have been made, for whatever reason, for William and John Dickens.

John Dickens would eventually work as a reporter, the power of his descriptive writing evident as early as 1822, in his piece published (anonymously) in *The Times* on the great fire in Chatham that took place that year. Such a level of articulacy would indicate a level of education that would perhaps not be the norm for most sons of servants. And some of the Yorkshire schools, despite their relatively low fees, aspired to provide a good standard of tuition and range of subjects; Woden Croft at one time even boasted a literary society for boys and masters.

The notoriety of the Yorkshire schools, and the scandalous circumstances depicted by Dickens in *Nicholas Nickleby*, are said by some to have been unfairly founded. Examining evidence of the abuses alleged to have been practised by these schools, however, from a range of accounts, it is a reasonable assumption to make that although Dickens may have exaggerated some of the details for literary effect, even by the standards of the time – and the equal prevalence of bullying and beating in many public schools in this period – boys were often badly treated in these 'academies'. They were deliberately distanced from their families, and forced to write home letters organised by the schools' staff in order to present a false picture of the conditions in which they were living, and their state of wellbeing.

It is known that William Shaw, the owner of Bowes Academy, was widely believed to be at least in part the inspiration for Squeers – but there is reason to think Dickens also knew about the Simpson family's operation at Woden Croft Lodge, and that details of the former regime at this school formed part of the research he undertook for *Nicholas Nickleby*.

Advertisements for Edward Simpson's establishment bore a distinct resemblance to the notice published by Squeers, as seen in Chapter Three, even referring to the same inn where the headmasters made themselves available to prospective patrons. Here is Dickens's version:

> At Mr. Wackford Squeers's Academy, Dotheboys Hall, at the delightful village of Dotheboys, near Greta Bridge in Yorkshire, Youth are boarded,

> clothed, booked, furnished with pocket-money, provided with all necessaries, instructed in all languages living and dead, mathematics, orthography, geometry, astronomy, trigonometry, the use of the globes, algebra, single stick (if required), writing, arithmetic, fortification, and every other branch of classical literature. Terms, twenty guineas per annum. No extras, no vacations, and diet unparalleled. Mr. Squeers is in town, and attends daily, from one till four, at the Saracen's Head, Snow Hill. N.B. An able assistant wanted. Annual salary 5 pounds. A Master of Arts would be preferred.

Compare this to an example of one of these advertisements in 1818, when Frederick Crewe Haswell was probably around twelve years of age (although he could have been accepted as a pupil from the age of six): from the *Morning Advertiser* of 9 July:

> At Mr. EDWARD SIMPSON's ACADEMY, Woden Croft Lodge, Yorkshire, near Barnard Castle, YOUNG GENTLEMEN are BOARDED and GRAMMATICALLY INSTRUCTED in the English, Latin, and Greek Languages, Writing, Arithmetic, – Merchants' Accounts, and the most useful branches of the Mathematics, on the following terms; Entrance, 10s. 6d.; from 6 to 9 years age, twenty guineas; and from 9 to 12, at twenty-two guineas per annum; a limited number of Parlour Boarders admitted. The French Language, Drawing, and Music, moderate extras. No vacations. Mr. Simpson is now in town, and attends daily, from twelve to three, at the Saracen's Head Inn, Snowhill, and having conducted the establishment for more than 25 years, will render perfect satisfaction to applicants, referring them to the Parents and Young Gentlemen who can speak from experience.

Simpson's advertisement certainly seems to show a closer resemblance to Squeers's version than this one in January 1818, for Shaw's academy at Bowes:

> EDUCATION, by Mr. SHAW, and able Assistants, at Bowes Academy, near Greta Bridge, Yorkshire. Youth are carefully instructed in the English, Latin, and Greek Languages, Writing, Common and Decimal Arithmetic, Bookkeeping, Mensuration, Surveying. Geometry, Geography, and Navigation; with the most useful Branches of the Mathematics: and

are provided with Board, Clothes, and every Necessary, at TWENTY GUINEAS per Annum each. No extra charges whatever. No vacations, except by the parents' desire. —N.B. The French Language Two Guineas per annum extra. —Further particulars may be known on application to Mr, Davies, Carpenter, Lower Eaton-street, Pimlico; Mr. Seaton, 91, Whitecross-street, St. Luke's; Mr. Annison, 10, Bedford-court, Covent-garden; Mr. Mattison, 30, Church-row, Pancras; and Mr. Bulman, 9, Cross-street, Finsbury-square, who is Agent, and will give the most respectable references to the parents of others at the above Seminary, as well those who have completed their Education there.

Mr. SHAW may be seen daily at the George and Blue Boar, Holborn, between eleven and one o'clock.

Other details which suggest that Woden Croft, as it was during Edward Simpson's time, was a specific point of interest for Dickens include not only the documented accounts of the school's issue of brimstone and treacle – (although this was also a feature of other similar establishments) – and the possible derivation of some of the circumstances of poor Smike and his attempt to run away from Dotheboys Hall in the tale of *Nicholas Nickleby*, but also various other details unique to Woden Croft. There is, for example, an awful tale connected with this school regarding a boy who ran away like Smike (the 'repudiated' son of Ralph Nickleby), was caught and returned, only to be punished by being stripped naked, tied to a door with ropes, and carried to where the other pupils were in bed, to be mercilessly flogged in front of them. An account of this incident, asserted to have happened to the 'original' Smike, was published in 1919, in the *Methodist Recorder*, given by a Thomas Cooke, whose father, Bold Cooke, was at Woden Croft from the tender age of six – he started there in 1804, so not so many years before Frederick Crewe Haswell.[3] When asked if conditions were as bad as those at Dotheboys Hall, his son confirmed that this was so, using as an example the description of the shortage of soap and towels, as detailed by Squeers, to Nicholas Nickleby. Thomas Cooke stated: 'Now, at Woden Croft, they had neither soap nor towels. The boys had to go to a well a little way from the house to wash, and for soap they used a sort of marl or clay which surrounded the well; they dried themselves on their garments.'

There have been comparative studies made of the mortality rates at the Yorkshire schools and claims by some that the number of deaths among pupils were not in any way above average, compared to figures for the North Riding at this time. But this is arguably a false comparison, as one might expect middle-class boys of the ages attending these establishments to have had a higher expectation of life: and many of those who died are likely to have been buried elsewhere.

Edward Simpson died in January 1824, only days after John Crewe's will was written. Frederick was then around seventeen years old (his exact date of birth is unclear) and according to the will had been living with Simpson at Woden Croft. It would appear that there was no sense of urgency in recalling him from school and clearly he had remained there, despite any doubts about the Yorkshire academies that might have arisen from the previous year's notorious court case, reported in *The Times*, involving William Shaw and his negligent supervision of boys at the Bowes Academy. Shaw was found to be responsible for causing boys to lose their sight as a result of infection from insanitary conditions: he was obliged to pay substantial damages, reports of which were later studied by Dickens.

The identity of the mother of Frederick Crewe Haswell is not certain, but there is a record of the baptism of a Frederick Crewe, on 3 August 1806, at St Marylebone parish church, to John and Charlotte Crewe – Charlotte's name first being given wrongly and crossed through. More interestingly, among the records of several amended entries for St James Piccadilly's registers, there is a statement dated 1836 by Charlotte Mills, formerly Haswell, spinster, of Bakers Cottage, Stroud Green, who declares that she used the name Charlotte Haswell when she married a John Mills at the parish church in 1812. It would seem likely, therefore, that Charlotte was the mother of Frederick Crewe Haswell – and that either Lord Crewe or his son John was the father. It may even be the case that Charlotte was an earlier example of a woman tricked into taking part in a bogus wedding ceremony, and that, at the time of the baptism of her son, she believed that she and John Crewe were husband and wife.

It is not impossible, in theory at least, that Frederick was Lord Crewe's son: he would have been in his sixties when the child was born, which perhaps makes it less likely – although we are expected to believe that John Dickens's father was of a similar age when he married and fathered two sons, shortly before his death.

What is significant, in any case, are the arrangements to make provision for the boy's education – while keeping him at a safe distance: in other words, there was a sense of responsibility for Frederick's support, but not a duty to acknowledgement by the Crewe family, or any chance of closer relations with him.

Chapter Eight

Playing the fool

Is it really a credible idea that Mr Crewe's housekeeper had a child, or children, by her employer? It might seem unlikely, based on what little we know, or think we know, about Elizabeth Dickens's character. She made a late marriage at the age of thirty-six, and was evidently a strong and capable woman, trusted to run a large aristocratic household – at the same time as bringing up two sons with no father. She would appear, from her length of employment, her financial transactions, and the careful arrangements of her will, to have been careful and sensible, disciplined and reliable. Would she have been reckless enough, earlier in life, to risk her position, and her security, by engaging in some sort of liaison with John Crewe? Or with one of his friends? Willingly or not, it may be so. Women in service were vulnerable and often powerless to refuse the attentions of an employer. And we think of Elizabeth through Dickens's eyes, and the memory of a child, in awe of an elderly and formidable grandmother, forgetting that once she was a younger woman, living on the margins of a privileged and unconventional circle of aristocrats and society figures.

Is it at all possible then, that, as some have wondered, Richard Brinsley Sheridan was the father of John Dickens? Is he likely to have fathered a child by a servant? In fact, at the time her sons were born, Elizabeth Dickens, who was only three years or so older than Frances Anne Crewe, had not been promoted to her later position of authority, and so may have been easy prey for a libidinous house guest – and, as we shall see, it is important to note that Sheridan was certainly recorded as having pursued at least one other employee of the Crewes – and fathered a child in the process.

Although what are commonly held to be Dickens's representations of his grandmother focus on the depiction of an older woman, he is careful to remind us that Mrs Rouncewell, the housekeeper in *Bleak House*, was a handsome woman, even as he portrays her impeccable loyalty to the Dedlocks, and dutiful submission to her responsibilities in their household.

It does seem unusual that, if it is true that William Dickens was in his sixties at the time of his marriage, he had then, at that advanced point in his life, taken a younger wife and then fathered two children, one of them in the last twelve months before his death. William Dickens is said to have been born in 1783, although we must rely on his date of baptism, as stated two years later, for this information. John Dickens was born in 1785, apparently just weeks before his father's death. The boys' joint baptism, interestingly, took place only two days before the Crewe family's departure abroad, in November 1785. It is tempting to wonder if this is entirely coincidental and we need perhaps to consider another line of speculation about the paternity – or maternity – of John Dickens, even if it may seem rather unlikely at first glance.

The affair between Frances Anne and Sheridan continued at this point, as Sheridan's wife Elizabeth noted wryly in a letter to a friend, which is said to have been written in November 1785, again just before the Crewes were to leave London for the Continent: 'S is in Town – and so is Mrs Crewe. I am in the Country – and so is Mr Crewe – a very convenient arrangement, is it not?'

The Crewes had decided to travel first to Spa, and Brussels, before moving on to Paris. The choice of their first destination is interesting: Spa was then popular with the fashionable classes for social reasons, but clearly primarily for those in search of the perceived health-giving properties of the waters. For women taking the waters at Bath, or Spa, or several similar venues, this was often because they were trying to become pregnant (Georgiana, Duchess of Devonshire and her husband had visited Bath for such a purpose) – or for those recovering from childbirth. Was Frances Anne Crewe in a delicate state of health? She appears, from comments made in her journal, and at least one letter, to have been recovering from some sort of illness. In Paris she refers to a cold, but that is unlikely to have been the reason for travelling weeks earlier to Spa, and more possibly a pretext for remaining, as she did, reluctant to engage in any particularly hectic social activities on her first arrival.

Once she arrived in Paris, we have a good account of her stay from the journal that has survived and which was published for the first time in 2011,[1] with a foreword and notes by Michael Allen. Did Elizabeth Dickens travel with the family? We do not know, but it is not impossible – certainly they took some of their servants with them.

The diary, as Allen concludes, is likely to be based on letters written to Sheridan. The intimate tone and artful liveliness of these letters is certainly compatible with the idea of a woman writing to a lover whose interest she wants to retain, someone she must impress with her thoughts on theatre, the arts, and social customs, feeding him with details she thinks he will enjoy, with literary and many theatrical quotations: flattering him as the 'wise friend', filling her correspondence with tantalising snippets of Parisian gossip – and reviews of plays and performances that she had seen.

Frances Anne's long affair with Sheridan, in truth, was nearing its end, and probably in the last year or so of its duration. Although they would continue to be close friends, perhaps here we see evidence of her attempt to maintain the relationship as it was, intimate and central to her emotional life.

That the letters which were later copied (and presumably edited to remove any indiscreet personal details) were meant for someone with whom her relationship is not one that can be openly acknowledged is evidenced by the diary entry of Friday, 23 February, which begins in teasing fashion, but makes an admission that is telling:

> An Actress should not be Italian, or French, or English. She should be a Woman and nothing more – how pleasant it is to write to you upon all this! and certain I feel that you will explain to me much better what I really think upon this Subject – To say the truth you were often in my Head when I wrote my Spa and Brussells Journal, but as I knew other People would see them I did not feel quite so secure as I do now …

'Other people' might have included her husband, John Crewe, who had accompanied his wife to Spa, and Brussels, and went with her to Paris, but returned from there to England after three weeks or so. Frances Anne alludes to her state of health, at the beginning of the diary, in a way that implies the recipient would know that she had not been in good health. It may be significant that although the letters from the period of her time abroad that was spent in Paris were transcribed, there would appear to be no surviving copies of the journals kept in the earlier part of her travels, that is to say during the month or so that she spent in Spa and then Brussels, during which time we know she was unwell. As Allen notes, this was reported by the son of Edmund Burke, who wrote to his father on 25 December that he had just been at Mrs Crewe's, recently arrived in Paris, who had been ill at Brussels, but was 'quite recover'd'. The journal entries suggest that on arrival she continued to be keen on resting, rather than rushing into the bustle of social engagements, and then appears to have 'a Cold', which she says necessitates the eating of boiled chicken quietly at home, due to fatigue.

There is another possibility, perhaps, which should be considered here regarding the paternity of John Dickens – and possibly his brother, no matter how extraordinary it might seem. Bearing in mind the rumours reported by Gladden, that both John Crewe and his wife had illegitimate children, one might need to consider, however unlikely it may appear at first: that John Dickens may have been the son of Sheridan, not by Elizabeth, but by Frances Anne Crewe.

It is interesting to note that the date of birth of both William and John Dickens, if accurate, would mean that they were both conceived during the time of year in which the Crewes traditionally retired to their Cheshire home, Crewe Hall: William in mid-December and John in November. This was when Sheridan – and usually his wife – would make their annual visit. There are newspaper accounts that report Sheridan had an unfortunate habit of suffering accidents during his stays, which confirm his presence there: on 9 October 1787, for example, the *Chester Courant* explained that, 'Richard Brinsley Sheridan Esq. has received a violent Fall from his Horse, and is confined at present at Crewe Hall, the seat of Mr Crewe …' On 30 October, the same newspaper reported that, 'Mr Sheridan is quite recovered from his late Accident at Crewe Hall'. Sheridan was there again in January and early February 1788, writing his speech for the trial of Warren Hastings.

On 1 February 1790, a short piece in the *Caledonian Mercury* noted that Mr Sheridan was confined to quarters due to a 'leg injury'. Quite how he received this injury is not clear – but his confinement to quarters appears to have happened too late, on this visit, to avert another unfortunate event, as we shall see, involving him and a member of the Crewes' female servants.

It is true that occasionally parliamentary duties may have required the attendance of John Crewe at Parliament, and therefore residence in London, at a time when usually the family would be in Cheshire: but then so was Sheridan, whose political career had begun in 1780, after being elected as MP for Stafford, not so far from Crewe. From 1784 to 1791, Sheridan lived at Bruton Street, conveniently close to the Crewes' townhouse in Lower Grosvenor Street.

It is clear, therefore, that the lives of Frances Anne Crewe and Sheridan allowed plenty of opportunity for them to sustain a frequently intimate relationship, and it would seem perfectly possible, if not probable, that at some point in their decade-long affair Frances Anne might have become pregnant as a result. What did other women in her level of society do in such circumstances?

A range of unusual solutions were at the time being found to foster the inconvenient children of such liaisons within the circles favoured by Frances Anne and her friends. Various examples are recorded in which arrangements were made for the discreet removal – and sometimes later reintroduction to the household – of children fathered by lovers, or children fathered by husbands with their mistresses, arranged often enough with the tacit agreement of their spouses. These children might eventually discover their true parentage, or they might not: in some cases, any regular contact with their parent would be explained as the interest of a godparent, or distant relative.

The history of the Devonshire House set includes several examples of illegitimate babies born abroad, or in seclusion elsewhere, fostered and then taken back within the wider family household, sometimes as wards, or even foundlings: and notably, in one case, one such child is known to have been born as a result of events that took place at Crewe Hall, and involving the lover of Frances Anne Crewe.

Although the Crewes had had four children together since they had married in 1766, no more seem to have been born to the couple after 1780, the year before William and Elizabeth Dickens married. Frances Anne was only thirty-two, and there was no obvious reason why she and John Crewe would not have had further children, if they were still sexually intimate. Perhaps they were not: the affair between Mrs Crewe and Sheridan was at its height and seems to have become a central part of the established pattern of their lives. When Sheridan and Frances Anne Crewe were involved with each other, as two sexually active, healthy adults with children by their respective spouses, it would perhaps be unusual if their intimacy over the course of so many years did not result in pregnancy at some point. It might even be questionable as to whether her daughter, Emma, born in 1780, was the child of John Crewe, or Sheridan. If the latter, it would appear that Crewe accepted her as his own and, of course, the birth of a daughter, in a dynastic sense, was not of the same importance as a son and heir, or second heir. After her birth, however, when Frances Anne's affair with Sheridan would have been continuing and perhaps had caused a cessation of any intimate relations with her husband, any further pregnancy would clearly not have resulted in a child he would be likely to acknowledge. And although a long-standing affair appears to have been tolerated by John Crewe, there must have been an acceptance, by all parties, that he would not tolerate any public scandal, should it become common knowledge and pose a risk to his own reputation.

This dilemma, the birth of a child to a married woman by her lover, was one faced by a number of other aristocratic and fashionable households of the time, even beyond the immediate bounds of the Devonshire House circle. It might seem far-fetched to speculate that such a child might have been fostered by trusted servants – but extraordinary solutions to similar dilemmas were demanded – and were found – in several other cases involving children born to women in this set, including friends – and employees – of Mrs Crewe. And as we shall see, there is some evidence that suggests an illegitimate child of her son John was informally adopted and brought up by senior servants in another aristocratic household.

Pregnancy, at this time, was much easier to conceal, due to the loose-shaped gowns of the period, but only up to a point: and once that point was passed, a solution had to be found that in most cases involved a secret birth, often abroad, and discreet arrangements for the fostering of inconvenient children. In one case that was a slightly different version of this solution to extramarital, aristocratic pregnancies, we know that a great deal of effort was made to conceal the birth of a child born as a result of a liaison with Sheridan: one that took place during one of his many visits to Crewe Hall.

Several sources – contemporary and more recent – allude to this incident, when the governess to little Emma Crewe was found in a compromising situation with Frances Anne's erstwhile lover while he was on a visit to Crewe Hall only a year or so after their relationship had come to an end and soon after the revelation, in the summer of 1789, of Sheridan's affair with the Duchess of Devonshire's sister Harriet, then Lady Duncannon, later known as Lady Bessborough.

It was an affair that had threatened to trigger a sensational divorce case. Within a few months of this narrowly averted action, Sheridan was already moving on to new conquests. His wife, Elizabeth, whose usual tolerance of her husband's philandering was wearing rather thin, reported in a letter to her friend Mrs Canning,[2] in January 1790:

> … at the moment almost in wh he was swearing and imprecating all sorts of Curses on himself on me and his Child, if ever he was led away by any Motive to be false to me again, he threw the whole Family at Crewe into Confusion and Distress, by playing the fool with Miss Fd [Ford] (little Emma's governess) …

'Fd' here appears to have been interpreted as short for Ford, as quoted in Claire Tomalin's biography of Dickens,[3] but in my view it would seem to be a misread transcription of what should be 'Td' for Townsend, as the governess charged with the care of the Crewes' daughter Emma was a Caroline Townsend – whose father Thomas had been for many years steward to Earl Spencer, father of Georgiana, Duchess of Devonshire, and Harriet, Lady Bessborough. Thomas Townsend remained an intimate and essential part of the family's household, relied upon at moments of crisis, a trusted, loyal and discreet servant.

Sheridan, when no longer Mrs Crewe's lover, had remained her friend, even as he turned his attention to Georgiana's sister Harriet, but he seems to have been happy enough to risk offending Frances Anne – as well as his wife – by taking advantage of her hospitality and indulging in a sexual dalliance with a trusted member of her own household staff.

That he was used to consorting with the Crewes' extended household, and even the local tenantry, is suggested by one anecdote repeated in Fintan O'Toole's biography of Sheridan.[4] Sheridan was fond of staging practical jokes to tease his hosts, when enjoying their hospitality, elaborate deceptions often involving the use of disguise, and with predictably farcical consequences:

> At Crewe Hall, when the owner expressed a desire to meet his friend Joseph Richardson, he announced that he had invited him and that he would visit the next day. When he arrived, Richardson's language seemed disgustingly lewd and vulgar, his manners disturbingly odd. Only when the visitor had sufficiently unsettled his hosts did Sheridan reveal that he had in fact paid one of Crewe's tenants to impersonate Richardson.

In a rather more serious incident, Sheridan is reported to have been caught in flagrante with the governess – a woman described by the biographer of the Duchess of Devonshire, Amanda Foreman, as 'intelligent, but plain' – in a bedroom in Crewe Hall.[5] In her letter, Eliza Sheridan, whose beauty Fanny Burney stated to be unequalled by anyone's other than Mrs Crewe, and who was on amicable terms with her husband's former mistress, describes the exposure of Sheridan's involvement with Miss Townsend with as much disapproval for the lack of discretion, as anything else:

> … contriving so awkwardly too, as to be discovered by the whole House, locked up with her in a Bed Chamber in an unfrequented part of the House … this last instance of his duplicity, the apparent want of all feeling for me, of all sense of Honour, Delicacy, Propriety, considering

> the Person, the Place, and the Time when he indulged so unwarrantable an inclination, provok'd me so much beyond all bounds …

Whether or not the incident with the governess was as part of a consensual liaison is not known – Sheridan was known for a somewhat unscrupulous approach to seduction, so it may not have been. Whatever the truth, the pursuit of Miss Townsend resulted in one particularly unfortunate consequence for her: she became pregnant.

Georgiana, Duchess of Devonshire, and her sister Harriet would also bear children fathered by lovers, born in secret, before sending them to be cared for elsewhere: Lady Elizabeth Foster, intimate friend of Georgiana, mistress (and future second wife) of her husband, the Duke of Devonshire, had already resorted to this plan of action in regard to the arrival of her daughter by the Duke, Caroline St Jules, who was born in Italy in 1785 – and then her son Augustus Clifford, born in France three years later.

Georgiana and Harriet now arranged for the unfortunate governess, the daughter of their father's steward, to have Sheridan's baby abroad, and later introduced the child into the Devonshire household as a 'foundling', whom they named 'Fanny Mortimer'. According to Foreman, the child remained there, 'inhabiting a nether world between the servants' quarters and the nursery'. When it was necessary, not so long afterwards, for Georgiana to flee to France with Harriet in order to have her baby by Charles Grey, in secret, and then handed over to others to rear – by a neat turn of events, it would be the same governess's father, Thomas Townsend, who accompanied them.

Turning to the suggestion that Elizabeth Dickens might have given birth to John Dickens after some sort of encounter with Sheridan: if he had been interested in an apparently plain governess in the Crewe household, it is likely that he had previously tried a similar approach to other female servants in the past and may have done so with Elizabeth if she had caught his attention. However, she was hardly of the age that he seemed to prefer, and it is hard to imagine a woman in her position, and from the little we know of her a cautious and steady woman, willingly engaging in such a liaison. But then female servants, and indeed women of all classes, were always at risk of forced sexual relations with male employers, or their guests.

In his biography of Sheridan, O'Toole makes the point that, as a consequence of a childhood in which he was frequently estranged from his family, Sheridan felt strongly that the bond between parent and child was precious: 'When he had children of his own, he worried incessantly about them, so much so that Charles Grey advised him to put his son in a glass case. He hated his children to be left in the care of servants, even for a day or two.'

That would be the Charles Grey whose own child by the Duchess of Devonshire, Eliza Courtenay, was born in Montpellier, in southern France, and was eventually brought up by his parents as his much younger sister. Sheridan's daughter with Caroline Townsend was protected by his former lover Harriet, Lady Bessborough, and her sister Georgiana, although the child's status within the household was reportedly ill defined. However, she had certainly been well looked after, if not acknowledged by him: he would no doubt have made some effort to help any other child that he had fathered.

If, as some have concluded, John Dickens really was his child, it might explain the efforts said to have been made by Sheridan to secure for him, in 1805, a promotion in the Navy Pay Office, where he had been working as a clerk, reportedly after the Crewes' friend Canning, who had preceded him as Treasurer to the Navy, had obtained a post for him: a persistent rumour that is worth further investigation.

Chapter Nine

John Dickens and Thomas Powell

In January 1807, during the short period that Sheridan was in post as Treasurer to the Navy, John Dickens was promoted to 'Fifteenth Assistant clerk for the general business of the Pay Branch'. And here is an intriguing story: in his book about Charles Dickens's childhood, Michael Allen reports that around the same time John Dickens was sent on a trip to Portsmouth, to carry a despatch to the Chief Clerk of the Pay Yard – and to escort back to London the wife of the Paymaster of the Forces – Mrs Richard Brinsley Sheridan.

He cites as his reference the article by the writer Thomas Powell, published in 1887, in *Frank Leslie's Sunday Magazine*.[1] This article, with the title 'Leaves from my life', has to be read with some caution, as Powell and Dickens had fallen out many years earlier, despite once being close friends: Powell was the manager, at John Chapman & Co., of Charles's black sheep younger brother, Augustus. It became apparent, at one point, that Powell, who was an accomplished forger, had swindled an astonishing sum of £10,000 from his employer – and after attempting to feign madness to escape the consequences of his criminal activity, eventually ended up in America where, in 1849, from a safe distance, he began to cause trouble for Dickens, who was eventually obliged to take action to keep him quiet: Powell knew far too much about Dickens's family and personal life.

Seventeen years after Dickens's death, and in the year that would be Powell's last, here he is, writing about his life, and passing on anecdotes about Dickens, and his family – including Charles's father John, whom he claims to have known, describing him as:

> a very handsome, portly man, of courtly and genial manners … He was as fond of good living, including brandy-and-water, as his son's great creation Mr Pickwick, and like most genial and courtly men, he was of a kindly disposition, and ever ready to help a friend, and also to be helped by one. He was the original of Wilkins Micawber, who was a very indulgent, shiftless husband, and always waiting for something to turn up.

Powell continues:

> Old John Dickens was a very pleasant, companionable man, and full of anecdote. In his early manhood he had been a clerk in the Paymaster's Office, Somerset House, London, and was there when that brilliant wit, author, and orator, Richard Brinsley Sheridan, who was also an impecunious scamp, was, mirabile dictum, Paymaster of the Forces. He told me several anecdotes of the author of the *School for Scandal*, characteristic of that brilliant wonder. I will endeavour to relate one which shows his fertility of resources when he was hard up.
>
> One morning, as John Dickens was adding up two and two, and trying to make them four when they are really twenty-two, the messenger of his department informed him that Mr Sheridan wanted to see him in his private office. As he was Sheridan's favourite clerk, John Dickens went to him, thinking it was on some trifling matter, such as filing a letter, or finding one. He was, therefore, somewhat surprised when Paymaster Sheridan told him that he was going to send him to Portsmouth on some very important business; in point of fact, to carry a private despatch to the Chief Clerk of the Portsmouth Navy Yard.

Powell claims that Sheridan gave John Dickens an order for £60 to accomplish his mission, and as he dismissed him, his clerk, 'out of reverence for the hand that had written *The School for Scandal*, raised it to his lips and kissed it'. He continues '... so terribly had dissipation shaken the nerves of the Cabinet Minister, that this simple act of homage from a young admirer drew tears to his eyes'.

As John Dickens was leaving, we are told, Sheridan called him back and asked him to accompany Mrs Sheridan, who was then at Portsea, near Portsmouth, back to London, and that he would ask her to meet him at the 'Clarence Head' in order to travel back with him. Powell claimed that Sheridan was using his position as Paymaster to use the public purse to pay for his wife's journey and pocket a few quid for himself at the same time.

Setting aside the fulsome language and remarkable wealth of imaginative detail offered by Powell's story, it is not entirely impossible that there might be a grain of truth in this anecdote. Sheridan was Paymaster to the Navy for just over a year, from February 1806 to March 1807. He had the very generous salary of around £4,000 a year – although he would only enjoy this appointment for thirteen months, and as he was continually under financial pressure, it may not have helped much with his level of expenditure.

His new post came with the right to a set of apartments at Somerset House. Although Sheridan is hardly likely to have immersed himself in any of the day-to-day organisation of Naval payment processes, letters from the period show that he did use his rooms at Somerset House, where John Dickens worked. About a third of the former palace was then occupied by the Navy Pay Office: Dickens's maternal grandfather, Charles Barrow, had been allocated his own set of rooms there, after his promotion around five years earlier from clerk to 'Chief Conductor of Monies in Town'– his son Thomas had started work there too, with John Dickens, and it was through their friendship that Elizabeth Barrow first met Dickens's father.

Sheridan did have family connections with the wider area around Portsmouth: his second wife Esther Ogle was from nearby Southampton and his letters show that they often spent time there, visiting family, or for their health, sometimes sea bathing: Sheridan was also fond of sailing around the coastline in this area in his small cutter *Phaedria*.

It is not clear what Powell meant by the 'Clarence Head', but there was a Clarence Hotel in Portsmouth: in fact, two – one in the second half of the nineteenth century, well after Powell had left for America – but there was an earlier hotel of this name in the Georgian period, definitely still in 1814, as there is a report in the *Hampshire Telegraph* of that year of Marshal Blücher staying there.

It might just be the case, therefore, that Powell's story is not entirely fictional, and that John Dickens had escorted Mrs Sheridan back to London on one of his visits to Portsmouth: he would be moved to a post there within the next year. If so, how curious a tale this is, if only because of the connections between the Crewes, their servants, Elizabeth and William Dickens, and the Sheridans. Even more interesting, of course, if the rumour about Sheridan was true, and John Dickens was his son. Perhaps he had found it amusing to allow his wife to meet the boy, if this really was the case.

John Dickens may have met Sheridan in the course of his employment at Somerset House, and told Powell about it: if so, Powell would seem not to know of the Crewe connection, or if he did, chose not to allude to it: in that case, if he did know of any rumours that connected the Crewe family, and Sheridan, to John Dickens, the telling of this story may well have been an act of mischief – and one that would have been characteristic of his trouble-making tendencies.

In his biography of Dickens, Peter Ackroyd appears to have taken Powell's tale of Sheridan and John Dickens at face value, although without attributing it to him, suggesting that Dickens's father is 'mentioned' in his first published story – *A Dinner at Poplar Walk* – which includes a red-whiskered 'smirking man' who had been 'endeavouring to obtain a listener to some stories about Sheridan', 'that truly great and illustrious man ...'. The main character, Mr Augustus Minns, is visiting his cousin Mr Budden, a clerk at Somerset House, which may indicate Dickens's line of thought, if indeed his father was in the habit of relating the Sheridan tale, repeated by Powell. Or perhaps John Dickens had hinted at a rather closer link with him, a suggestion that Charles Dickens is unlikely to have ignored and may have relished.

Dickens's father was twenty years old when he was given his post at the Navy Office: what had he been doing before then? Did he support himself? His later history would suggest that this is unlikely. It would seem clear that he felt entitled to a standard of living to which he would appear to have had no claim by rank, and no means of achieving by his own efforts.

As Claire Tomalin comments, whether Sheridan, or Lord Crewe (or any man other than William Dickens), really was the father of John Dickens is less important, perhaps, than that John, and perhaps his son, may have believed it to be true – or wished it so – and perhaps encouraged others to think the same. It should be noted, perhaps, that he had chosen to name his eldest daughter Frances Elizabeth – Frances before his own mother's name, Elizabeth. This may have been to incur favour from Frances Anne Crewe, for whom his mother was still housekeeper at this point in 1810 – or to imply some sort of closer association. What is clear, in any case, is the extent of the impact and influences upon John Dickens, the young boy, and the young man, in growing up attached to the Crewe household, yet not of it. The sense of being on the edge, as only an outsider, an observer, of a glittering world of wealth, political intrigue, and literary fame; where some of the most brilliant figures of the age, beautiful, clever women and influential men, lived a life of ease and privilege, clearly left its mark. If he felt he belonged there, he must have struggled to contain a sense of resentment, as well as an appetite for a standard of living that, as it would for his son's character Micawber, would always be beyond his means, and so often lead on to the road to poverty, debt – and even imprisonment.

As Michael Slater observed of John Dickens:[2]

> John favoured a richly orotund style in speech and writing on which Dickens later modelled Mr Micawber's idiolect, and Forster states that no one could know John "without secretly liking him the better for these

> flourishes of speech, which adapted themselves so readily to his gloom as well as to his cheerfulness".

According to Forster, Dickens – at least in later life – appeared to find his father's way of speaking amusing and passed on several examples of his 'rhetorical exuberance'.

John Dickens's grandiosity in speech might well have been his attempt to ape the oratorical style of the circle of politicians and society figures that frequented the Crewe household: Sheridan's wit and flamboyant style of repartee being one example. The peculiar affectation in manner of speech of the Devonshire House set is well documented: distinguishing them as members of an elite circle of power, within the wider network of fashionable society. Those on the sidelines, looking on, would not think of seeking to emulate the language and customs of their superiors: unless they felt, perhaps, that they too should be a part of the same circle, but for a mischance of birth.[3]

Did John Dickens pass on to Charles a suspicion, or perhaps inspire a self-constructed fantasy, that Sheridan, or Lord Crewe, may have been his father – or even that Frances Anne may have been his mother? Perhaps it was something that could be hinted at, and left unexplored, on the pretext of discretion. Subconsciously, Charles Dickens may have felt he was more naturally entitled to be the grandson of a writer, and politician, than of a servant: a sort of psychological annexation of a preferred ancestry, unacknowledged, hence the interest in Sheridan, his work – and even his family, as we will explore.

There is, of course, an alternative, if somewhat more prosaic, explanation for the generosity of the Crewe family to William Dickens, his widow and her sons – an explanation that is possibly more likely.

Placed as they were at the heart of the household of a socially prominent couple whose intimate lives and private affairs were, if not exactly unusual in terms of their peers, certainly remarkably relaxed in terms of marital fidelity and sexual impropriety, it must have been imperative that servants such as William and Elizabeth Dickens were reliably loyal, discreet, and that they remained dependent on the goodwill of their employers.

The affair between Frances Anne Crewe and Sheridan lasted many years, perhaps more than a decade, possibly from as early as 1775 to around 1787: and it is unlikely that the intimate nature of their relationship was something that would have gone unnoticed by their household staff. Affairs may have been commonplace in the circle in which the Crewes moved, but discretion and an appearance of respectability were of paramount importance, and indeed becoming increasingly so, in the subtly changing standards of morality of the age. It is unlikely that within the family's households, however, the indiscretions of their employers and their guests could remain unobserved. Taking an interest in the welfare and comfort of their more senior servants, therefore, would have been crucial to the maintenance of such a façade. Loyalty and silence may have been rewarded by the promotions we know they received – and what would appear to be years of generous financial payments, and support for their children. In short, the rather privileged position of Dickens's grandparents may literally have been secured by a long-running performance of 'what the butler saw'.

Just as the loyalty of Thomas Townsend, the former steward of Earl Spencer, was relied upon to facilitate the flight of the Duchess of Devonshire and the secret birth of her baby in France, his own grandchild, little Fanny Mortimer, the child of Sheridan and his daughter, the Crewes' governess, would be raised as part of the Devonshire household, even if in that 'nether world' between nursery and the servants' quarters. A bond of trust and interdependence between such servants and their employers hid many secrets in these circles at this time.

In the next generation of the Crewe family, moreover, there would appear to have been another example of an illegitimate child being fostered by senior servants, a circumstance naturally highly dependent on their loyalty and cooperation.

It is believed by some descendants that a cleric with the name of the Reverend John Griffiths, born – or at least baptised – in Byford, Herefordshire, in 1813, was really the son of the younger John Crewe, fostered and brought up by a John Taylor Griffiths and his wife, Ann. Significantly, perhaps, in terms of a potentially similar background to the early life of John Dickens, John Taylor Griffiths was the much respected and long-serving butler to a Sir John Geers Cotterell, twice elected MP for Herefordshire, a landowner of substantial means, and resident at the family estate of Garnons, near Byford. John Taylor Griffiths died after more than fifty years' service and was said to have been 'an old and faithful servant', 'highly respected and esteemed' for qualities such as his 'sobriety, integrity and zeal', and his death was felt keenly by his employer.

This butler's son, adopted or not, was fortunate enough to attend Christ Church, Oxford, after which he was ordained and followed a career in the Church: one that was largely spent in India, where he was eventually appointed senior chaplain to Madras Cathedral. India, of course, was always a favoured destination for problematic family members: younger sons, or sons marked by the stigma of illegitimacy.

Reverend John Griffith's children were all born in India, including a son who was christened, in 1855, as Talbot Monckton Milnes Griffiths: the middle two names being clear references to the Crewe family – Annabel Crewe, daughter of General John Crewe, had married Richard Monckton Milnes (a close friend of Charles Dickens) four years earlier.

Sources claim that Annabel and other family members were aware of, and perhaps even engaged with, the two illegitimate children of their brother, their half-sister and half-brother. Perhaps the decision to identify Talbot Griffiths in this way was some indication of an acknowledged connection. Talbot, who followed his father into the ministry, and would also undertake many years of service in India, would give his own son Theodore, born in 1886, the middle name of Houghton: of course, Annabel Crewe had become Lady Houghton when her husband was elevated to the peerage in 1863.

The pattern of names used within the Griffiths family would certainly seem to confirm at least that they believed there was a close association with the Crewes. And closer inspection of the record of Talbot Griffith's career would appear to suggest that there may well have been a tacit recognition between the two families of some sort of kinship.

By the time of the 1911 census, Talbot and his wife were now in England. After service in India, he had taken up the position of Rector at Warmingham, only 4 miles or so from Crewe Hall. The appointment to Warmingham was in the gift of the Earl of Crewe, who was the son of Annabel, Lady Houghton – and grandson of General John Crewe; Talbot's entry in *Crockford's Directory* for 1908 also reveals that he had become Honorary Chaplain to the Earl of Crewe, four years earlier. Was Talbot Griffiths a cousin of the Earl of Crewe, and like his patron, a grandson of the disgraced John Crewe? The circumstantial evidence for this argument is compelling: and if this was the case, parallels with the favoured position of John Dickens, the apparent son of the Crewes' own faithful butler and housekeeper, might well be of significant interest: was this another, earlier example of an illegitimate member of the Crewe family brought up by senior servants as their own child?

Chapter Ten

Will and Sally: Uncle William Dickens and Sarah Latham

Whether or not the parents of John Dickens were William Dickens and his wife Elizabeth, there remain many unanswered questions about John's early life, and that of his older brother William: not just the matter of their education – or their employment when old enough to earn their own living. Now, we have new information that gives us some idea at least of Uncle William's occupation, at least in the latter years of his life.

Perhaps, like Mrs Rouncewell's son, in *Bleak House*, he had become a soldier: not an unlikely career move for a young man in the early years of the nineteenth century, and the continuing conflict with Napoleon's army in Europe, and beyond. It is perhaps significant that William married in late December 1815, only months after Waterloo, at the age of thirty-two. Had he returned from service abroad, met Sarah, and decided to settle down?

William died in 1826, only forty-three years old, and only two years after his mother's death. His immediate address is given in his will, written the year before, as 16, South Molton Street, which is but a step away from Oxford Street. There is a record, however, at the London Archives, of a fire insurance document for a 'William Dickens, Gent', at number 20, South Molton Street, for the year 1817[1] – which means (assuming this is the same William Dickens, which seems probable) that his association with this street is much longer than previously thought.

It seems an extraordinary thing to contemplate that Dickens's uncle, while in South Molton Street, was for some years a close neighbour of the visionary artist and poet William Blake, who lodged in two rooms, on the first floor, at number 17, from 1804 to 1821. We don't know when Uncle William moved (if the change was not a matter of renumbering), but it may have been while Blake was living next door, and according to one source, in the habit of pinning works like the now lost 'The Last Judgement' to the wall adjoining No. 16: in one recorded instance, to display to a French woman who was a fellow lodger.[2] Whether his other neighbours were aware of his work is not known, although late in life Blake cut a somewhat eccentric figure in appearance and must have been the matter of some speculation by those living in the area.

Did Charles Dickens ever visit his uncle in South Molton Street, when William Blake was resident? It is not impossible: the Dickens family were living not so far away, in Norfolk Street, near Fitzroy Square, when Charles would have been round four years old.

As a somewhat precocious and observant child, perhaps he noticed or at least heard about his uncle's somewhat unconventional neighbour, whose literary wanderings through the 'charter'd streets', nearby the 'charter'd Thames', would be revisited by Dickens in the later configuration of his own London landscape – as well as literally in the trail of his night walks.

On 28 December 1815, Dickens's uncle William had married a woman named Sarah Latham at St George's church, Hanover Square. The witnesses to his marriage were friends, rather than family members: surprising, perhaps. His mother may have been at Crewe Hall – or perhaps did not approve of the match – but his brother John and family, including the three-year-old Charles, had returned to London from Portsmouth at the beginning of the year.

William Dickens's death eleven years later was announced in the *Morning Post*, on Thursday, 7 December 1826, in a simple notice, immediately below that for the elderly daughter of a long-dead Baronet: 'On Tuesday last, in South Moulton-street, Mr William Dickens, aged 43 years.' One might suspect, after the notices placed in the *Morning Post* and elsewhere for the birth of his first son, that John Dickens may have been responsible for this announcement.

William may have described himself in his will as 'Gentleman', but, of course, he and his brother were the sons of servants. For the Dickens family, however, aspiration was always more important than reality: the marking of his brother's death in this way would have mattered to John Dickens, if no one else.

A relatively young age, forty-three, but it may have been that his health was not good, as his mother Elizabeth's will, only two years earlier, had been careful to state what should happen to her bequests should William predecease her. A woman of her advanced years would not generally expect to outlive her son.

In his will, written in April of that year, William Dickens is stated as being of South Molton Street, but 'late of Lower Grosvenor Street': originally, he had written 'of Oxford Street', but crossed it through. Had he and Sarah perhaps spent time living with his mother? The Lower Grosvenor Street address is interesting and it might seem likely that at one time he had been employed in the Crewe household. Perhaps his insistence in mentioning an old address was because he felt this was more impressive, even if it had not been his most recent lodging.

In South Molton Street, at No. 22, at this time, were hatters John and James Hunt: it seems likely that the friend, Mrs Sarah Hunt, mentioned in William's will, was the wife of one of these men. Sarah Dickens's sister Elizabeth Latham, before marriage, appears to have been listed as a hatter in Little Bell Alley in a London directory for 1822: the association with hat makers and the wider family circle of William and Sarah Dickens may explain perhaps the choice of lodgings in the same street.

Looking at the witnesses to his marriage to Sarah, we see the name of one George Reid. This helps identify William as a witness at a trial at the Old Bailey on 21 April 1819,[3] of one Evan Thomas, who was accused of stealing two and a quarter yards of silk serge – a fabric used for the linings of gentlemen's coats – from his employer, a tailor named George Reid, who was in partnership with a James Milne. 'Messrs Milne and Reid' were 'tailors and habit makers', whose place of business was at No. 8, Lower Grosvenor Street – just a few houses along from the Crewes' townhouse where Elizabeth Dickens worked.

The transcript of this hearing includes the evidence given by Dickens's uncle:

> WILLIAM DICKENS. I am the prosecutors' clerk. On 4th of February I went with Plank, and stationed myself at the corner of King-street – I had a view of Snaith's house, which is in King-street. In about ten minutes I saw Thomas cross the street, and go into Snaith's shop. We went round a little way, and then went into the shop, Plank told Snaith that a tailor in the neighbourhood had been robbed repeatedly, and he suspected the stolen goods were sold to him. I saw a piece of serge on the counter with our private mark on it, and told Plank that that was the piece which had been stolen that day …

At this point, therefore, William Dickens was working as a clerk for George Reid, and not as a coffee house keeper, or servant. Perhaps whatever education he and his brother had had did include book-keeping, after all: and perhaps some inkling of his uncle's bending over the ledgers of Messrs Milne and Reid became a half-formed notion in the younger Charles Dickens of the life of quiet drudgery such an occupation entailed as a basis for innumerable fictional clerks in his later work.

Uncle William, then, and Dickens's grandfather, would appear to be eminently respectable, modest, trustworthy and conscientious people: men you could rely upon to give evidence in court: steady and reliable.

John Dickens, on the other hand, although undoubtedly charming and good company, was not content to fit the family model of service and modest expectations: he had other aspirations, and fitted in more easily with the family of his wife, the Barrows, whose ambitions, often disappointed, were to escape the limitations of class and a dependence on the prosperity of those you served, and who had reason to be discreet about their own background.

Charles Barrow, like John Dickens, was unable to live within his means, and spent the last years of his life in exile to avoid prosecution for fraud. Curious that his daughter should marry a man whose mistakes so neatly resembled those of her own father – or perhaps Elizabeth Barrow found that such a match in some way fitted her expectations of married life.

John Dickens's relaxed attitude to matters of financial economy and his enjoyment of the finer things in life would appear to be in sharp contrast to the disciplined outlook of his mother and his older brother. Or so we would imagine. It maybe, however, that as ever the truth was more complex. In the case of Uncle William, for example, the closer one looks, the more questions arise.

George Reid died in 1833 and left a will to which one of the witnesses was a James Parnell. In the records of the King's Bench Prison for 1810–12[4] there is listed a William Dickins who owes a debt to a James Parnell and another creditor. Could this possibly be Dickens's uncle, enjoying the hospitality of a debtor's prison long before John Dickens so famously entered the Marshalsea unable to pay his own debts? Or is it another William – perhaps a member of the family living in the Grosvenor Square area?

Another interesting detail in Uncle William Dickens's will is the bequest he left to the committee of management of a chapel in Robert Street, also in the Grosvenor Square area. Robert Street, also previously known as Chandler Street, is now named Weighhouse Street, and runs between what are now Duke Street and Davies Street. In 1813, a chapel formerly operating as a Methodist place of worship was replaced by an independent congregation and in 1824 by a new building under the charge of the 'London Association for Extending the Gospel in the Metropolis and Its Environs'. This was exactly the sort of dissenting body whose practices were loathed by Charles Dickens: as early as 1836 he had written about the subject in *Sunday with Three Heads*, a pamphlet published under the name of 'Timothy Sparks'. It was a piece written in reaction to an attempt to introduce a Parliamentary bill to forbid working and recreational activities on Sundays:

> The preacher enters the pulpit. He is a coarse, hard-faced man of forbidding aspect, clad in rusty black, and bearing in his hand a small plain Bible from which he selects some passage for his text, while the hymn is concluding. The congregation fall upon their knees, and are hushed into profound stillness as he delivers an extempore prayer, in which he calls upon the Sacred Founder of the Christian faith to bless his ministry, in terms of disgusting and impious familiarity not to be described. He begins his oration in a drawling tone, and his hearers listen with silent attention. He grows warmer as he proceeds with his subject, and his gesticulation becomes proportionately violent. He clenches his fists, beats the book upon the desk before him, and swings his arms wildly about his head …

Dickens's work includes a disproportionate number of canting, hypocritical preachers: physically repellent, gluttonous, with a malign influence on their congregants. Stiggins in *Pickwick Papers* and Chadband in *Bleak House* are just two examples, and indeed *Bleak House*, which, as we will see, uses the experience of the Dickens's family background directly, expends a notable amount of effort on depicting the sanctimonious and self-serving behaviour of several characters who are influenced by evangelical or missionary Christian practice: Mrs Chadband, the former Mrs Rachael, Mrs Snagsby, Miss Barbary, Mrs Pardiggle and Mrs Jellyby.

The dislike of such clerics, their acolytes and their hysterical congregations seems to be of an intensity that must necessarily have been informed by personal experience, and one might wonder if he, as a child, had been taken to the Robert Street Chapel, or at least associated this type of evangelical fervour with his uncle. Such piety and sermonising would have appeared as a sharp contrast to the more relaxed approach of his parents, and John Dickens certainly exhibited a dislike of such religious leanings.

Perhaps Uncle William had been 'born again' and had taken to the revivalist movement in his middle years, or after he had met his wife. If so, it may perhaps have caused a certain distance with his brother's family, especially once John Dickens's rather more liberal lifestyle and financial indiscretions followed their course, and the family found themselves in straitened circumstances.

Whatever Dickens's uncle William was doing before he took up his post with George Reid, we do know that he managed to save significant amounts of money – including £100 in three per cent consols, in 1804, when he turned 21, and he continued to invest sums of money, as well as being entrusted with £750 from his mother in 1813. When Elizabeth Dickens died, in 1824, she had left £950, giving more to William than to John, as the latter had already had sums of money from her during her lifetime. When William died only two years later, he then left an estate of £1,300, a not unsubstantial amount of money for a man in his circumstances.

Charles Dickens was around fourteen years of age when William Dickens died, so presumably his uncle must have played some role in his childhood, but until now little has been known about him, or his wife, Sarah Latham, who lived on for much longer – and whose second marriage was to benefit Charles's family by returning to them the legacy of her first husband, which of course had included the estate of Dickens's grandmother.

Sarah's background, in fact, is worth a closer look, as it tells us more about the Dickens family's connection with the Crewes. Latham is a Cheshire name and found in abundance in the area immediate to Crewe Hall, to the extent that untangling the several families with this surname is almost impossible due to repetition of first names and the absence of details of mothers on baptismal records. We know that Sarah was born in Wybunbury, only 3 miles or so from Crewe Hall, around 1784, due to her details in census records. She was the daughter of a tenant farmer, William Latham, and his wife Mary Turner: the eldest of a large family. It seems likely that employment in the household of the Crewe family was the way in which they met.

Ten years after the death of William Dickens, Sarah remarried, to William Warder, a comfortably placed widower twelve years her senior, who had had a hat shop in Oxford Street. This marriage meant that the legacy left by her first husband reverted to the family of Charles Dickens, following the terms of his uncle William's will.

William Dickens described himself in his will as a 'gentleman': John Dickens also considered himself to be of this rank: was it because the brothers believed they had some right to belong to this class, by some connection to the Crewes, or due to their distant Dickins ancestors – or was it simply an affectation?

The origins of the Lathams would have been seen by the Crewes as being that of an ancient and worthy local family; solid yeoman stock in the main, but one branch of the family lived at nearby Bradwall Hall, at Sandbach. Another member of the extended family was the architect George Latham, who was summoned in 1836 to make alterations to Crewe Hall – although shortly dismissed in favour of another. But there is another interesting family member whose connection to Charles Dickens has perhaps been overlooked – or at least not seen in full context.

By curious coincidence – or a deliberate choice, perhaps – a member of the Bradwall Hall Lathams came to purchase Dickens's former home at Gad's Hill, twenty years after his death.

Francis Law Latham, born in 1837, a retired High Court judge, and a former Advocate General of Bombay, bought Gad's Hill in 1890, and lived there until his death in 1923. According to an obituary in the *Dickensian* of July that year (which made no note of any family connection), he was 'an ardent student of Dickens' and visited constantly by strangers wanting to view the property, to whom he was remarkably welcoming. The judge was perhaps aware of a distant family relationship with Dickens's aunt Sarah: Sarah's father, of course, had lived until he was over ninety, dying as late as 1851. Perhaps knowledge of the Latham connection with Dickens had survived, therefore, in the remaining families in the area around Crewe Hall.

Chapter Eleven

Bleak House revisited

Perhaps now we should return to *Bleak House*, and the secret at the core of the plot of this novel, first serialised in March 1852. This secret concerns a child born to Lady Dedlock, and given to foster parents to raise, her origins disguised. The reality of a 'natural' child fathered by an aristocrat, although barely acknowledged, was hardly uncommon: that a woman of this rank might have an illegitimate baby was far less so: how curious that *Bleak House*, Dickens's personal exploration of the world inhabited by his grandmother, father and uncle, should feature this particular indiscretion. What gave him the idea? Did it emerge from the story of Frederick Crewe Haswell, the boy who was sent to a Yorkshire school, and supported by John Crewe? Was it inspired by the story of the daughter born to the son of Lord and Lady Crewe? Or was it some sort of exploration of a closer family connection to the Crewe family?

Gilian West's article in the *Dickensian* in 1995[1] discusses some of the ways in which the history of the Crewes and even the physical descriptions of Chesney Wold are reflected in the story of *Bleak House*. West points out the many similarities between Chesney Wold and Crewe Hall: each surrounded by woods and an ornamental lake, both properties with a red-bricked courtyard and stables, and a 20ft-high gateway (Crewe Hall's original magnificent stonework arch being later demolished). Most telling is the interior description of Chesney Wold, with references to the old oak panelling and a dominant staircase. The use of heraldic creatures and escutcheons in the Dedlocks' home is easily identifiable as a dominant feature of Crewe Hall. If Dickens had not visited the house and estate as a child, he certainly may have done so as an adult: if not he may have seen the engravings which feature all these characteristics.

The article also mentions the husband of Mrs Rouncewell being buried in the Dedlocks' churchyard – we know from Hinchcliffe that loyal servants of the Crewes were buried at their church at Barthomley. Mrs Rouncewell, like Mrs Dickens, has two sons, one 'industrious', and the other estranged. That George Rouncewell, the 'lost' son of the housekeeper, has run away to become a soldier reminds us that the soldier son of the Crewes is their own family black sheep, cut off from the family – and eventually disinherited. (It might also support the theory that Uncle William Dickens's missing years were spent in military service.)

The Crewes' errant son, of course, like Lady Dedlock, had an illegitimate daughter: in Crewe's case by the young woman with whom he conducted a bogus marriage ceremony – just as Captain Nemo, whose real name was Hawdon, had fathered Esther with Lady Dedlock. He appears to have fathered other children out of wedlock too, of course.

The legitimate children of the Crewes' son would become wards of Chancery, just like Ada and Richard in *Bleak House*.

Mrs Rouncewell forgives her errant son and visits him in prison, where he is detained under a false accusation of murder. He had also been in trouble over a debt owed to a usurer, just as John Dickens had: it might be, as West suggests, that Mrs Dickens visited her son John in the debtors' prison, the Marshalsea, shortly before she died, perhaps to forgive him – or that Charles Dickens wished that it had been so.

The Dedlocks are noted as being similar to the Crewes: see Mrs Thrale's observation, from 1777, of the elder John Crewe's 'frigidity', which may be seen to be reflected in the character of Sir Leicester. And the emphasis in *Bleak House* on Lady Dedlock's beauty and the iconography of her portraits – including a reference to an engraving, a copy of which is owned by Tony Weevle – could easily be an echo of the contemporary mythologising of the attractions of Frances Anne Crewe.

With new evidence about the Dickens family background we now need to revisit *Bleak House* and reconsider the text from a more informed perspective: it becomes clear, knowing much more about Charles Dickens's grandparents, father and uncle, exactly how the narrative and context of this novel are influenced not just by the Crewe family but his own family's part in their history. The relationship between the Dedlocks, their housekeeper, and her sons is central to the progression of the story. Almost always, the plot from the viewpoint of the Dedlocks is introduced through reference first to Mrs Rouncewell or other servants: we arrive at the family houses in Chesney Wold, or London, and follow a powdered 'Mercury' into the presence of Sir Leicester or Lady Dedlock.

There are more than forty references to these 'Mercurys', in fact: silent witnesses to the sequence of unfolding events. Mercury was a mediator between the gods and mortals: as part of the structure of Dickens's depiction of the Dedlocks' world, and like many of the servants in Sheridan's comedies, these servants play an essential, if unspeaking role, acting alternatively as a channel or a buffer between their employers and all others.

More importantly, quite apart from the obvious significance of Mrs Rouncewell and the association with his grandmother, it cannot be coincidence that before he was promoted to butler Dickens's grandfather William was once one of these 'Mercurys', a porter, almost certainly liveried and in powdered wig, stationed by the door in attendance on arriving and departing members of the household and their guests.

Included in the somewhat random conversational journeys of Inspector Bucket when seeking to elicit information from potential sources is an interesting diversion that he takes when talking to one of the Dedlock Mercurys, trying to encourage him to answer questions about Lady Dedlock and confiding that his own father had been in service:

> My father was first a page, then a footman, then a butler, then a steward, then an inn-keeper. Lived universally respected, and died lamented. Said with his last breath that he considered service the most honourable part of his career, and so it was.

Page, footman, butler, steward, inkeeper: reminiscent of the career path of both William Dickens, his friend Joseph Bott – and the Shropshire Dickins family in service in the Grosvenor Square area.

As soon as we meet Lady Dedlock, in Chapter Two, we immediately find reference to her journey to Paris, which prompts a reminder of Frances Anne Crewe and her Parisian journal: could Dickens have known about this trip, or this diary, or come across references to it?

Dickens refers to Weevle's engraving, taken from a portrait of Lady Dedlock, 'in which she is represented on a terrace, with a pedestal upon the terrace, and a vase upon the pedestal, and her shawl upon the vase, and a prodigious piece of fur upon the shawl, and her arm on the prodigious piece of fur, and a bracelet on her arm'. Pedestal, terrace and vase was a common enough background for eighteenth-century portraits, but this might encourage one to think of the engraving of Frances Anne Greville, as she was, as a young woman holding a vase, rather than standing next to it, taken from Reynolds, and which would probably have been easily available as a reproduction, or indeed the mezzotint of Mrs Crewe and her friend Mrs Bouverie, from another portrait of Reynolds, circa 1770.

At the beginning of Chapter Twelve, as Mrs Rouncewell waits at Chesney Wold for the return of Lord and Lady Dedlock from Paris, we are introduced to the estate recovering from the rainy weather, as the 'clear, cold sunshine' moves over the woods and the park, and looks in at the windows, touching the ancestral portraits, and notably, 'Athwart the picture of "my Lady", over the great chimney-piece, it throws a bend-sinister of light that strikes down crookedly into the hearth and seems to rend it'.

This suitably oblique reference to 'bend-sinister' is code for indicating, in heraldic terms, a legacy of illegitimacy: a hint of the secret hidden in Lady Dedlock's past. Here we are reminded that Dickens, despite his use of a coat of arms to which he was not entitled, was well enough acquainted with the language and rules of heraldry even as he chose to ignore them in his own case. Later in the book, in fact, he notes the number of armorial bearings on the carriages who attend the funeral of the Dedlocks' 'legal butler', Tulkinghorn.

But there is something else that needs acknowledging: the coat of arms, which, in slight variation, he deployed as some sort of affectation, vaguely signalling to the people with whom he mixed at the height of his success that he too was a gentleman, is similar to the Crewe coat of arms.

Dickens used crests that showed a lion and a cross: the armorial bearings of John Crewe, the first Baron Crewe, employer of Dickens's grandparents, also display a lion and a cross. It would seem unlikely that Dickens was not aware of this, and yet he chose – or his father had chosen – to use a bogus coat of arms that also displayed these features. Was it because John and Charles Dickens wanted to imply some connection with the Crewes?

Apart from the evidence of the portraits, and the tributes to her beauty, we read that 'Lady Dedlock is always the same exhausted deity, surrounded by worshippers, and terribly liable to be bored to death, even while presiding at her own shrine …' Like Mrs Crewe, she is surrounded by a circle of brilliant and charming admirers, and the Dedlocks are deeply entrenched in political matters and the activities, factionalism and electoral extravagances of Lord Coodle, Sir Thomas Doodle, the Duke of Foodle, and even Zoodle: homage, perhaps, to the heady political engagement of the Whiggish set to which the Crewes belonged.

Dickens cannot wait to undermine the attitude of studied indifference that Lady Dedlock assumes, with the observation that all those in service to her, behind a façade of obedience, are in fact controlling her:

> She supposes herself to be an inscrutable Being, quite out of the reach and ken of ordinary mortals – seeing herself in her glass, where indeed she looks so. Yet every dim little star revolving about her, from her maid to the manager of the Italian Opera, knows her weaknesses, prejudices, follies, haughtinesses, and caprices and lives upon as accurate a calculation and as nice a measure of her moral nature as her dressmaker takes of her physical proportions. Is a new dress, a new custom, a new singer, a new dancer, a new form of jewellery, a new dwarf or giant, a new chapel, a new anything, to be set up? There are deferential people in a dozen callings whom my Lady Dedlock suspects of nothing but prostration before her, who can tell you how to manage her as if she were a baby, who do nothing but nurse her all their lives, who, humbly affecting to follow with profound subservience, lead her and her whole troop after them …

Here is not just a challenge to the power of the aristocracy, and to any sense of inferiority he might have inherited from his Dickens grandparents and father: part of a rejection, you might argue, of the class system itself, paradoxically at a time when his increasing success meant that he was extended a privileged membership of the circles of the most influential and powerful members of society, including members of the aristocratic family with whom his grandparents had been in service.

In Chapter Seven, we return to the story of the Dedlocks, and find ourselves at Chesney Wold, their country estate, and in the company of Mrs Rouncewell, who we learn has worked for the Dedlocks for more than fifty years – Elizabeth Dickens had perhaps been employed by the Crewes for nearly as long, or at least known to them from the date of her marriage in 1781 to her retirement in 1820:

> She is a fine old lady, handsome, stately, wonderfully neat, and has such a back and such a stomacher that if her stays should turn out when she dies to have been a broad old-fashioned family fire-grate, nobody who knows her would have cause to be surprised.

There are several references to Mrs Rouncewell as having a handsome face, belied perhaps by the descriptions of her iron casing, and stately bearing, which were not entirely as a result of corsetry but a projection of Dickens's memories of an upright, disciplined woman: the attribution of handsome features, still notable in old age, indicates a woman who had been attractive enough in her younger days to provoke attention, welcomed or not, from Mr Crewe, or indeed one or two of their visitors, such as Sheridan, the seducer of Miss Crewe's governess.

Mr Rouncewell, who like his wife had come from the local market town, appears only in retrospect, as one who had died long ago: 'sometime before the decease of the pretty fashion of pig-tails, and modestly took his own (if he took it with him) in a corner of the churchyard in the park near the mouldy porch.' Gone and all but forgotten, then: remembered only for his (probably bewigged and powdered), eighteenth-century hairstyle, a man with local roots, and leaving a young widow: just like William Dickens.

The name Rouncewell is interesting: Rounce is the name of a handle that when turned moves the paper and plates on a printing press. A tacit acknowledgement, perhaps, by Dickens, of the imprint on his imagination left by such influences as he had from his family's background in service to the Crewes, from a grandson whose published work would elevate him so far beyond any success they could have imagined, which would be produced by exactly such a process.

Another name of significance in *Bleak House* is the name of Captain Nemo, former lover of Lady Dedlock, and father of Esther Summerson. Nemo, of course, itself means 'no one', or 'nobody', but Hawdon, his real name, carries more than a hint of connection to the Crewe family story. Rumours that Lord Crewe had an illegitimate son by the name of Robert Hawgood Crewe would seem too coincidental to be an accidental choice.

The significance of the name Dedlock is more obvious: it indicates Dickens's view of the aristocracy; an immoveable lock, or a state where progression cannot be made: the damp, melancholy surroundings of Chesney Wold, and the sense of decline at the end of the book, when Sir Leicester, who has no heir, is 'invalided, bent, and almost blind', and his wife resting in the mausoleum in the park, indicates the fading power of the aristocracy.

As Orwell pointed out, Dickens's portrayal of this class is generally more focused on 'not so much the great aristocracy, who hardly enter into his books, as their petty offshoots, the cadging dowagers who live up mews in Mayfair, and the bureaucrats and professional soldiers …' In *Bleak House*, however, Dickens makes the exception for the Dedlocks, with a degree of interest that was undoubtedly driven by his own family's experience.

The two sons of Mr and Mrs Rouncewell, and in a different sense the grandson Watt, clearly reflect the family of Mr and Mrs Dickens: George, who falls into debt and has been estranged from his mother for many years, is yet her favourite child: his unnamed brother, the ironmaster who has prospered through his own hard work, is less favoured. He had rejected the path expected of him by the Dedlocks and his mother: 'Her second son would have been provided for at Chesney Wold and would have been made steward in due season.' Steward was not so far away from butler in some households.

The degree to which the housekeeper's sons are considered to exist within the orbit of the Dedlock household and engage with their mother's employers is perhaps significant if it reflects the extent of the close relations with the Crewe family enjoyed by John and William Dickens in overseeing their choice of occupation, or as is commonly believed, their education.

It is impossible to see Rosa now and not think that she is likely to be a version of Sarah Latham, who married Dickens's Uncle William. Sarah, like Rosa, was from a respectable local family: perhaps she was educated at the 'convent' school for girls that Frances Anne Crewe had established on the estate: she 'bettered' herself by marrying someone associated with the Crewes who considered himself a gentleman and left her well looked after when she was widowed.

There is a curious reference at the end of Chapter Forty-one in *Bleak House* after Lady Dedlock has visited Tulkinghorn in his turret room to confront him over his intentions regarding the disclosure of her secret. Dickens describes the sun rising and its light falling on Chesney Wold:

> Also into rooms high in the roof, and into offices in court-yards, and over stables, where humbler ambition dreams of bliss, in keepers' lodges, and in holy matrimony with Will or Sally. Up comes the bright sun, drawing everything up with it—the Wills and Sallys, the latent vapour in the earth, the drooping leaves and flowers, the birds and beasts and creeping things, the gardeners to sweep the dewy turf and unfold emerald velvet where the roller passes, the smoke of the great kitchen fire wreathing itself straight and high into the lightsome air.

The Wills and Sallys: this choice of names – Sally being a diminutive of Sarah – is surely significant; is this a coded reference to William and Sarah? The lodge is where Lady Dedlock used to watch the keeper's child at play, and the place where she met her secret child in the rainstorm. Now it will be the place where the 'trooper' George Rouncewell lives.

George Rouncewell, the favourite son of the housekeeper who, once returned to favour, assists the invalid baronet after the flight of his wife, is clearly more acceptable to the Dedlocks and viewed with pride by his mother, their loyal housekeeper. Like his mother, he is loyal to the status quo and the established order, whereas his brother, rejecting their patronage, offers their servant an opportunity for her own advancement and so represents the threat of radical social change and the emergence of a newly confident, newly powerful meritocracy. As a loose interpretation of Dicken's own family background, all of this is very interesting: the self-defined, later re-casting of his father and uncle, the sons of the Crewes' housekeeper, as of the rank of gentleman was certainly a similar example of social aspiration, albeit one that exhibited the desire to join and preserve the social order rather than challenge it.

Chapter Twelve

Dickens and the Sheridans

Charles Dickens was clearly familiar with Sheridan's work: much has been written about the influence of his experience of reading in the 'sentimental tradition' of the eighteenth century, and his own reflection or revision of that tradition in the depiction of his characters and the fictional worlds they inhabit as the nineteenth century moved on. The extent to which the setting of much of his work retreats to an age before the one in which he was writing is also notable, and in terms of his creative process the forces that worked on his imagination necessarily included those experiences that shaped his parents' and even his grandparents' lives and characters. The age of Sheridan, and the position of his family on the edge of that world, cannot but have left its traces on Dickens, not just as a literary influence but as something that had personal meaning for him: whatever that meaning was.

Valerie Purton comments of Dickens that whatever misreading he had of other eighteenth-century writers such as Sterne and Goldsmith, 'at some deep level he *understood* Sheridan'.[1]

She also notes:

> References to Sheridan's plays too continually resurface in the "Letters". *The Rivals* (1775), Sheridan's first play, is a particularly potent presence. Fag's "I was sly, Sir, devilishly sly!" re-emerges as a verbal tag of Major Bagstock in *Dombey and Son*. Many references are linked to performances of Sheridan's plays. Dickens's first sight of Macready on stage was in *Pizarro*; he saw *The Duenna* and *The Critic* and refers twice to Lord Burleigh from that play. There is a reference in a cancelled paragraph of *The Old Curiosity Shop* to Sir Benjamin Backbite from *The School for Scandal*, and Dickens probably saw that play with Macready in 1841.

The marks of his influence are obvious: the comic characterisation, and the formulation of characters' names, for example – but also evident in his work are distinct echoes of Sheridan's writing. It is interesting, too, that Dickens included a reference to Sheridan in his very first published work, *A Dinner at Poplar Walk*.

When Dickens was driven to write *Nicholas Nickleby* and chose to draw attention to the issue of the Yorkshire schools, including the establishment where Frederick Crewe Haswell was placed, he chose, in his description of Squeers, to allow distinct echo of a line from *The Rivals*. As Dickens puts it:

> Mr Squeers's appearance was not prepossessing. He had but one eye, and the popular prejudice runs in favour of two. The eye he had was unquestionably useful, but decidedly not ornamental: being of a greenish grey, and in shape resembling the fan-light of a street door …

In *The Rivals*, Captain Absolute remarks of his requirements in a wife: 'though one eye may be very agreeable, yet as the prejudice has always run in favour of two, I would not wish to affect a singularity in that article'.

When editing the memoirs of the clown Joseph Grimaldi, in the early years of his career, Charles Dickens included in the final text many references to Sheridan, and examples of his kindness. One might speculate on the conversations he may have had on the subject with his father, to whom he is said to have dictated much of his editorial contribution to this work. Regardless of any speculative paternal connection, presumably John Dickens would have had much to say on the subject of Sheridan and the Crewes – and may even have had memories of him, as a boy, or stories passed on from his mother.

It would seem likely that Dickens would have been interested in Sheridan because of his family's association with the Crewes: whether he knew of any potential personal connection with his father, we cannot be sure. It is certain, however, that early on in his career, Dickens actively sought connection with the Sheridan family.

In a letter written by him in 1837 to Madame Sala[2] he apologises for not being able to accept an evening invitation where he would have met Caroline Norton, one of Sheridan's granddaughters – a strikingly beautiful woman and a talented writer. She was also to become a political activist and a powerful advocate for the rights of separated wives and mothers after suffering appalling treatment by her estranged husband, an experience that became the focus of a scandalous court case the year before in which her private life was exposed to public view in the most humiliating way. The case was reported by Dickens for the *Morning Chronicle*.

That Mrs Norton was a subject of notoriety and for many years would be shunned by society appears not to have deterred Dickens from seeking to make her acquaintance and remaining on close terms with her family, even though as a young man newly married and still in the early stages of forging his own reputation as a successful writer and public figure he might have been expected to be more circumspect.

In the letter to Madame Sala it is evident that Dickens is very keen to emphasise his interest in meeting Mrs Norton – and indeed in meeting her uncle, Charles Sheridan, the son of the playwright, born in 1796 during his second marriage:

> I shall be exceedingly happy to know Mrs Norton; and regret this circumstance the more, because it is only a few weeks since I was prevented from meeting her at another friend's house.
>
> If you see Mr Sheridan you will perhaps have the goodness to communicate my address and inform him that I shall be happy to see him if he will call upon me, Or, you can if you please tell Mrs. Norton from me that as I am a most unceremonious person, and most anxious to have the pleasure of her acquaintance, I shall be happy to call on her, if she will communicate the when and where.

Dickens had reported the sensational hearing held in June 1836, at the Court of Common Pleas, of 'Norton v Melbourne', brought because Mrs Norton's husband George had sought to prosecute the Prime Minister Lord Melbourne for 'criminal conversation'– sexual relations – with his wife. This accusation was stoutly denied, even though it was clear that there was an intimate and sexual relationship between the pair over a period of some years. George Norton lost the case, but Caroline's reputation was in ruins and for some years she was allowed no access to her children.

Melbourne was much older than Caroline and had been a friend of her father, Tom Sheridan, and of her grandfather, Richard Brinsley Sheridan. Tom was born in 1775 – probably the year in which his father began the long affair with Frances Anne Crewe: Lord Melbourne was born in 1779. His wife had been the infamous Lady Caroline Lamb, daughter of Sheridan's other long-term mistress, Lady Bessborough. As part of the hopelessly entangled relationships of the Whig faction's circle, Lord Melbourne's brother, George Lamb, had married Caroline St Jules, the illegitimate daughter of the Duke of Devonshire and his mistress and later wife, Lady Elizabeth Foster.

It is not hard to see why Dickens, someone whose family had been linked, even if in service, to the Crewes and the Devonshire House set, might be intrigued by the Sheridan family: especially if he entertained the thought that he might be in some way related to them. If Sheridan had been his grandfather, of course, it would have meant that Caroline was his niece, and Charles his uncle.

After making a sustained effort to meet Caroline, Dickens maintained a close friendship with her and her family, and they had many mutual friends, including Richard Monckton Milnes – later Lord Houghton and the husband of Annabel Crewe. In May 1842, Dickens sat next to Caroline at a dinner party held by the poet Samuel Rogers, much to the envy of his friend, the artist Daniel Maclise (who also painted her), referring to her in a letter as the 'Heavenly Norton'.[3]

It would seem from Diane Atkinson's study of Caroline Norton that Dickens's admiration for her was also at risk of turning into something more profound:[4]

> Once at a supper party Dickens and his wife Catherine were attending he was asked whom he thought was the most beautiful of the Duchess of Sutherland and Mrs Norton. His fellow guests were startled when he replied, "Mrs Norton perhaps the most beautiful, but the duchess to my mind is the more kissable person". He sounded infatuated with Caroline when he wrote to an American that Caroline and her sister Georgy were "sights for the Gods", as they always have been.

The nature of Dickens's attachment to the Sheridan family, however, was not simply as an admirer of Mrs Norton: he appears to have cultivated the friendship of the wider family – as Forster recalled in 1846 when Dickens was in Paris and had had a letter from his father telling him of his sister Fanny's serious illness as a result of the tuberculosis that would end her life within a couple of years. He compared her illness to that of Caroline's younger brother Charles: 'In the same letter I heard of poor Charles Sheridan, well known to us both, dying of the same terrible disease …'

According to Diane Atkinson: 'At the end of November Charles Dickens wrote to friends from Paris that he had seen Charlie Sheridan, who was "dying of a consumption". Dickens knew Charlie "very well": he had enjoyed seeing him in amateur productions of his grandfather's plays, and in the past they had gone sightseeing together …'[5]

Forster later noted a dinner attended by Dickens in 1849, where among his fellow guests was Lady Graham: '… than whom not even the wit and beauty of her nieces, Mrs. Norton and Lady Dufferin, better represented the brilliant family of the Sheridans; so many of whose members, and these three above all, Dickens prized among his friends.'

In November 1853, Dickens wrote a letter to Angela Burdett Coutts in which he referred to the rather surprising marriage that had taken place between Caroline Norton's son Brin and a young woman in Capri, supposedly the barefoot daughter of a fisherman: of Brin, Dickens remarked:

> He was described to me as usually sitting on a rock, translating Longfellow's poems for the entertainment of his wife, who has not the least desire to hear anything about them. He appears to be a Young Ass, with certain incoherent inherited ideas concerning the Mantle of Sheridan …

There might be said to be a certain amount of suppressed resentment here: the resentment of one who had inherited nothing but the burden of (the wrong sort of) relations, in service to a family close to the Sheridans: one who perhaps felt in some way closer to the genius of Sheridan than his acknowledged heirs – and indeed who could boast of a close friendship with Longfellow – looking at the indulged great grandson of the playwright, playing the role of a lover of the arts, while he, born with no privilege, worked so hard to achieve and sustain his own literary reputation.

Whether or not Dickens indulged in the idea that Richard Brinsley Sheridan may have been his grandfather, he clearly felt in some way that he was worthy to inherit his 'mantle' – or certainly was more worthy than his rather feckless great grandson.

It would seem that it was *The School for Scandal*, first performed in 1777, and dedicated to Mrs Crewe, rather than *The Rivals*, that most intrigued Dickens. As noted by Purton, he commented that this play 'is … usually considered the most impracticable and difficult play in the whole Theatrical Calendar, the parts being without exception "characters" which require very delicate manipulation'. To another correspondent he wrote: '*The Rivals* is more droll, as a mere piece of drollery; but *The School for Scandal* is a more delightful piece of comedy'.

Perhaps he noted the prominent roles played by servants in *The School for Scandal*, and indeed in *The Rivals* – in which their actions are integral to the dialogue, as well as the plot – and wondered about the way in which his own servant grandparents would have been seen, or not seen, in the course of their employment by the Crewes.

In the staged world of these characters, the relationship of master or mistress and servant is not exactly what one might expect, in fact: their exchanges are made on a basis of intimacy and mutual dependence. Sheridan's servants are not silent walkers on, but active participants with their own opinions, which they do not hesitate to express. They have their own motivation, and sphere of influence. The maid Lucy, in *The Rivals*, for example, acts as a 'simpleton' while profiting financially from the tangled intrigues of her employers and their associates, and Fag, servant to Captain Absolute, is perfectly able to tell his master what to do while pretending to be subservient to his wishes.

In *The School for Scandal*, Rowley, who is in the service of Sir Peter Teazle and who was formerly the steward to the father of the two Surface brothers, converses with his new 'master' with ease and mutual respect – and is privy to the sort of admissions and discussions that might normally be exchanged with a close friend. Trip, who is servant to Charles Surface, appears to enjoy, as Sir Oliver suggests, 'a pleasant sort of Place here, I guess' as well as a very generous salary – Sheridan perhaps overestimated the pay of footmen in allowing him to boast of his £50 a year. This is, however, not enough for the needs of Trip, who attempts to try the visiting moneylender for a loan, secured by insuring his 'place', his life and possibly using some of his master's clothes as sureties. Sir Oliver looks on indulgently at 'Mr Trip's Negotiation', remarking: 'An annuity! ha ha! a Footman raise money by annuity – Well done Luxury egad!' Dickens's former footman grandfather and his housekeeper grandmother, as we know, both invested money in consols, or consolidated annuities.

When Dickens took part in a selection of scenes from *The School for Scandal* in an amateur theatrical performance while staying with his friends the Watsons at Rockingham Castle in November 1849 there would be no servant role for him, of course: he played Sir Peter Teazle.

It would seem that Sheridan took note of the character and behaviour of the staff at the aristocratic houses to which he was invited – presumably including the Crewes and the circle around Georgiana, Duchess of Devonshire. The governess at Crewe who bore his child was after all not only an employee of the Crewes but the daughter of the Spencers' trusted steward. William Dickens, as porter and then butler to the Crewes, must have admitted Sheridan frequently to their establishments in Mayfair and Cheshire: was the playwright, frequent visitor to the household and intimate companion of Mrs Crewe, as easy and familiar with him as the masters and servants in this play?

Arguably the fictional world of Charles Dickens, as it evolved, offered a way through the limitations of the old world, the world of Chesney Wold, or Crewe Hall, and through to a society where a middle class were feeling increasingly confident and ambitious: an emboldened bourgeoisie, where self-advancement, not privilege, was what counted, but where every step of the way was marked with potential failure and humiliation.

PART TWO

Blacking and Blackmail

Chapter Thirteen

Ravensfield

Air we in possession of a sinful secret, and doe we require corn, and wine, and oil – or, what is much the same thing, money – for the keeping thereof? Probably so, my friends!

The Reverend Mr Chadband, *Bleak House*

The Burroughs forms part of the old village of Hendon, formerly in Middlesex but now in north London, much of it now the main campus of Middlesex University. On one side of the road here is now a rather tired-looking, wooden-framed, box-shaped, pre-fab office block bearing the name 'Ravensfield House'. This property, however, is an imposter, appropriating the identity of a vanished historic house that once stood nearby on the other side of a turning still lined with the trees that formerly marked the boundary of its grounds, to mislead and confuse generations of future local historians.

A few years ago, papers relating to the old Ravensfield House were passed to me by a friend who lived nearby. She had mentioned casually that these documents included some sort of mortgage agreement, with three signatories, one of them a 'Chas Dickens', of Tavistock House – and passed the papers on.[1]

The Ravensfield document is in the form of fifteen large-scale pages of ageing typewritten material, approximately A3 in size: two pages with hand-drawn maps, the rest apparently carbon copies of transcript documents relating to the property and various transactions regarding its ownership. The last transaction was in 1923 and the transcription would appear to date from then.

There are very few surviving photographs taken of Ravensfield House, taken in the Edwardian period just before the demolition of the building while it was known as Ravensfield Manor and was used as a nursing home. Three postcards from this period show the property as it was in the Edwardian period with some later additions to the original building, which might appear to date from the early to mid-nineteenth century: however, some earlier maps seem to indicate some form of building was on the site in the late eighteenth century. Newspaper reports speak of a serious fire in 1874, so how much of the house was rebuilt by the time of these photographs is hard to say. Judging from the view taken from the side, the central section of the house pre-dated later additions, built at some point to the left- and right-hand sides of the property.

The earlier provenance of this material was unclear, except that it had been included with the other documents related to the history of the row of small eighteenth-century terraced cottages that still stand in the Burroughs, only a short distance – a couple of minutes' walk – from the location of the site of Ravensfield House.

According to the transcript, bound together with rusting staples and seemingly typed some years ago, before the age of photocopying, the information is taken from a small collection of original documents, including one of particular interest agreed and signed on 28 January 1853.

This is a mortgage or loan to the value of £1,500, which had been arranged on behalf of a man named Patrick Rouse in order to purchase the freehold of Ravensfield House, then a substantial property with grounds. There were three parties guaranteeing the mortgage: three names – Francis Lovell, Claudius Francis du Pasquier … and Charles Dickens.

Although there has not previously been any knowledge of the Ravensfield mortgage, or its association with Dickens, after a good deal of research it was possible to verify the identity of the first two signatories and substantiate the connection. However, that process itself raised more questions than perhaps it answered and it has led to a trail of new material that not only leads to an unexpected link with Charles's relationship with his youngest brother Augustus but reveals previously unknown information about Dickens himself. This information may even change our perception and understanding of him and the secrets of his early life, the consequences of which pursued him even through the years of his spectacular success until the very end.

The Ravensfield loan is not the only previously unknown property associated with Dickens that has come to light in recent years.

In 2009, Bonhams auctioned some papers connected to a house in Wanstead, a detached villa with grounds situated at 18 Grove Road, now Grosvenor Road. Dickens appears to have had an interest in this property from 1860 and the auctioneers speculated that this was in some way due to his increasingly close relationship with Ellen Ternan. The house is gone now, replaced with flats, but there is still a pair of old chestnut trees looking on to the street that may have marked the old turning into the older building. Rather interestingly, a former home of Sheridan is a short distance away, just around the corner, next to the old manor house. A search in the archives of the Charles Dickens Museum in Doughty Street, London, shows that after his friend's death, John Forster retained an interest in a house in this road: no. 36. And perhaps it is significant that the Wanstead dealings were not dealt with by Dickens's lawyer Frederic Ouvry but G.F. Hudson.

The fact, however, that Dickens's association with the Wanstead property was completely unknown until so recently reminds us that he was adept at concealing aspects of his life and activities – as he appears to have done so successfully with Ravensfield House.

To try to confirm the authenticity of the Ravensfield mortgage, the first step was to try to identify the co-signatories to the agreement and to establish what association, if any, that they may have had with Charles Dickens.

Claudius Francis du Pasquier can be traced, with little difficulty, through a range of records and sources: he was a man of impeccable social standing, the son of a naturalised Swiss courtier, also called Claudius du Pasquier, who was a senior page to George IV and evidently an intimate and trusted member of the Royal household. His son, born in 1811, became a physician and apothecary to the Royal household after serving his apprenticeship and later entering into partnership with John Nussey – brother of Charlotte Bronte's friend, Ellen.

Francis Lovell was easy to find through the marriage of his sister Harriett, who married Charles's Dickens's youngest brother, Augustus Newnham Dickens, in 1848. Francis was her half-brother, a surgeon who spent most of his life in Chelmsford, Essex, and died relatively young.

There would appear to be no firm evidence of an earlier connection between du Pasquier and Dickens, but it is interesting that the former's father was a senior servant in the Royal household at the same time as members of the family of Dickens's grandfather's friend and best man, Joseph Bott.

Claudius du Pasquier is referred to as a friend in the will of Harriett's father, also named Francis Lovell, who died in 1836. The elder Francis lived for many years in India, trading in jewellery and silverware and acquiring a substantial fortune.

Harriett's brother Francis and Claudius du Pasquier feature together in only one other document associated with Charles Dickens, apart from the newly discovered Ravensfield agreement. The other document that binds all three men together is the marriage settlement of Harriett, an arrangement made before her marriage to Augustus. Details of this settlement can be examined in papers held at the British Library among the papers of the Mitton Collection, documents associated with Dickens's lawyer and close friend, Thomas Mitton. As we will see, there are also surviving papers from du Pasquier's nephew, who was a solicitor, in the archives of the Charles Dickens Museum, which relate to Harriett's financial affairs after the death of her estranged husband some ten years after his desertion of her: Harriett's family's determination to protect her inheritance proved to have been a sensible precaution.

Du Pasquier, Francis Lovell and Charles Dickens were charged with the responsibility of overseeing this settlement and safeguarding the security of funds invested for Harriett Lovell when she married Augustus in 1848: it is significant, however, as we shall see from the details of his bank account, that it was Charles Dickens who took the main responsibility for overseeing Harriett's investments until the death of his brother.

For some reason, the same three signatories on Harriett's marriage settlement were brought together again five years later to sanction a large loan – £1,500 – to a previously unknown party in order for him to purchase Ravensfield House in the village of Hendon.

Who was the beneficiary of this generous arrangement? A man called Patrick Rouse. Was he connected in any way to Charles Dickens? Not that one could see at first glance: in fact, research soon proved that Mr Rouse was a man who might well be unlikely to have been trusted with a loan of such an amount: he was a bootmaker – an Irishman, who had been living in Hendon in modest circumstances but now would take advantage of his new status as a man of property after the loan from Dickens and his fellow trustees to rise, almost overnight, to the self-proclaimed rank of 'gentleman'. And the closer one looks at this arrangement, as we shall see, the more extraordinary it becomes.

Why did Dickens, du Pasquier and Francis Lovell involve themselves with this man and provide him with the funds to buy Ravensfield House? What connection, if any, did this investment have with the subject of their other arrangement, that is to say Francis's sister, and Charles's sister-in-law, Harriett Dickens?

And why was the mortgage agreement terminated after five years and three months in the middle of what was the most tumultuous week in Charles Dickens's life: when he was separating from his wife Catherine and thrown into a maelstrom of family argument, scandal, and prurient public interest in his domestic affairs?

We can only examine the facts and consider a choice of potential explanations, or invite the reader to form their own conclusion based on those facts. And to begin an investigation of the mystery of Ravensfield House and the new material the process of examination will uncover, we must start with a new look at the life of one member of the Dickens family: Charles's youngest brother, Augustus Newnham Dickens.

Chapter Fourteen

A brilliant scapegrace: Augustus Newnham Dickens

Most biographies of Charles Dickens refer to his brothers only in passing as a source of concern and an unwelcome distraction for him – although, in happier times, playing their part in the strictly edited narrative of his family life and as willing partners under his command in his theatrical performances; clearly sharing his lively character and sense of fun: qualities no doubt inherited from their parents. A sense of fun, for Charles Dickens, however, ran along aside an irresistible desire to control the lives of others around him as if they were characters in a fiction of his making: his brothers and sisters did not escape this fate, one that was perhaps unavoidable as he stepped into the role of head of the family long before his father's death in 1851: a role confirmed by his phenomenal success as a writer and the material rewards that it brought him.

The story of Augustus, the youngest child of the Dickens family, has attracted a little more interest from biographers, at least regarding his later life, partly because of the belief that Charles deliberately designed his reading tour of America to avoid any association with the family of this troublesome younger brother. The embarrassment Charles was so keen to avoid was due to the decision of Augustus to flee England some years previously, having abandoned his wife Harriett shortly after she had become blind – and settling in America with his mistress, Bertha Phillips, and their three children.

The sensational press coverage in America of the story of Charles Dickens's black sheep brother provided plenty of unwelcome publicity at the time and has overshadowed the wider context of his relationship with Charles. The really significant events in the life of Augustus Dickens do not begin and end in America: his career and activities, the circumstances in which he found himself before his departure – and the reasons for that flight – are all far more interesting than anyone has previously suspected.

In 1994 a book written by Sidney P. Moss, and Carolyn J. Moss, *Charles Dickens and His Chicago Relatives, a Documentary Narrative*, gave the first account of the story of the life of Augustus Dickens in America.[1] They describe the amount of information about this latter period as 'voluminous' but stated that material relating to events in England was 'fragmentary'. Since then, however, access to many records has greatly improved and it is clear that there are further sources to examine, of vital significance, especially in regard to the motive for his flight and the actions Charles Dickens took in order to mitigate the risk to his own life and reputation from the scandal that would become attached to his youngest brother and family.

Augustus was born on 10 November 1827, the youngest child of John and Elizabeth Dickens – some fifteen years younger than his brother Charles, who had just months before started work as a junior clerk with the solicitors' firm of Ellis and Blackmore. No doubt because he was the youngest member of the family, Augustus would appear to have been looked on with great affection, particularly by his eldest brother. He was known as 'Boz', a family nickname derived from 'Boses', his version of 'Moses', who is the rather naïve son of Dr Primrose in Oliver Goldsmith's *The Vicar of Wakefield*.

According to the records of St Pancras parish church, where he was baptised on 7 December 1827, the birth of Augustus Newnham Dickens took place in Johnson Street, Somers Town: a rented house from which they were temporarily evicted while Elizabeth was pregnant.

The choice of 'Newnham' as a middle name is significant for all the wrong reasons, perhaps, taken as it was from one of the more patient and generous benefactors of the Dickens family, Richard Newnham, a neighbour from the Chatham days, whose friendship – and generosity – was tested in the course of a loan to John Dickens, part of a burden of debt that was the inevitable result of his financial mismanagement. That Augustus was to carry the additional name of Newnham in recognition of his father's obligations to a former creditor was an ominous beginning in life, perhaps, for any son of such a father.

By now Charles Dickens had left his clerical posts behind, taught himself shorthand and begun a new career using his newly acquired skills as a reporter at the ecclesiastical courts known as Doctors' Commons. He moved on to work for his uncle John Henry Barrow at the *Mirror of Parliament*, where his father was also employed; for a new paper – *The True Sun*, and then the *Morning Chronicle*. He had begun to write stories and sketches.

In 1834 Dickens moved to his own lodgings in Furnival's Inn, joined by his younger brother Fred, and in August of that year he had first signed himself 'Boz': his life as a writer had begun. The original Boz was left behind with his parents, sisters and brother Alfred in what must have continued to be a chaotic household, and one that was now without the mediation and steadying influence of the eldest son. Curious, perhaps, that Charles chose to take the name Boz with him and not leave it behind with his brother where it belonged.

As Charles's writing career began to flourish and he achieved a degree of prosperity, there was a period of some years of relative ease for John Dickens, his wife and younger children. This was not to last, however, and by 1839, when Augustus was twelve, Charles had decided the best option for distancing himself from the problems caused by his father was to move him far away from London into rural exile, hoping that a quieter life in the country would provide less opportunity for incurring debt and minimise the distraction and embarrassment caused by the constant difficulties in which he found himself and in which his son was almost inevitably required to intervene.

A suitable retreat was found in the village of Alphington in Devon: Mile End Cottage, which Dickens described to Thomas Mitton, with a certain amount of proprietorial satisfaction, or as Michael Slater suggests, as a writer who had 'written the (idyllic) end of their story'.[2]

One of the benefits of moving there was that Augustus could attend a school near to home: Mount Radford College, founded in 1826 and about 3 miles from Alphington. Augustus appears to have remained happily enough there for some time, even after his parents had returned to London. But return to London, and his family, brought new challenges.

For Augustus, whose nickname 'Boz' Dickens adopted for his own work, there might seem to have been left by that very act of annexation no hope that he might develop his own identity in some way, and a conclusion drawn that he would always be dependent on the patronage of his elder brother. Why did Charles choose to take the nickname of his youngest brother and use it for his own purposes when publishing his first work? He would abandon the name after a few years, but by then he had apparently taken to referring to Augustus as 'Shrimp', even to his employer, as if to maintain a tradition of demeaning his brother's status.

This is a subject addressed by Robert L. Patten in his study of Dickens's writing as 'Boz', and he considers the possibility that he 'may have started out concealing his name to protect against failure', and that the choice of 'Boz' was simply due to Dickens's reverence for Oliver Goldsmith; particularly because of 'the association of feckless son with unfortunate father' in *The Vicar of Wakefield*.[3]

Patten also points out, however, that the arrival of Augustus in 1827 was in the same year in which Charles Dickens was obliged – for the second time – to enter employment, albeit in very different circumstances, in order to secure additional income for his family, who were ejected temporarily in that same year from their lodgings and were as usual struggling to live within their means.

Perhaps Charles had taken over the name of Boz because the writer had unresolved – and unacknowledged – feelings of jealousy at the arrival of Augustus, just at the time when he was sent out into the world once more to earn a living. And he may still have retained a sense of injustice at the unequal treatment of his younger siblings by his parents from the time when Charles was removed from school and sent to work while the family paid for his sister Fanny to study at the Royal Academy of Music. A pseudonym protected him from failure as an aspiring writer but the assumption of his brother's name might suggest a more complex motivation than might first appear to be the case.

It might be argued that the psychological impact of this appropriation of his identity, as the youngest child, the focus of his family's attention and indulgence, and by his eldest brother, was keenly felt by Augustus – and perhaps formed an underlying sense of inadequacy that drove him, eventually, to assert his independence and turn his back on his own family while creating a new one beyond the reach of their influence: of his brother's influence.

Forster describes Augustus's career as follows: 'Augustus was now placed in a city employment by Thomas, which after a little time he surrendered, and found his way to America, where he died.' A somewhat tight-lipped summary, clearly, and omitting any detail of the trouble in which Augustus would find himself, why he left for America, or the circumstances in which he lived.

When Augustus was seventeen, Charles had written to city businessman Thomas Chapman and asked if he might have a place for his younger brother. Chapman obliged and Augustus settled down to what he may have found a somewhat tedious form of employment as a shipping clerk, work lightened by the entertainment he would have pursued outside of his duties, for example taking part in Charles's theatrical performances. Just before Augustus's wedding to Harriett Lovell, however, Charles Dickens had written to suggest to Chapman that it might be better for his brother to drop 'these theatricals'. For a young man about to be married that might have seemed a sensible idea but it is significant that Charles, still so watchful over his younger brother's interests, should raise the matter with his employer.

Some sources have wrongly stated that Augustus worked for Dickens's publisher Edward Chapman – in fact he was employed by John Chapman & Co., a company based in Leadenhall Street in which Thomas Chapman was a partner. Their businesses were associated with shipping, ship-owning and insurance. It has been claimed that Thomas Chapman was the model for Paul Dombey. The genesis of characters in Dickens's work is always complex, however, and as we will see it would appear to have been overlooked that the life of his great uncle John Barrow had a large influence on this novel and the character of Dombey.

But there was something else that had occurred, only three years before Augustus's marriage: another issue that had required a certain amount of discreet discussion in August 1845 with Thomas Powell, the manager at John Chapman & Co., who appears to have been charged with the supervision of young Augustus before being exposed as a fraudster. Charles's eighteen-year-old brother had, it seemed, formed some sort of romantic attachment to an unknown young woman. Concerns were raised but Charles did not take this seriously and advised that nothing need be done.[4] In retrospect, and in the light of new evidence that we will later consider, one might speculate as to the extent of this intrigue and the identity of the young woman – and if it hinted at the trouble that was to follow over the next few years.

The close terms of the relationship between Charles Dickens, his family and Powell at this point is seen in the exchange over the matter of the unnamed subject of Augustus's romantic attachment early on in his time at Chapman's: Dickens wrote to Powell: 'I have sounded out my brother Fred; and he seems to think the Virgin may be "only joking". She may be a Platonic Virgin, perhaps. Who knows?'

Intimate, and rather racy: clearly Dickens trusted Powell with personal family matters – or at least Dickens took the trouble to make him feel he was a trusted friend in order, perhaps, to ensure his younger brother's position was secure – at the same time as knowing Powell knew much about his family's background that would prove embarrassing, at the very least, should the information become public knowledge.

A search of Freedom of the City Admission Papers[5] show that Augustus became a Freeman of the City of London on 4 June 1853. He is described now as a ship agent 'of Gracechurch Street'. Quite a step up from the position of a humble clerk in a post secured by the intervention of his famous brother.

Within a few days of his induction as a Freeman, on 9 June, Augustus is included in a published list of guests attending a 'Conversazione' held to promote science and art, given by the Lord Mayor and Lady Mayoress at the Mansion House. Also in attendance were such notable figures as Gladstone, Sir Joseph Paxton, and the Master of Harrow School. Although other guests were noted as attending with their wives, Augustus is not.

In September of the same year there appeared a notice in *The Times* including him among a list of 'Persons admitted to act as brokers within the City of London and liberties thereof ...' In order to act as a broker, at that time, it was necessary to be a Freeman but still the fact that he was able to acquire these qualifications is perhaps significant. And here is another new and crucial piece of information, one that indicates another route for preferment and advancement in business in the City of London: in November 1855, Augustus was initiated into membership of the Universal Lodge of Freemasons.

The lodge he joined, No. 212, appears to have been a fairly exclusive one, with members on the same page as Augustus generally describing themselves as 'gentleman' and including a barrister, two solicitors, another ship broker. There are no payments, it should be said, in Augustus's name noted after 1855, and his active membership must have been of a short duration. The reason for that will become clear. Once in America, it seems, from a recent enquiry made to the guardians of Masonic records now held by the Grand Lodge in Illinois, he did not continue in membership.

Some of Augustus's most trusted business partners were fellow masons, and such connections would appear to have been a significant benefit to him as his life began to drift into dangerous waters. But there are also other curious aspects of his membership, however short lived, of this Lodge.

Chapter Fifteen

The eyes you have trusted in: Harriett and Bertha

My dear blind daughter, hear me and forgive me! The world you live in, heart of mine, doesn't exist as I have represented it. The eyes you have trusted in, have been false to you.

The Cricket on the Hearth, 1845

Much confusion has been caused by the various accounts of Bertha Phillips's background: her own son, Bertram Dickens, in 1912, had claimed that she was the daughter of the famous lawyer Charles Phillips. The truth, as perhaps one might expect, was rather less interesting. Although Bertha's father was indeed a solicitor, his name was James Phillips; he was born in Monmouthshire circa 1790 but lived for much of his life in Grove Lane, Camberwell, with his wife Mary and their children. James Phillips worked, as he described it on one census return, as an attorney in 'all the superior courts'. There are references in various court reports in newspapers during the 1840s to a James Phillips who specialised in marine insurance cases, which may well be the same man, and may explain in part the suggestion in some sources that he was an insurance agent.[1]

No one really knows how Augustus Dickens and Bertha met: there was a vague idea that it may have been through her brothers – a closer look now suggests that this may have been Edwy Phillips, who worked as an 'average stater', an occupation that was connected to marine insurance. Augustus had been working as a clerk for a shipping company that also dealt with insurance, so it seems highly likely that he and Edwy were acquainted and that this led to the introduction of Bertha to Augustus.

Edwy Phillips was married twice, and his second marriage to Emma Browne had produced a daughter, born in May 1850, whose name was Malvina Dickens Phillips. The choice of middle name would presumably have been in honour of a godparent or family friend and it seems probable that that friend or godparent was Augustus.

The date of Malvina's birth, and the adoption of Dickens as a middle name, would therefore suggest that the association between the two families was earlier than we might have thought – could this even mean that perhaps the young woman with whom Augustus was said to be romantically involved when he was a young clerk working for Chapman's was Bertha?

On the same page of the masonic lodge register that lists his membership there are other names which stand out. His brother Alfred Lamert Dickens, for one, eight names below his, joining in April 1856, and then, ten names below Alfred, we find George Augustus Sala, the writer, friend of Charles Dickens, and a contributor to his journals. But the real point of interest is the name immediately after Sala. And that is Edwy Phillips, the brother of Bertha Phillips, who would become Augustus's American 'wife'.

Quite extraordinary, one might think, when considering the date of Edwy's initiation, which was in April 1860 – in other words, about four years after Augustus Dickens had eloped with his sister, and while she was living with him, as his common law wife, with those illegitimate children that Edwy and his siblings chose to abandon and leave to their own fate when they were orphaned only a few years later.

It seems Edwy joined this Lodge from another, the Old Kings Arms Lodge, into which he was initiated in 1854. Why on earth he would want to join one associated with the man who had seduced his sister and was living with her and their illegitimate children, and a Lodge to which Alfred Dickens still belonged (although he would die later that year) is a complete mystery.

It may be that Edwy thought his sister and Augustus were legally man and wife. This would require a complete absence of knowledge of the existence of Harriett Dickens, however, and a belief that Bertha and Augustus had been married either in England or on arrival in America. If on the other hand, as would seem more likely, he was aware that Augustus's wife was still living and that Bertha was not married, could not be married, to him, this would raise many questions. Bertha's brothers, of course, were not subject to the same moral code as their sister: a cursory examination of the private lives of her own brothers reveal a rather less than exemplary standard of conduct in their own personal lives. Edwy Phillips, for example, married his first wife Margaret Browne in September 1838, only days, it would seem, after the birth of their first son, James Tobias Phillips. This child was, most unusually, baptized only several years later – presumably because of his illegitimacy – a lapse that would appear to have had no moderating influence on Edwy's attitude towards Bertha and her children in the ensuing tragedy of their later lives.

Henry Druit Phillips had married, in 1865, a young woman named Thurza Saunders, eleven years his junior. Which is not so unusual, except for the fact that at least four years earlier, according to the census returns of 1861, he was noted as already living with her as man and wife, in Queen's Square, Holborn – and with a five-year-old son.

We should also consider the case of Bertha's youngest brother, Pearce Phillips, later also known as Frank Pierce Phillips, who was not only a serial bigamist but ended up in court in New Zealand in 1882. Pearce, who had been a midshipman in the Merchant Navy, claimed in court that his first wife, whom he married when he was nineteen, was a prostitute. His last attempted marriage was to a girl who was fourteen when they met: he was then her schoolmaster.

Edwy Phillips's second marriage to Emma Browne had produced a daughter, born in May 1850, and her name was Malvina Dickens Phillips. The choice of middle name, of course, is highly significant: it would seem likely that it was in honour of perhaps a godparent or family friend and probable that that friend or godparent was Augustus.

The date of Malvina's birth and the adoption of Dickens as a middle name would therefore suggest that the association between the two families was earlier than we might have thought and may suggest that the young woman with whom Augustus was said to be romantically involved when he was a young clerk working for Chapman's was Bertha. If so, why he married Harriett, rather than a young woman with whom he had already formed an association, is hard to guess. It is possible, however, that Harriett's wealthy family background was a temptation he found hard to resist.

One aspect of the story of Augustus and Bertha has been greatly overlooked, and that is the account of events from the point of view of Harriett, his abandoned wife.

The settlement made on behalf of Harriett Lovell at the time of her marriage to Augustus Dickens was a common enough arrangement in this period, when a woman's ability to hold property or funds in her own right or to exercise the management of her investments was so strictly limited. The only way of safeguarding the inheritance or funds settled on a woman entering into marriage was by a carefully worded agreement and by the appointment of trustees to act on her behalf.

It was just as well that such caution was shown before the marriage of Harriett and Augustus. Within a few years, Harriett had become blind and Augustus had fallen in love with another woman, and at this most vulnerable point in her life, deserted his wife, leaving her utterly dependent on the protection of her brother-in-law and his management of her financial affairs. If Augustus had not been prevented by the terms of the trust from having access to his wife's inheritance, there is little doubt that she would have been left with no financial support.

Augustus fled to America, accompanied – or at least followed – by Bertha Phillips, the young woman whom he had met in London, and who, in their new life together, would become Mrs Augustus Dickens in name, if not in law. Only after the death of Augustus, and the consequent publicity that ensued on both sides of the Atlantic, was Bertha was exposed as his mistress and their three surviving children proven to be illegitimate. For Harriett, the death of her estranged husband was an opportunity to assert some control of her own life, for so long managed on her behalf by Charles Dickens and nominally, it would seem, her brother Francis and Claudius Francis du Pasquier. In her widowhood, at last, she found some independence and a greater affirmation of her identity than had been the case as a wife, if only in the margins of her late husband's family.

Harriett's continued presence within the family circle is quite clear from the evidence of Dickens's surviving letters. There are occasional references to Harriett, for example on 27 September 1866, when writing to his sister-in-law Georgina from the office of *All The Year Round*, sending his love to 'Letitia and Harriett', and on 2 January 1867, to Letitia, from Gad's Hill, suggesting tickets in the stalls for one of his public readings, on the 15th of that month – three months after Augustus's death.

Clearly Dickens felt a duty to protect and support Harriett: it is also true that he could hardly do otherwise if he wanted to minimise the risk to his own reputation posed by Augustus's desertion and his adulterous domestic arrangements in America.

It is not clear, in truth, exactly when Harriett realised that she had been abandoned, as it seems her husband's flight to America and his intention to settle there with Bertha may not have been recognised as such at the time. Charles Dickens was himself unsure of his brother's movements during this period and the exact circumstances. From Harriett's point of view, the only evidence we have of the acknowledgement of her change in circumstances is that according to the 1861 census she was then living with her widowed mother, Elizabeth Lovell, and the children of her sister Julia, in Chepstow Villas, Kensington. Harriett is described as a 'fundholder in trust'. She would outlive Dickens and spent quite a few years of her widowhood in lodgings with his sister Letitia. Harriet died in Dulwich in 1901, living as a boarder among strangers.

Harriett's role throughout her married life, and before marriage, was one destined to follow the line set out for her by others, from the supervision of a father and a brother to that of a husband – like so many other dutiful Victorian wives and daughters. However, in her case, her lack of independence was even more acute as a result of the abandonment by Augustus – and of course her blindness made her utterly reliant on the goodwill and assistance of friends and family alike.

Her means of support and every circumstance of her life – at least until she was widowed – became subject to the decisions of those male relatives and guardians given control of her money: from the point of the marriage settlement made on her behalf, and, significantly, at the very moment of her wedding to Augustus, when her own timid signing of the marriage register entry, below a casual misspelling of her Christian name, is overwritten by the flamboyant signature, so determinedly underlined, of her new husband. Her name would also be misspelled by her brother-in-law,[2] and in at least one census entry made on her behalf ('Harriette', in 1871), even as her married surname and status as 'Mrs Augustus Dickens' had been appropriated by the woman who had fled to America with her husband.

No photograph or portrait of Harriett has come to light: it is fitting, perhaps, that we have no image of her: another invisible woman, like Ellen Ternan, for so long marginalised and obscured in the wider narrative of the Dickens family history. The extent of Harriett's invisibility, of course, is made even more poignant by her own sightlessness and lasting experience of a world unseen, translated for her through the interpretation of others – those who managed and controlled the circumstances of her life.

At the time of the 1851 census, Augustus is recorded at two separate addresses: at home with his wife Harriett at 5 John's Terrace, Lewisham village, but also at a house in Bloomsbury, the home of a physician, with other members of the family attending their dying father, John Dickens. The duplicate census listings may be due to confusion by Harriett as to whether a temporary absence from home should be counted – or it may suggest that that their living arrangements were already somewhat irregular.

In the census entry in Lewisham, Harriett is stated to be living with her husband, described as a merchant's clerk, and two servants. She is not listed as blind, although there was provision for this, which would seem to contradict the story generally accepted that she had lost her sight within a couple of years of their marriage. It is not until the 1861 census, by then deserted by Augustus and living with her mother Elizabeth in Kensington, that Harriett is described as 'blind not from birth'.

Harriett and Augustus appear not to have had any children, although some biographers such as Claire Tomalin[3] have suggested that they may have done so. No children are mentioned in any records relating to family wills or settlements, and there appears to be no trace of any birth or burial records of children born to the couple.

Clearly Augustus went on to have several children with Bertha: two sons and a daughter, as well as triplets who died soon after birth, so one might assume that Harriett was infertile, or that they did not cohabit for very long. It is also just possible, perhaps, that her failure to bear children, aligned with her development of blindness after a few years of marriage, was because she was one of many Victorian wives who contracted a sexually transmitted disease from their husbands. A significant percentage of nineteenth-century men were infected in this way at the time of their marriage, presenting a potentially fatal, or at least life changing, risk to the health, childbearing ability and wellbeing of their wives – and the health of any surviving children.

Pure speculation, but it is interesting to note that Bertha's health was also poor, and she was to lose four of the seven children she had with Augustus: not such an unusual statistic then, but possibly significant, especially in view of her husband's early death, at the age of thirty-nine. However, it is true to say that Dickens's two other brothers, Alfred and Frederick, died at a relatively young age, from pulmonary-related illness – in Frederick's case aggravated by alcoholism, a factor that may also have contributed to the death of Augustus within only a few years of fleeing to America.

Chapter Sixteen

Amboy and Chicago

From a number of references to his younger brother in surviving letters, it would appear that Charles Dickens was still in communication with Augustus and on good terms with him until at least the year before he left for America. In May 1855, for example, we know he wrote to his younger brother in response to some sort of enquiry, seemingly about a journey he was planning.[1] 'I cannot think of anyone on that route which is quite out of my beat. If I should recall any useful personage in the course of tomorrow, I will write again.' He signed himself: 'Affectionately always ...'

There appears to have been a good deal of confusion about the date of the elopement of Bertha and Augustus, but this letter should have suggested that it was later than was previously accepted, and certainly not as some would imply soon after his marriage to Harriett.

In the Post Office Directory for 1856, Augustus Dickens is listed under 'ship and insurance' at the Gracechurch Street address, and also Lee Terrace, Blackheath. We know from other documentation that he lived at number 6, Lee Terrace – presumably still with Harriett, but it is unclear. This was, after all, the year in which Bertha most probably became pregnant with their first child.

On 7 May 1858, however, a notice in the *London Gazette* confirms that the residence of Augustus was now Amboy, Illinois: it announced the dissolution of a partnership between him and one Henry Warren, based at an address in Gracechurch Street, regarding a business formed as 'Ship and Assurance Agents and Merchants'. The date of the dissolution is noted retrospectively as being as of the first day of February 1857. By 4 June 1857, an advertisement in the local press reveals Augustus's new venture – the 'People's Cheap Store' – in Amboy: the first proof of his residence in America. There is now reason to suspect, in fact, that he had arrived in the country in the previous year.

Bertram Dickens, the eldest son of Augustus and Bertha Phillips, was born on 9 June 1857, so was conceived around September 1856 – and it would seem reasonable to assume, therefore, that his parents' elopement to America may have taken place sometime in that year, or early in 1857. It may be that if the relationship was already an intimate one, Bertha's pregnancy had necessitated the flight from England.

This may not be the sole reason, however: there are references in some sources to 'a dishonourable act' committed by Augustus, which may have caused him to feel his family would never forgive him and persuaded him to leave for America.[2] This may have been interpreted by most as relating to his seduction of Bertha, and the heartless abandonment of Harriett, but shameful though his behaviour may have been, and no doubt it was part of his reason for leaving, the act that forced his departure from England was something else entirely – a matter relating to his previously unknown business life back in England, as will be revealed.

A sense of uncertainty within the family about the exact date of their flight would seem to be suggested by Charles in a letter of 1859 written to his sister-in-law Helen in which he discusses Augustus, who 'had not been in America three months (I think) when he wrote asking me to correspond with some man or other who had done something for him, and who would write to recommend me to advance him a sum of money ...'

In this letter he explains that he had chosen not to communicate with his errant brother for fear of encouraging him to use his name for advancement or to secure a loan. He says the more 'conspicuous' he is, the less he can risk the involvement of others in Augustus's schemes, or expose himself to criticism of 'the fools and knaves who are always panting to yelp at a public man ...' Here we see clearly the priority for Dickens was his own reputation and the risks raised by the threat of publicity surrounding his brother, rather than any need to help him out.

Whatever his lack of certainty about the exact circumstances and timing of Augustus's arrival in America, it must be significant that, according to a Coutts's archivist quoted by Moss and Moss, the first payment of money to support Harriett was made on 26 October 1857.[3] This must mark the point at which her abandonment was acknowledged, presumably after formal verification of some sort.

In his early days in Amboy, it is reported Augustus had handbills signed 'Boz' distributed in the city to announce his plans to give a lecture, or lectures, on Shakespeare.[4] If true, the use of his own former nickname would be a telling act – not just an attempt to cash in on his famous brother's name, but a determination to reclaim his own identity and independence, his own nickname, at the furthest possible distance from his old life.

Amboy was a new town in a farming area about a hundred miles west of Chicago that had grown along with the expansion in the 1850s of the Illinois Central Railway: the company's divisional headquarters would be built there. By 1856, there was a population of around 2,000 residents: only in March of the following year, the year in which Augustus arrived, was the name formally adopted. The new Mr and Mrs Augustus Dickens, as they presented themselves, had chosen to settle in a pioneering small town in mid-western America and begin a new life. For a while, they managed to live quietly and happily enough.

Within two years of the birth of Bertram, another son was born – Dudley, who died in infancy. Adrian Charles Dickens arrived in 1860, to be followed two years later by Amy Bertha. In 1865, Augustus and Bertha were to become the parents of triplets: Lincoln, Violet and Ophelia, but these babies survived for only a short time, a loss that must of course have been immensely difficult, especially for Bertha, and perhaps contributed to the tragedy yet to unfold.

In 1860, as detailed in the Federal Census, Augustus Dickens was a farmer in May township, Lee County, Illinois, a settlement that in 2010 had a recorded population of only 304 residents. Here he worked a 40-acre farm – a one-horse farm; 22 acres of the land were listed as 'unimproved', the rest 'improved' and growing wheat, Italian corn, and oats. It would appear that, like the store, farming was not destined to be a successful enterprise, however, for Augustus. Newspaper reports of the period refer to particularly hard weather conditions, including, on 3 June, a widely destructive tornado, and this may well have made his new venture unviable.

Whatever the reason for leaving Amboy, later in the same year as the census he moved to the North Clark area of Chicago, where he worked as a clerk for the land department of the Illinois Central Railroad. He had asked Charles, via their sister-in-law Helen, wife of Alfred, to assist in obtaining a post, but this had not been successful, or apparently necessary. He gained promotion to the level of 'correspondent' and he and Bertha seemed to enjoy a good life, living in a two-storeyed, gabled 'frame cottage', entertaining a range of visitors, holding musical soirees, and impressing their new friends with their cultured tastes, and amiable nature.[5] In 1866, an article in the *Chicago Tribune*, published after Augustus's death, describes him as 'highly esteemed by all with whom he came into contact. He was a man of that happy, cheerful, kind-hearted disposition which endeared him to his friends, and made but few enemies …'[6]

In 1876, an article in the *New York Sun* quoted a man called William Munt who claimed to have been a friend of Augustus and Bertha, describing the couple as he had known them:[7]

> Mr and Mrs Augustus Dickens won the respect and affection of their neighbors in Chicago. Mrs Dickens was cultured, refined, and amiable, and an affectionate wife and mother. Mr Dickens was somewhat addicted to drink, but otherwise he was an affectionate husband. He had a fair education, but he exhibited no remarkable talents. In one respect he seems to have resembled his distinguished brother, namely, in his turn for humor. He was good company, and, like the great novelist, was given to caricaturing. He quickly detected anything grotesque in persons whom he met and his talent for caricaturing such persons made his company much sought. He was volatile and wayward, but he attended to his duties as record and report clerk in the land office of the Illinois Central Railroad to the satisfaction of his employers, and kept the place by his merit until his death. He was generous to a fault, giving without stint to every beggar who approached him.

Some sources claim that the house in North Clark was bought with money sent by Bertha's family; that her family believed her to be his wife and maintained some sort of communications with her. Perhaps they had been told, as some were, that Augustus had obtained a divorce and married Bertha in the US: records from this period were destroyed in the massive Chicago fire of 1871, so it is unlikely that this can be verified, nor perhaps the assertion in a letter to his daughter in 1865 by Dickens's friend, the actor Charles Kean, that Augustus had become an American citizen.[8]

Certainly there was still communication with both the Dickens and Phillips families to some extent – on 14 February 1861, news from London reached Bertha that her mother had died. Augustus immediately cancelled invitations sent to friends for that evening, explaining in one letter that the news of Bertha's loss 'has quite prostrated her & turned our abode from that of jollity into the house of mourning'.[9] It is certainly possible that Bertha received some sort of bequest then, as well as on the death of her father in 1867. By that point, of course, she was in desperate need of financial support.

On 4 October 1866 Augustus Dickens died from tuberculosis. He was only forty years old. Augustus, his brothers Alfred and Frederick, and his sister Fanny, all died relatively young, apparently from pulmonary-related conditions: perhaps their poor health and susceptibility to disease was a consequence of the circumstances of some of their childhood years. In the case of Augustus, as his illness was said to have lasted only four weeks it may be that other factors were to blame, including perhaps some underlying disease – but several accounts suggest that he drank heavily and that this was really the cause of his early death.

With no religious ceremony, Augustus was buried, on a Sunday, in the plot in Graceland Cemetery in which lay the three babies lost in previous years.

On 21 October, Charles Dickens referred to the news about his brother in a letter to his assistant William Henry Wills: Moss and Moss state that he 'expresses no grief', but his comments are prefaced with an admission of some regret: 'Poor fellow! A sad business altogether.' He then continued: My mind misgives me that it will bring upon me a host of disagreeables from America.' Whether or not he was referring to the demands of Augustus's 'wife', or the emergence of new criticism from the American press about his conduct to his brother's family, it might appear, again, that his concern was as much about the impact on his life, in terms of reputation, or nuisance caused, as any sadness about the fate of Augustus.

Bertha did her best to continue their life in Chicago, within the limits of their new circumstances. She moved her family to the back of their house and reportedly, for a while at least, let the other rooms to relatives of her late husband, Emily and George Lawrence. Emily Lawrence was the daughter of John Henry Barrow and a first cousin to Charles and Augustus, and in the light of her own family background, should have been sympathetic to the unorthodox domestic arrangements of her cousin and his mistress: her own parents were not married. Emily was one of the children of Dickens's uncle and Lucina Pocock, an illegitimate, probably Anglo-Indian, daughter of Captain Luke Pocock, a wealthy, former East India Company man.

In later life, Emily Lawrence sought to distance herself from the part she had played in the lives of Augustus and Bertha, and in particular her failure to support their orphaned children after their mother's death. In truth none of the children's English relatives did much to help them.

Just over a year after his brother's death, Charles Dickens arrived in America to begin a five-month reading tour, which he hoped would prove a profitable venture. He would encounter the sort of fevered attention that is a familiar part of contemporary celebrity culture – verging on the hysterical, accompanied by an unparalleled intensity of coverage by the press.

Dickens's health was to prove barely able to meet the demands of this gruelling tour, and as a consequence, or perhaps using it in part as a pretext, he amended his proposed schedule of readings and decided to exclude certain western cities, including Chicago. This was to cause a good deal of offence and then unwanted speculation as to why he was 'avoiding' such a major venue. In February, the *Chicago Tribune* and other papers begin to draw attention to the writer's personal link to the city – and to the fate of his late brother's family.[10]

> One of the principal reasons for Mr. Dickens' coming to the United States, we are assured, was to visit the grave of his brother, and to comfort the heart of the widow and her orphans with the sympathetic offerings of a brother's heart. Those who see Mr. Dickens merely on the platform, and know of him only as the recipient of thousands of dollars for each evening's performance, scarcely imagine that while he is before them, the delineator of the joys and sorrows of his own creation, his thoughts are far away upon the shores of Lake Michigan, where lies the unmarked grave of the playmate of his early days.
>
> While he reads to his audiences in Boston, New York and elsewhere the story of the Nickleby family, it is impossible to suppose that, like Ralph of that name, he would forget the widow of his brother, whose young children would have been suffering ere this for want of food, but for the charity of Mr. Augustus Dickens' American friends …

According to Moss and Moss, it was a report from the London correspondent of the *Boston Daily Advertiser* that resulted in an article suggesting, on 22 April, that the widow of Augustus Dickens was not Bertha, but a woman in England, in 'feeble health'. Around this time, the other 'Mrs Augustus Dickens', living in Chicago, also began to suffer from ill health, some sort of illness that appears to have led her to become dependent on morphine. That this dependency began at the time of her exposure as an unmarried woman, and the mother of three illegitimate children, cannot reasonably be considered coincidental. From now on, Bertha's attempt to rebuild her life began to unravel – by December, the signs were clear that despite the kindness of neighbours, and the financial support offered to her by former colleagues of Augustus, she was no longer able to cope with the new circumstances of her life.

On Christmas Eve, Bertha sent her children to visit their Lawrence cousins, on the west side of the city. Another letter purportedly from Bertha, published subsequently to events that now were unfolding, explains to Emily Lawrence why the children will be visiting without her:

> Dear Emily:
> After seeing you yesterday, somebody relieved me of my purse and its contents. The affair has worried me so that I have concluded not to accept your invitation for myself, but to let the children come. Please see them safely to the cars; or, if too late after your festivities, keep them all night; but be sure and send them home early in the morning as we are anticipating a merry little dinner to-morrow.

The next day, Christmas Day, 1868, two years after the death of Augustus Newnham Dickens, Bertha was found dead in her bed by neighbours, alerted by the children that there was no response from the house when they returned.

As reported by the *Chicago Tribune* representative who attended the inquest held the same night, Bertha had been found lifeless on her bed, 'her head resting on one hand, the other lying on the counterpane. Her face was composed and as natural as if she were in a deep sleep, and so it proved – that she was in the sleep that knows no waking.'

A neighbour, it was reported, had been asked by Bertha on Christmas Eve to buy her some more morphine from the druggists and had done so. Yet it was said she had been 'in good spirits, cheerful and bright' when visiting another friend, Mrs Pease, that night. And it was noted: '… she had made every preparation for Christmas dinner; the turkey was in the sideboard ready for roasting, the children's candy, and the raisins, and other ingredients for plum pudding were in the house'.

The *Tribune* reporter continued: 'The scene that took place when the little ones, who came home to partake of Christmas fare, and found they had no mother any more, may be imagined.'

It was concluded that Bertha was the victim of an overdose of morphine, 'administered by herself while in a state of mental aberration'. This explanation neatly avoided the emphasis on motive and helped to offer a degree of ambiguity that allowed family and friends to mask what may have been an act of suicide with the possibility of accidental death.

Despite the failure to reach any proof of deliberate self-harm, however, reports in the press both in America and abroad would be quick to present the death as the result of a deliberate overdose: a suitable ending to a story involving a shameless woman who had lived with a man already married to another. For her children, so soon after the death of their father, the death of their mother was, of course, particularly hard: and came with such cruel timing. And the irony of the close association of the season's sentimental festive celebrations with the work of their famous uncle was a point that did not go unremarked in the *Chicago Tribune* reporter's coverage:

> Charles Dickens did not write a Christmas story this year because "others imitated his productions" but a discarded member of his family, 4,000 miles away, who shines like the moon by light reflected by him, has furnished the subject of a Christmas story that in pathos and all the elements of a sorrowful fate cannot be imitated by anyone or produced by Charles Dickens himself.

It was claimed that at the time of her death Bertha was reading a book about the effects of morphine and may have been considering taking an overdose – or it may have been merely that she was interested in knowing more about the effects on the human body. She had been taking the drug, ostensibly, to alleviate the 'neuralgia' that had started, coincidentally or not, around the time that her unmarried status had been revealed in the press and she had become exposed to condemnation by those who had previously assumed she was the rightful widow of Augustus Dickens. The ignominy of her position and that of her children, now revealed as illegitimate, in a world so intolerant of sexual immorality must have weighed heavily on her spirit. Perhaps she thought her children would be treated better as orphans, left to the care of strangers, than as the bastard children of a shamed mother.

Had she become dependent on morphine? It would seem so. She may have depended on it as a temporary escape from an increasingly problematic reality. Whether by accident or design, anyway, death removed her forever from what must have seemed to be a place of no hope. Poor Bertha.

Her funeral took place on Sunday, 27 December, and she was laid to rest with Augustus and the triplets who had died in the year before their father's death. But what fate was to befall her three surviving children now? The eldest child, Bertram, was about twelve years old (his exact date of birth is unknown): Adrian was eight, and Amy only six. After returning temporarily to the care of the Lawrence cousins, it was thought by some, or at least assumed by the *Tribune* reporter, that the children would be sent to England, where their nearest relatives were on both sides of the family. Unfortunately, neither the Dickens nor the Phillips family would show any interest in giving a home to the orphaned children.

Charles Dickens had been the subject of much critical coverage from the American press regarding his apparent indifference to the plight of his Chicago relatives and accused of avoiding the city on his tour of America. Charles did eventually provide some financial support for his brother's children: but he did so quietly, and without informing the editors of the American press, who therefore formed their own conclusions and criticised his perceived indifference to the plight of his nephews and niece despite the very handsome profits made on his recent reading tour – clearing a very satisfactory figure of around £19,000. The limited financial support given to his nephews and niece was a fairly typical response by Dickens when his reputation was at stake: the use of money to resolve the risk of personal embarrassment.

Arrangements were made by a court to award guardianship of the children to a former friend of Augustus, and then American census records show that two years after the death of their mother, twelve-year-old Amy was living with a family by the name of Keeling, while her nine-year-old brother Adrian was two households away with a local physician, Edmund Travers, and his wife. Bertram's whereabouts are a mystery: presumably at school elsewhere.

After the death of Charles Dickens in 1870, it was clear no provision had been made to continue payments to the children: they were abandoned to the care of strangers, deserted by their families in England.

Chapter Seventeen

Other people's money

"If the money I have sacrificed had been all my own, Mr Rugg," sighed Mr Clennam, "I should have cared far less."

"Indeed, sir?" said Mr Rugg, rubbing his hands with a cheerful air. "You surprise me. That's singular, sir. I have generally found, in my experience, that it's their own money people are most particular about. I have seen people get rid of a good deal of other people's money, and bear it very well: very well indeed."

Little Dorrit

Before the passing of the Married Women's Property Act in 1882, a woman had little control over any inheritance, money, or indeed property, but widowhood largely restored those rights – and Harriett Dickens also had the protection of her marriage settlement. Soon after Augustus's death, therefore, she or perhaps her family acted to claim her entitlement under the terms of her marriage settlement, as revealed now by the discovery of documents in the Ouvry Collection held by the Charles Dickens Museum archive. It appears her claim was dealt with by a Francis John Du Pasquier, a lawyer and the nephew of Claudius Du Pasquier, one of the two other trustees of her settlement. A letter was sent on Harriett's behalf in October 1867 about the transfer of funds: whether this was done, however, is unclear.

According to documents held at the British Library and in the Dickens Museum archives, Harriett Lovell had an inheritance of around £2,500, with annuities of £17 10½s. It would appear the latter amount represented a rate of three per cent return on the invested sum, originally held in stocks and other 'property'.

There are other papers held by the Dickens Museum relating to the trust funds created by the marriage agreement for which Charles Dickens was one of the guardians: it was noted at the time that the bank annuities' share of the fund 'by change of investment' now accounted for £1,534 10s 6d. Interestingly, this was around the same amount of money that had been lent to Patrick Rouse in order for him to purchase Ravensfield House, with a loan extended to him by the same three men who were trustees of Harriett's marriage settlement: Charles Dickens, Claudius du Pasquier and Francis Lovell.

Is this mere coincidence? Had there been a withdrawal of funds, perhaps a cashing in of stocks and transfer of money to some other investment, during the years in which Charles Dickens, her brother Francis and Claudius Du Pasquier had unchallenged control of her money? Or had the money been used elsewhere – perhaps as a mortgage to Patrick Rouse – and returned in the form of annuities at some later date?

Harriett's brother Francis Lovell, one of the three original trustees of her settlement, had died just a month before Augustus, in September 1866, leaving Charles Dickens and du Pasquier as the remaining guardians of her investments, although it seems that Charles was the active agent regarding this responsibility. It would appear significant that Harriett later chose to use the Du Pasquier family law firm to question the status of the investments made in her name.

Was the Ravensfield mortgage backed with money from Harriet's trust fund? If so, was that really a wise and safe use of such a large portion of her inheritance? Would stocks and shares, or some other form of savings, not have offered a more stable and orthodox way of safeguarding her financial security?

And why would Charles Dickens and Harriett's two guardians undertake such a risky venture, with money meant for Augustus' wife? Why make such an undertaking, at this point, in fact, five years after the marriage had taken place? Was this some indication of concern over her future, perhaps due to early warnings of marital problems and a need to change the scope of her investments? Or was Dickens using the funds in his control for another purpose?

Dickens had opened an account with Coutts in 1837, with the profits that had resulted from the success of *Pickwick Papers*. The bank's archives retain records of his financial transactions, access to which is only given to researchers with permission from the Dickens family: perhaps it is not surprising, therefore, that there appears to have been only limited analysis of the information provided in the details of his account. We know that in 1854–55 the account balance fell below £4,000.[1] If, therefore, the loan to Rouse came not from Harriett's funds but from his own money, it would have been a substantial investment to make at this time.

In 1838, to offer a point of comparison, his purchase of the Devonshire Terrace property had cost only £700, and in 1851 the cost of a forty-five-year lease on Tavistock House was also around £1,500, so equal to the value of the Hendon property; and later in his career, £1,500 was the amount earned by one reading tour. The purchase of Gad's Hill Place in 1856, an acquisition of such personal significance to Dickens, was to cost him £1,790: not much more than the amount lent to Patrick Rouse. If the Ravensfield loan was an investment on behalf of Charles's sister-in-law, Harriett, and her inheritance, it was certainly a very curious one, because the small amount of interest that would have accrued in the short time it took for the debt to be repaid was minimal, and would indicate a low return for a high level of risk.

A copy of the marriage settlement made on behalf of Harriett, held in the British Library, suggests that at least some of the inheritance from her father of around £2,574 was held in stocks – at that time a safe investment as annual returns from such funds were high during the period of Victorian industrial expansion and likely to be much higher than the return from any interest paid on the mortgage for Ravensfield House.

There is further evidence regarding the later form of investment for Harriett's fund: according to a statement by a former archivist of Coutts quoted by Moss and Moss, from October 1857, we read that Dickens was making payments to Harriett that were six-monthly dividends, 'probably on stock'.[2] It is suggested that there may have been two stocks involved, twice a year, amounting, for example, as shown in accounts for 1867 and part of 1868, to £23.0.6 and £14.11.6.

Charles Dickens's bank account records are kept in the Coutts Archives, at their offices in the Strand. By coincidence, this is only a short distance across the road from the location of the blacking manufactory where Dickens once worked as a young boy. The original Coutts building was further along the Strand in that period, at number 59, nearer to the Chandos Street site of the business to which he was transferred, where he was seen working in the window; but the young Charles must have passed the bank many times. Hard not to wonder to what extent his later friendship with Angela Burdett Coutts, or the opening of his own account with this bank, gave Dickens a sense of triumph over the adversity of his early years: and how extraordinary it would have seemed to him as a young boy that the currency of banks in the future would include the representation of his adult self, on a ten pound note, stuffed in the wallets and purses of almost everyone in the country.

The Dickens accounts are extensive but the entries not always easy to understand, and identification of some of the payments continues to elude even the most experienced of Dickensian scholars. It was just about possible to follow, however, the range of references – or lack of such – to funds relating to Augustus Dickens and then to his estranged wife Harriett.

As we know, Augustus and Harriett married in December 1848, and according to the terms of her marriage settlement her inheritance from her father should have been invested safely in stocks. Direct reference to payments regarding these investments, however, would appear to begin only in 1857, although there are a few minor disbursements from 1851 to a Mr A. Dickens, which may be Augustus, or perhaps their brother Alfred. This period coincides, more or less, with the years of the Ravensfield mortgage.

On 19 May 1857, there is an entry noting the payment of £13 11s 10d regarding 'Mr Augustus' Trust'. Presumably this was a reference to Harriett's trust, as Augustus was unlikely to have had his own. This was only three weeks before the birth of Bertram Dickens, his first child with Bertha, born in Illinois, on 9 June – we do not know if Charles knew about the impending birth: perhaps Augustus had asked him for money without disclosing the full circumstances of his flight to America. Alternatively, bearing in mind, as we shall see, that a notice had appeared in the press in February in regard to a meeting of Augustus's creditors, it may be that it had become clear that Augustus was not going to return to his wife, and the fund distribution was made not to him but to Harriett.

In the October accounts for that year there is the first mention of a payment that refers to a dividend (of £14 16s 9d) on a capital sum – £970 2s 10d – noted in brackets with the description '(F. Lovell & ors)', paid out twelve days later to 'Mr A Dickens' Trust'. That Augustus, now in America, had access to the trust seems unlikely, and it is probable that only Harriett could benefit from the funds, especially as her brother had been involved in the disbursement.

In April 1858, the 'Trust AD' produced another dividend of £14 2s 10d – and on 28 May a payment of £50 to the Trust was made. This is a highly significant date: the same day the Ravensfield arrangement was terminated. And, of course, it was in the week in which Dickens's personal life was in crisis, immediately after the separation from his wife, in the aftermath of the revelation of his involvement with Ellen Ternan.

Shortly after this momentous week, on 4 June, there is a payment noted to the account referring to '£1,000 New 3 pcts, £960'. For 8 June there is an entry stating, with no further explanation, that there has been an investment of £500. In what, or for whom, we do not know. Could these and other account entries represent a re-investment of £1,500 on behalf of the trust fund after the termination of the Ravensfield mortgage?

From now on it is evident that Dickens's accounts deal with the funds for which he was a trustee with regular entries, clearly defined as such. But not only does the pattern of entries change, there is a difference in the amounts accruing to the funds in the form of dividends: a difference that might suggest a change in scale of investment – or a more scrupulous form of accountancy.

As noted by Veronica Stokes, Harriett's inheritance appears to have been placed – when is unclear – into two separate stock investments, each yielding two six-monthly dividends of around £23 and £14. There are references to an investment – 'Consols' – worth £1,534 10s 6d, and another of £970 16s 9d: approximate in combined total to the amount left to her by her father. The smaller figure of £970 is first mentioned in October 1857, the second in September 1858. The obvious question, therefore, is this: if all or some of Harriett's money had been invested in stocks throughout the years before her desertion by Augustus, and during the period in which there was a loan made by her three trustees to Patrick Rouse, why were there not regular dividends, equal to the amounts that accrued from 1857–58, noted in the accounts?

Further questions: was some of the money not retained in stocks, but used by the trustees – or at least one of them – for part of the time? Was some of Harriett's fund, intended to produce annuities, 'resting' in Dickens's account as a capital sum, for some time, without being identified as such – or even diverted elsewhere? Is it a coincidence that the apparently later, larger total of stock investments approximates to the amount of money lent in the form of the mortgage for Ravensfield House?

It is clear from an inspection of Dickens's expenditure that although he made an awful lot of money, he spent perhaps more extravagantly than was wise: he enjoyed a high standard of living and chose to use his income accordingly.

On the subject of Ravensfield, if Patrick Rouse was making regular interest payments, and then, in May 1858, had paid off any outstanding capital owed, would this not show up in Dickens's accounts in some manner, either as a private arrangement, or as a trustee? Or was there an account elsewhere that managed this investment – or whatever it was? If so, why? Was it something with which he did not wish to be directly associated?

If the financial transaction regarding Ravensfield House was intended in some way to be to the benefit of Harriett's fund, why would Dickens and the two other trustees not invest the money directly, by purchasing Ravensfield House themselves, rather than lending the money to Patrick Rouse? They could easily have let the property and capitalised on their investment without the use of an intermediary. And such an intermediary: a common workman – an Irish bootmaker. Time to look closer at Patrick Rouse and try to understand why he became the recipient of Charles Dickens's extraordinary generosity.

Chapter Eighteen

The Arcade of Melancholy-Mad Bootmakers

Who was Patrick Rouse?

Census records indicate that he was born in Ireland, circa 1816. By 1841, he was living and working in London, and on 7 June of that year married Catherine Connolly, the daughter of an Irish weaver, in the Bavarian Chapel in Golden Square, Soho, a short distance from his lodgings at 43 Marshall Street, Soho. At the time of his marriage, Patrick is described as a shoemaker, the son of a clerk. After the birth of John Patrick Rouse in 1842, they moved to Denbigh Street, Pimlico, where daughter Mary was born in 1845. The birth was registered by Catherine Rouse: the entry is signed with her mark, denoting her inability even to write her name, in sharp contrast to her husband, who was literate and sported a confident style of handwriting on the surviving few documents connected with him.

Teresa Catherine Rouse, who would die in Hendon aged only ten years, was also born in Pimlico in 1847. At this point the family appears to have moved to Marylebone: Edward Rouse was born in St John's Wood in 1849. The youngest son, and last child, Joseph Ignatius Rouse, was the first and only one to be born in Hendon, in 1853.

By 1851, less than two years before Dickens so generously assisted him in the purchase of Ravensfield House, Patrick Rouse describes himself in his census entry as a master bootmaker, 'Carrying on Business in London', and he was living with his wife and children in a modest dwelling in the Hyde, on the western side of the parish of Hendon; his neighbours were a wheelwright and a road labourer. Just two years earlier, a temporary place of worship for Roman Catholics had been established by the Passionist order in a chapel in the Hyde and this may have been one of the reasons Patrick Rouse decided to settle in the area. A church for Catholics – Our Lady of Dolours church, in the Burroughs – was eventually built, in 1863, an achievement in which Rouse, by then a man of property, was 'instrumental', as we learn from a local obituary more than thirty years later.

According to rates records, by June 1852 Rouse had moved his family into another rented property, 'Stile House', on Church Lane, Hendon, close to Ravensfield House.

In January 1853, however, thanks to the help of Charles Dickens and his two co-signatories, the Irish bootmaker was to become the owner of Ravensfield House and from then on was a man of means: listed in the local directory as a gentleman, wealthy enough to support his son John Patrick in his studies for the priesthood and able to send Edward (who by 1871 was a law student) to a private Catholic school in Clapham. John Patrick Rouse rose eventually to the rank of Monsignor, and newspaper reports show him regularly celebrating Mass or weddings for the wealthiest and most well-appointed Catholic families of the time.

Patrick Rouse died while in Folkestone in 1894, from complications following a fall. His probate records describe him as a gentleman, of Ravensfield House, Hendon, and 12 and 13 Opera-arcade, Charing Cross. The estate was to be administered by his son, the Very Reverend Monsignor John Patrick Rouse, and amounted to £5,233 12s. Monsignor Rouse died in Switzerland in 1904, leaving his estate of more than £8,000 to a cousin. Two years later his property would be advertised for sale, by auction, on behalf of his executors – and was described as 'highly important and increasingly valuable, part of an estate of over nine acres, with two freehold houses' – the other being the neighbouring house "Fenella", which brought in a ground rent of £16 10s per annum, compared to the rent of Ravensfield itself, which was set at an annual rate of £120.[1] Clearly the Rouse family had done very well from the acquisition of Ravensfield House more than fifty years earlier.

Rouse had chosen not to live at Ravensfield House until the latter years of his life, but let it and lived in rented accommodation, first in Golders Green and then at Ivy House in Parsons Street – opposite the local rectory that was home to the infamous 'Sultan of Hendon', Reverend Theodore Williams. The Williams household is next but one below the Rouse entry in the 1861 census returns. In his own household entry, incidentally, Patrick Rouse declares, with evident satisfaction, that he employs one Ann Quin, described by him as a 'gentleman's servant'.

The Reverend Williams is unlikely to have formed a favourable opinion of his new neighbour Mr Rouse. Williams was notorious for his snobbery and temper, and had an apparently insatiable appetite for inciting controversy, a tendency fuelled by his confrontational manner with parishioners, his arrogance – and his personal extravagance, an indulgence that was to lead him into serious debt and eventually imprisonment.

As a biography notes, during his childhood in Hendon in the 1820s, Dickens's close friend Mark Lemon was well acquainted with Williams, living at the Farmhouse adjacent to the parish church. He was said to have been strongly influenced by his years in Hendon, and specifically by the literary and classical allusions of the Rector in his sermons.[2] Certainly the evidence from the catalogue of sale of his books in 1827 suggests that the range and depth of Williams's scholarly interests were exceptional and must have shaped the style and content of his oratory.

In 1844, during Lemon's tenure as editor, a reference was made in *Punch* to the combative minister whom Lemon had known in his younger days:[3]

> The Rector of Hendon – A Christian Peacemaker
>
> At the Edgware Special Sessions, the Rev. THEODORE WILLIAMS – a gentleman not unknown to fame – was charged with provoking a MR FOSTER SMITH, a neighbour, to a breach of the peace. The Rev. THEODORE, it appeared in evidence, "shook his fist" – his apostolic fist! – in MR. SMITH'S face; and with lips that are, doubtless, wont to drop oil and honey, said – "You are a very dirty fellow, a shabby fellow; you are a coward." The Reverend peacemaker then added – "You dare not fight." Truly, a severe reproach from the Rector of Hendon – from one who hath the cure of souls.

This description, with its allusions to lips that 'drop oil and honey', and his 'fat smile', might be seen as reflective of the characteristics of the equally unctuous, hypocritical Chadband, as described in Chapter Twenty-five of *Bleak House*:

> "Peace, my friends," says Chadband, rising and wiping the oily exudations from his reverend visage. "Peace be with us! My friends, why with us? Because," with his fat smile, "it cannot be against us, because it must be for us; because it is not hardening, because it is softening; because it does not make war like the hawk, but comes home unto us like the dove. Therefore, my friends, peace be with us! My human boy, come forward!"

Dickens must have been well acquainted with the behaviour of the Reverend Dr Williams: he certainly knew about his history as a debtor – Williams's release from jail in 1853 (despite the enormity of the sum owed, nearly £40,000) was reported in the *Household Words Narrative* for that year, the year in which the Ravensfield agreement was made.

Quite apart from the connection with Mark Lemon, Williams's antics had been widely reported in the press at the time he was a young reporter – for example this case in August 1837, which had ended up in the church court: Williams had reported one local man – a rate payer, so someone of relative means – to a church court for 'brawling' with him. The impertinent Mr Farlar had dared to inform the Rector:

> You fancy yourself the Sultan of Hendon, but I will teach you that you have not Turks to deal with; we do not live in Tartary ... You are more impudent than the Surrey parsons and your conduct is unworthy of a gentleman, and you are a disgrace to the name of a clergyman ...

Mr Williams is reported to have provoked such an outburst by telling him: 'Such tricks as yours may do at Kensington, but they won't at Hendon', and he had taunted Farlar for failing to pronounce the H, in Hendon: 'we call it Hendon, not "Endon" ...'

There is another Hendon link with Dickens that has apparently been overlooked, relating to the story of 'The Italian Boy' murder, which is the subject of a fascinating book by Sarah Wise.[4]

In 1828, Williams appeared as a witness at a scandalous court case that took place under the auspices of the Middlesex Sessions, in which three local young men were accused of breaking into a vault in Hendon's parish church and severing a head from one of the bodies – as the report in *The Times* described it – 'to the outrage of public decency'.[5] What made this worse was the fact that one of the defendants, a medical student named Henry Haley Holm, was the son of the woman whose body had been violated in this way: it seems he was a follower of the work of pioneering phrenologist Johann Spurzheim. Another of the accused was the son of the local sexton. Williams, rather oddly, seems to have intervened and enabled the young men to evade any heavy punishment.[6]

The practice of 'burking', bodies being stolen for dissection, was a widespread fear in this period, a fear that increased after the murder in 1831 of a young boy, Carlo Ferrari, by John Bishop and Thomas Williams, who had shortened the process of supply to their clients by the act of murder.

For some reason, when Bishop and Williams (presumably no relation to the Sultan of Hendon) were in custody for the murder of the Italian boy and then convicted of the crime, the Rector of Hendon visited them regularly in Newgate and encouraged them to make a full confession – an action mentioned in press reports of the trial at a time when Dickens was a young reporter. One might wonder if the Reverend Williams had some sort of unhealthy interest in the subject of dissection and grave robbing: in any event, Dickens, believed by some to have written reports of the Bishop and Williams trial, would have been aware of both cases – and would probably have noted the involvement in both of the local rector.[6]

There are, of course, references to burking in *Pickwick Papers*, and *A Tale of Two Cities*, and indeed to Bishop and Williams, in Dickens's sketch of 1836, *A visit to Newgate*, which describes the casts of their heads on display there.

Chapter Nineteen

Hendon

That Dickens was familiar with Barnet, Finchley, Hendon, Golders Green and Hampstead, in the present-day London Borough of Barnet, is a fact well established, although perhaps not very well known. There are references to all these areas in his fiction – Hendon and Barnet are mentioned, for example, in *Oliver Twist*, Finchley in *The Old Curiosity Shop* – but also there are other references in his letters and journalism that reveal a knowledge of Hendon and a fondness for the area, which was within walking or riding distance of the city itself, a quiet landscape of villages and farmland, offering a day away from the pressures of life in town.

In a history of Hendon published in 1932, author and resident N.B. James states that Dickens was reported as having often been seen there and having a fondness for the view from St Mary's Churchyard.[1]

Dickens's close friend Mark Lemon retained his fondness for Hendon and wrote about his memories of what had been an idyllic rural childhood. Just 250 yards across the way from Church Farmhouse where he had lived with his grandparents is the site of Ravensfield House: both Lemon and Dickens would have known the property, Lemon from his childhood and continuing family connections to the area, Dickens from his walks in the area, and probably from Lemon's conversations.

Another, newly revealed association of Hendon with Dickens lies in the background to the story of *Oliver Twist.* A book by Dr Ruth Richardson published in 2012 – *Dickens and the Workhouse* – argued that the inspiration for this book lay largely in the Cleveland Street Workhouse, which was close to one of the early homes of Charles Dickens at two distinct periods in his young life: around the age of three and then briefly again when he was working in Doctors' Commons as a young clerk.[2]

In the later stages of *Oliver Twist*, after his brutal killing of Nancy, Bill Sikes goes on the run, following a route that must have been familiar to Dickens, through Islington, to Highgate, Kenwood, across Hampstead Heath and the

Vale of Health, down to North End, where Dickens's father had stayed when he was also on the run – from his creditors. After sleeping rough, Sikes heads off towards Hendon, but the people there seem suspicious of him and he goes back to the Heath. Earlier in the story, of course, the scenes that perhaps linger the longest in the memory are those set in the workhouse in which Oliver has spent his childhood. No doubt Dickens was aware of the Cleveland Street institution and may well have been influenced by aspects of the place and surrounding area, but new evidence reveals that there might be a strong case that locations in Hendon, and possibly Barnet, also worked their way into his imagination: perhaps this reinforces the depth of Dickens's association with the area in a way that forms the background to the story of Ravensfield House.

Located at Burroughs Lodge, just a couple of minutes' walk along the road from Ravensfield, there was, at one time, the Strand Union's workhouse for infants – known as the Infant Poor Establishment. The practice of having a more rural location to house the infant inmates of a London workhouse was quite common, this being better for their health and wellbeing. The first years of Oliver Twist's life were passed in such a place, before being transferred to the workhouse proper. The Strand Union Workhouse itself, in Cleveland Street, which served the parish of St Paul's Covent Garden, was of course the same workhouse referred to by Dr Richardson.

One other notable feature about Hendon as a source of possible inspiration has been overlooked, however. Across the road from the Infant Poor Establishment linked to the Cleveland Street Workhouse there was the local Hendon Poorhouse, located in a row of cottages next to Burroughs House, on the spot where there is now a block of flats. This poorhouse served the parish until the requirements of the new Poor Law Act dictated the need for a union workhouse: newspaper reports show that this was in the planning stages by late 1838, by which time instalments of *Oliver Twist* had been in publication for more than a year: looking now at events that took place at the old Hendon institution reveals at least one particularly notorious incident that would appear to have influenced Dickens's new work, and it involved a figure we have already met – the infamous Reverend Theodore Williams.

As Rector of Hendon, Williams was also chairman of the local Board of Guardians and as such responsible for overseeing the conduct of Hendon's old workhouse. In November 1836, a shocking story regarding Williams's actions regarding one particularly vulnerable inmate was reported widely in *The Times* and elsewhere in the national press.[3]

Captain Carvick, one of the Guardians of the Board, and a local magistrate, whose name in some of the press coverage is spelled, in a suitably Dickensian manner, as 'Carwick', informed his colleagues that he wanted to make a statement about the treatment of a pauper named Alice Shepherd at the workhouse in Hendon.

Newspaper reports of the fate of Alice Shepherd, a consumptive woman punished with a two-week-long starvation diet merely for daring to ask to be allowed to take a walk, seem to show parallels with some of the early parts of Oliver Twist's time in the workhouse.

The captain said that on the previous Saturday night, the master of the workhouse had come to him 'in a state of great agitation' and said that one of the inmates, Alice Shepherd, had been acting outrageously and violently, 'in the most beastly manner'. The Master had been obliged, it was said, to put Alice in a 'straight waistcoat'. The Reverend Williams went to the workhouse to see Alice. He said that the medical officer had advised she be kept in the straitjacket 'a few hours longer'. He claimed to have 'soothed her' and restored order in the workhouse.

The next Monday Alice was brought before the Reverend Williams in his capacity as magistrate. He felt her 'disgusting conduct' was such that she should be committed to the House of Correction, 'but as she had never been in a prison, he would not take so harsh a step' and instead he ruled that she should be punished by the master of the workhouse by solitary confinement for twenty-four hours and kept on a diet of bread and water until the next meeting of the Board – which met only once a fortnight.

Captain Carvick took another view of the punishment forced on this inmate. He told the Board that by accident he had called at the workhouse while Alice was being punished in this way. He was asked to go and look at her. He did so and saw: 'a thin spare woman apparently suffering from consumption, and the last person he should have thought to whom such a punishment should have been inflicted'.

He left the workhouse, 'but the idea of the poor woman suffering 24 hours solitary confinement, and fed on bread and water haunted him, and he returned the next day hoping the punishment had been mitigated …'

The reaction to Oliver Twist's 'impertinence' in asking for more food is perhaps an echo of Alice's daring to ask to go out for a walk: a reasonable request met by fury by those whose job it was to enforce the unremitting authority of the Board of Guardians, by whose mercy the undeserving poor were granted the means of a life of such bleak subsistence.

Both Oliver and Alice were subjected to solitary confinement, and yet, as we learn, the parish boy's punishment was to be considered not so bad because he was allowed out into the stone yard to wash under the pump, just as the Reverend Williams pointed out – he begged it to be understood – that the room appropriated for the solitary confinement and starvation of Alice Shepherd 'looked upon the yard where all the other paupers were, and therefore, was not a very severe punishment …'

In mid-January, within weeks of this story being reported, Charles Dickens was writing to his publisher Bentley that he had 'hit upon a capital notion for myself, and one which will bring Cruikshank out' … In other words, the creation of *Oliver Twist* had begun, and indeed the first chapters would be published in February 1837, illustrated by the starkly graphic work of George Cruikshank.

Chapter Twenty

Arcadia

Among the tenants who rented Ravensfield House in the 1850s were, at the time of the 1851 census, the family of a dentist called Joseph Davis, his wife Jeanette, their six children, a governess, and a nurse with the name of Blumy Weiller: perhaps the first Jewish family to settle in Hendon. Joseph Davis may have known Rouse before arriving in Hendon: in the early 1840s, both were in business in Pall Mall – Rouse's shop was very near to where Davis's earliest business was established: a few steps across the road, at number 123. Dickens had been a member of the Athenaeum, just a little further along Pall Mall, since 1838.

We know from reference in one of his letters – to his friend Frank Stone, in May 1852 – that in this period, in the matter of footwear, Dickens gave his custom not to Patrick Rouse but to another local bootmaker – one Richard Hall, at the Quadrant, 97a Regent Street.[1]

Whatever the reason for moving to Ravensfield, at the time Patrick Rouse was taking possession of the property, Davis and his family had disappeared, leaving their rates unpaid.

Local rate records show the cost of renting Ravensfield House in the period when it was newly owned by Patrick Rouse to have varied slightly but averaging around £110 a year: not a huge sum, and of course he was paying a substantial amount of rent for his own family. One must question how, with the limited income of a bootmaker, and so many outgoing expenses, it was possible for Rouse to repay a debt of £1,500 within only five years. And we must bear in mind that during the period of the mortgage, he was supposed to pay interest at three per cent – so around £45 per annum – while he was also paying other rental costs of his own as well as supporting his family, educating his sons – and, of course, running his own small business, with all the expenses and variation in income that it entailed.

Since at least 1844, Rouse had been based in one small shop in the Royal Opera Arcade, a location once described by Henry Mayhew, in his work of

1865, *The Shops and Companies of London*, as 'the Arcade of Melancholy-Mad bootmakers'. Mayhew was, of course, a member of Dickens's circle, and co-founder of *Punch* with Mark Lemon.

Interestingly, Rouse originally only had one shop, No. 13, but expanded to No. 12 in 1858, the year in which the Ravensfield mortgage was apparently paid in full. In that year, for whatever reason, Patrick Rouse's financial circumstances were favourable enough to allow him to rent an extra shop: was that because he no longer had to pay the interest on his mortgage – although there would appear to be no record of any payments – or had the mortgage been written off?

As for the melancholy bootmakers – perhaps their gloomy outlook was because of the fall in trade caused by the competition from the huge number of boot and shoemakers in London in the mid-nineteenth century, and the looming threat to their business from mass production. The more select traders established in the St James's area, offering bespoke services, would have continued to enjoy the patronage of wealthy customers, although the reference to the atmosphere of the Arcade in the 1860s would suggest a degree of decline. The tiny size of shops in the Arcade would not have allowed for many other workers engaged in Patrick Rouse's business, so one must presume his output was limited in scope, which may not have helped to sustain a particularly profitable turnover.[2]

The location of Rouse's shop, in fact, is perhaps of significance in more than one way and may hold some clue to Rouse's connection to Dickens.

The covered walkway of the Royal Opera Arcade, connecting Pall Mall with Charles II Street, was designed by John Nash and George Repton, circa 1816 to 1818, and runs along one side of the theatre that was originally known as the Haymarket Opera House. It was the first arcade of shops of this type to be opened in London – and was just yards around the corner from Dickens's clubs in Pall Mall – and indeed also near to the home of Claudius du Pasquier, at 62 Pall Mall. Rouse's shop was also very near to where Ravensfield tenant Joseph Davis's earliest business was established and continued until 1846: opposite the point from where the Arcade meets Pall Mall – a few steps across the road, at number 123.

It is interesting to note that Her Majesty's Theatre, as the building was then known, was closed, for four years or so from 1852, apparently due to the competition from Covent Garden's opera company: this must surely have had an adverse effect on the traders situated in the Arcade – a period that began just before the Ravensfield mortgage.

The Opera Arcade was virtually part of the theatre itself, on the corner of Pall Mall and the Haymarket: the length of the back of the building opened straight out into the arcade, and was evidently a well-used route of exit after night-time performances; a point to be considered in the context of the infamous character of the area, particularly in the evenings. An article from *Punch*, published in 1842, gives some idea, within the limitations of a respectable publication, of the furtive nature of the Arcade, alluding to its darkness and anonymity:

> The place is tenanted by a proud race of merchants, who are chiefly above their business – for they live in the little cavities over their shops; and it is supposed that they prefer this spot that they may carry on their trade without being publicly seen, – for if an article happens to be purchased in these dark recesses, it is impossible for the features of the vendor to be recognised by the purchaser.

Darkness and anonymity may well have been useful for some of the night-time activities of this area, just around the corner from the Haymarket, a centre of prostitution in the West End. One study specifically depicts the louche nature of the Arcade, describing it as follows:

> a place around the Opera House where people met before and after performances, and gathered during the intervals. After midnight, when the performances were over, the streets around the theatres, especially the Haymarket, were the parade of prostitutes. The Royal Opera Arcade, with its spatial connection to the Haymarket through the theatre lobby or via the external colonnade became the evening promenade for prostitutes looking for clients.[3]

In line with Victorian ideas on the influence of architecture, for good or evil, on the conduct of society, it was also felt that the very nature of arcade design encouraged immorality, offering an easy and convenient cover for the practice of prostitution. Such was the extent of this belief that at least one arcade, the colonnaded Quadrant in Regent Street, was pulled down in 1848 because of the number of women who would take shelter there in the course of their work. Burlington Arcade, like the Opera Arcade, had small rooms above the shops, which were said to have been used for immoral purposes.

In a study of 'Arcadia', published in Dickens's own journal *Household Words* in 1853, the same year as the Ravensfield arrangement was made with Patrick Rouse, there are references to Burlington Arcade, Exeter Change and the Lowther Arcade – 'an Arcade of desolation, silence, despair' – but not the Opera Arcade. A curious omission.[4]

Chapter Twenty-one

Nightly wanderings

Charles Dickens took a keen and active interest in the issue of prostitution, as described so well in Jenny Hartley's *Charles Dickens and the House of Fallen Women.*[1]

In this book we find an exploration of his attempts to run 'Urania Cottage', an innovative idea forged with Angela Burdett Coutts, his patron and partner in philanthropy, with the noble aim of rescuing young women from a life of crime, or a life on the streets, giving them a home; reforming, educating and preparing them for a new and better life in the colonies.

An article about Urania Cottage appeared in *Household Words* only a few weeks after the Ravensfield mortgage was signed. It may be that the timing of the article was significant, putting into context, as it does so carefully, and at this period in his life, the charitable work undertaken by the editor regarding these unfortunate young women. Dickens's personal commitment to this project was tireless, intense, and intimate – it was also demonstrated in one particularly high-risk activity: he is recorded as having targeted and pursued young women in the streets, and perhaps elsewhere, in order it seems to recruit them for his project.

As Hartley suggests, Dickens may fairly be accused of 'trawling the streets' in the course of his enthusiasm for identifying women to save, and on 12 April 1850, he wrote to Miss Coutts to tell her about exactly this form of activity. Hartley notes that Dickens has been 'pitching for the Home, with emigration as the selling point'.

The letter itself makes it clear that he is indeed actively looking for young women who might be suitable for the home:

> I cannot think of any better plan for finding inmates for the Home, than getting a room near the Magdalen on their Receiving-Days, and seeing the girls whom they cannot take in. Will you think of this? In the course of my nightly wanderings into strange places, I have spoken to several women and girls, who are very thankful, but make a fatal and decisive confusion between emigration and transportation.[2]

The Magdalen was a hospital in Southwark established in the eighteenth century for 'the Reception of Penitent Prostitutes'. The idea of Charles Dickens taking a room nearby to 'rescue' those unfortunate young women denied a place at this institution strikes rather a curious note, let alone his admission of approaching others during his own nocturnal activities.

Hartley continues:

> Encounters of a rather different kind are suggested by a letter written within a fortnight of this one, this time to his old friend Daniel Maclise. The two men had been out together the night before, and Dickens had been waylaid, But "the young lady was not interesting, and I was after you in three or four minutes". What kept him the three or four minutes, and what did he mean by "interesting"?

'Interesting', in this context, is an ambiguous term, a word that at the time might mean several things, including simply 'attractive'. These admissions, however, clearly demonstrate that, at this period of his life, Charles Dickens did approach women of the streets directly and engage with them. Such behaviour, even if entirely innocent and merely the act of a man looking for new recruits for his philanthropic project, may well have been misinterpreted by observers, thereby putting himself at risk of exposure – or the threat of it. Is it just possible that Dickens was seen in such a compromising situation – however innocent – and recognised? This is certainly possible: he would not have been the first high-profile figure of his age to be caught out in this way.

Jenny Hartley reminds us that as well as Charles Dickens, another prominent public figure was wandering the streets of London at this time in search of fallen women: William Gladstone is well known for his interest in this form of activity. 'Benevolent stalkers' is the term she gives them, while acknowledging that both individuals found the process 'exciting'.

Checking the *Household Words Narrative* shows that there is a report, published in perhaps rather surprising detail, in the 'Law and Crime' section for May 1853 – so only around three months after the Ravensfield mortgage had been arranged – describing an 'unfortunate misunderstanding' and an attempt at extortion in regard to William Gladstone, then serving as Chancellor of the Exchequer, as he had been walking home one night from Covent Garden having dismissed his carriage. Quite why Gladstone wanted to walk home is not clear, but he is known to have had a history of seeking out fallen women, ostensibly to give them moral and religious guidance.

> On his way he was accosted by a young woman; and while he was listening to her story, a man came up and calling him by name, threatened to "expose" him if he did not make it right with him, or promise him a government appointment.

Gladstone stated that the attempted extortion had taken place while he was in conversation with a young woman who was 'walking by my side' and had clung to his arm for protection when she spotted the alleged blackmailer 'just below' Coventry Street and Oxendon Street – both in the immediate proximity of Haymarket.

Streets surrounding the Opera Arcade and the Haymarket catered for the trade in prostitution, as recorded by Mayhew in 1861, with 'accommodation houses' in Oxenden Street and James Street, rooms let for the purposes of the women entertaining their customers.

From the publicity that resulted from this case, another story soon emerged in the form of an anonymised letter to *The Times*, in which it was revealed Gladstone had also been involved in an incident in the Haymarket in the previous year involving another two 'unfortunate' young women, to one of whom he gave money and then was 'unremitting' in his efforts to try to reclaim her – although it would appear unsuccessfully.

Mayhew also made the following observation:

> Men in a certain position avoid publicity in their amours beyond all things, and dread being seen in the neighbourhood of the Haymarket or the Burlington Arcade at certain hours, as their professional reputation might be compromised …

It was obviously a high risk to reputation for any man in danger of being recognised to walk through this area at night and engage with young streetwalkers – for whatever reason. By the 1850s, increased literacy and an increase in popular reading material, including publications that carried engraved illustrations, meant that the public were more familiar with the appearance of well-known political and social figures. Gladstone clearly attracted attention by his unorthodox missionary work, and Dickens too. Gladstone was the victim of attempted extortion – it is not unreasonable to suggest that Charles Dickens may also have been recognised in the course of his 'nightly wanderings' and similarly compromised.

Chapter Twenty-two

My bachelor state

In order to consider one possible explanation for the arrangements that existed between Dickens, Rouse and the Hendon property, it is necessary to examine the state of his family and domestic life in the years immediate to this curious affair. The year 1851 had been a particularly hard one for Charles Dickens and his family. As well as experiencing the loss of his father, his infant daughter Dora died suddenly while both parents were away from home; Catherine was spending time in Malvern, recovering from a period of ill health, undoubtedly the result of the wearying cycle over the years of her marriage of perpetual pregnancy and childbirth. In March 1852, less than a year since the death of Dora, Edward was born. There would be no more additions to the family.

Lilian Nayder's study of the life of Catherine Dickens offers a highly detailed account of the Dickens marriage and a sharp assessment of the balance of power between the writer and his wife.[1]

Nayder undertakes an assiduous investigation into the most intimate areas of the relationship between Mr and Mrs Dickens, going to the point of noting the high level of Catherine's fertility and the regularity of their sexual activity. Clearly Catherine became pregnant very easily, a consequence that her husband, while generally a loving father, came to regret.

The fact that no more children were to be born after 1852 would suggest, in an age when the use of any form of contraceptive practice amongst married couples was rare, that their intimate life may have ended around this time, some while before he fell in love with Ellen Ternan and felt the need to nail shut the door between their bedrooms. It is hard to believe, if one reviews the evidence, that he spent the next few years in a state of complete chastity. The earliest stage of Dickens's estrangement from his wife would appear to coincide with the period in which the Ravensfield mortgage was being arranged, and the mortgage was paid off in the week in which Dickens formally separated from Catherine.

Dickens's involvement with Urania Cottage would last from 1847 to 1858. His interest in active recruitment, as well as the other ways in which he oversaw the management of the young women at the home, clearly brought him into regular contact with the realities of sex work – and potentially offered a cover for any more personal engagement he may have had. As early as 1841, as noted by Clare Tomalin, he is known to have written to his friend Maclise (to whom he would later report the discarding of the young woman who was not 'interesting') in coded terms about certain services available to him should he join the Dickens family in nearby Broadstairs: 'There are conveniences of *all kinds* at Margate (do you take me?) and I know where they live.'[2]

Tomalin also points out the period in 1859 – after leaving Catherine and before his relationship with Ellen Ternan would appear to have become a sexual one – when Dickens complained to his doctor that: 'My bachelor state has engendered a small malady on which I want to see you …'

Dickens told both Collins and Forster of a lingering illness, which he hoped might be restored by the sea at Broadstairs, remarking to Collins: 'Perhaps a tumble into the sea might – but I suppose there is no nitrate of Silver in the Ocean?'[3]

Silver nitrate was, of course, a treatment for gonorrhoea at the time. In Tomalin's biography of Ellen Ternan we also read:

> From the early 1850s he had made what he called a "gipsey camp" in two rooms above the Household Words office at 16, Wellington Street, off the Strand, so that he could be free to remain there overnight when he chose. It was convenient for his nocturnal walks, his bachelor dinners and also his clubs, the Athenaeum and the Garrick, still more so for his frequent visits to the theatres clustered around the area – the Lyceum, Adelphi, Olympic, Covent Garden and Drury Lane, as well as the Surrey and the Victoria …[4]

And perhaps Her Majesty's, across the road from the Athenaeum, and round the back of the Haymarket – and adjacent to the Opera Arcade?

Dickens frequently socialised or took holidays with groups of male friends: association with men like Wilkie Collins, Augustus Egg, Maclise and others gave him plenty of encouragement for sexual adventures, if he had wished, long before the official separation from Catherine.

Dickens parted from Catherine in May 1858, only three weeks or so after Augustus Egg had first exhibited his best-known work at the Royal Academy, a narrative triptych now titled 'Past and Present'. This depicts the story of a 'fallen' woman, the final picture showing her clutching a dead or dying baby as she takes shelter in the Adelphi arches by the river. No one has realised, seemingly, the full significance of the notice pasted on the wall behind her, a playbill for performances at the Theatre Royal, Haymarket: the headline act is *Victims* – a comedy in which Dickens's mistress, Ellen Ternan had appeared in the autumn of 1857, presumably when the artist was completing his trilogy. This must surely have been a deliberate inclusion by Egg; perhaps a sly joke from a friend who knew more about Dickens's private life than most.[5]

We should include, as well, perhaps, the earlier period of Dickens's life, in the early 1840s, when he was a member of the Parthenon Club, or when he was a member of the set that hung around Mark Lemon's public house, the Shakespeare's Head, in Wych Street, not so far away from Wellington Street, and the 'gipsey camp'. No one appears to have remarked upon the nature of the location of the business of his close friend Mark Lemon, or its location in Wych Street. This was, however, a thoroughfare as disreputable as the neighbouring Holywell Street – both notorious as the centre of the publication and sale of pornographic books and prints – and Wych Street also boasted several brothels.

Did Patrick Rouse, whose business was right in the heart of London's most notorious market in sexual services, obtain his generous loan through some form of blackmail – implied or overtly?

Would Patrick Rouse have recognised Dickens? Well, yes, probably: if not from published illustrations, from somewhere they both knew well: perhaps from the Pall Mall area, but possibly from Hendon. If so, did Dickens find himself approached for a loan, and then persuade the other trustees of Harriett Dickens's marriage settlement that the Ravensfield mortgage was a sound investment? Or did they leave all the financial transactions to Dickens to arrange, without involvement?

There are no references in any of the standard biographies of Dickens, or usual sources, to Claudius du Pasquier, or to Francis Lovell, let alone to the property itself, or to the fact that Charles Dickens and Harriett's guardians were signatories to such a financial transaction. They were marginal and discreet connections, dependent on Dickens's goodwill.

At this point there remain many questions. Was the mortgage intended to be directly for the benefit of Augustus's wife? Why then was it arranged four years after the marriage and years before her husband deserted her for Bertha Phillips and ran off to America – some four years before his departure – and why was it ended, most probably, as much as a year after Dickens knew that his brother had left the country? If intended to benefit Harriett, for whatever reason, at any point, what would justify such a risky and short-term investment? Or is it a coincidence that the two other signatories were involved? Were they simply trustworthy acquaintances, outside Dickens's immediate circle, who relied on his goodwill in order to protect their charge's best interests and could be expected to be discreet about his business affairs?

Is the amount of £1,500 from Dickens's own account, and not, as the agreement states, from a joint account held by him and Harriett's two other trustees? In which case, it is odd that this expenditure has not previously been noted by other Dickens scholars, and it is curious that he should choose to use his sister-in-law's trustees to witness the transaction.

Even more curious is the fact that the Ravensfield papers show that the arrangement with Patrick Rouse was terminated in May 1858, in a week in which Charles Dickens's private life was in absolute turmoil and he was at the most critical point of his adult life: his separation from Catherine had taken place, was increasingly the subject of public comment, and he was now trying to negotiate a settlement with his wife, while desperately trying to avoid the threat of a divorce petition from her.

The Ravensfield mortgage was signed off on 28 May 1858: the sum of £1,500 was due, but it is stated that all interest had been paid – and now, after apparent payment of the full sum, the property was transferred to Patrick Rouse. On that year 28 May fell on a Friday: it had been only three days earlier, on the Tuesday of that week, the 25th, that Dickens had written the infamous 'violated letter', an extraordinary statement about the circumstances of the separation from his wife and a rebuttal of any speculation about his involvement with 'a young lady for whom I have a great attachment and regard' – this was, of course, Ellen Ternan. Between 26 and 28 May efforts were under way to agree terms of settlement with Catherine and to address the risk of trouble from her mother and sister Helen, who were said to be spreading rumours about his association with Ellen. He was also keen to end the speculation about an alleged relationship with Catherine's sister Georgina, who had chosen to remain in his household after the departure of his wife.

Dickens was no doubt aware that Catherine could have made application to the new Court for Divorce and Matrimonial Causes and raise the most unwelcome spectacle of the intimate details of their personal lives being exposed to public knowledge. The damage to his reputation would be irreparable. He had made himself vulnerable to such a process through his involvement with

Miss Ternan and because of the suspicions raised about his connection with Georgina, his sister-in-law. In that week, however, he managed to avert such a crisis by the extraction of statements from the Hogarths denying any credence in the rumours and leaving him able to dictate his own terms of separation.

On 29 May, the day after dealing with the Ravensfield mortgage, Charles Dickens collected the signed agreements he wanted from his mother-in-law and Helen Hogarth stating that there were no grounds for believing the allegations that had been made by some regarding his behaviour:

> Certain statements have been circulated that such differences are occasioned by circumstances deeply affecting the moral character of Mr. Dickens and compromising the reputation and good name of others, we solemnly declare that we now disbelieve such statements.

Quite extraordinary, one might think, that in this week of such unprecedented upheaval in his private and public lives he should be able to make time to bring the mortgage arrangement with Patrick Rouse to a sudden end. Can it be entirely a matter of coincidence? Or did the reason for entering into the agreement no longer have the power to keep him tied to whatever sort of commitment had required the parties to become involved with the property?

That the Ravensfield agreement was brought to a sudden conclusion in this week, in the midst of so much urgent and critical negotiation, serves only to emphasise the significance, for whatever reason, of the arrangement, and suggests that it was in some way linked to Dickens's personal or financial affairs, rather than a matter directly relevant to Harriett Dickens or Augustus. It is stated that the full amount of £1,500 was paid at this point, which perhaps might be seen as a premature conclusion of the loan – how did the bootmaker find the cash? Had he been saving up over the last five years? If so, was the income from his shop and the modest rent from letting Ravensfield House sufficient to allow him £300 a year to set aside for this purchase, as well as cover the interest?

Or was the sum of £1,500 simply written off, as a matter of convenience to all parties concerned – and perhaps most notably for the benefit of Dickens, placed as he was at a moment of such intense and increasing scrutiny and vulnerability in regard to his reputation and career?

On Christmas Eve 1852, just a month before the Ravensfield mortgage agreement was drawn up, Dickens wrote a letter to Mark Lemon in which he rather cryptically described himself to be … 'in the Forlornest Mess I ever saw' … Was this just a light-hearted joke, about some minor matter, or a reference to something more serious, a problem of unprecedented concern?

At the time he was writing *Bleak House*, a work that is so deeply rooted in his own family history and is redolent with mystery and dark secrets – including a woman with a former lover, and an illegitimate child that she had hidden from her husband. It is also the story of someone whose reputation is vulnerable to the exposition of a shameful past, and who becomes the target of blackmailers. That term, of course, was not recognised in the way we would perceive it now, or as a criminal offence. But the fear of reputational damage from the public knowledge of private weaknesses has always provided a profitable opportunity for those in possession of such information.

Lady Dedlock, of course, has a secret, an illegitimate child, and becomes subject to the fear of exposure of that secret when she realises, belatedly, that her past life has been the subject of investigation by her own lawyer, Mr Tulkinghorn, whom Dickens, tellingly referring to the position held by his grandfather in the Crewe household, describes as 'the steward of the legal mysteries, the butler of the legal cellar, of the Dedlocks'.

Tulkinghorn's exploitation of the knowledge he holds leads to his murder: perhaps Dickens rather enjoyed the thought of blackmailers coming to a bad end. But it is also interesting that the odious Reverend Chadband, surely inspired by Hendon's Reverend Williams, along with the Smallweed party, then attempts to extort money from Lord Dedlock – and Inspector Bucket's suggestion to Lord Dedlock is that he should 'buy this up'.

If we return to the falling out between Charles Dickens and the fraudster Thomas Powell and the way in which Dickens sought to silence his commentary from the safety of his new life in America, we again see how anxious Dickens was about the risk of reputational damage, or even the potential risks from such quarters. Although his pride may have been piqued by any literary criticism, from Powell or anyone else, the real point of worry for him was what Powell knew about his family, and his family's background, and what must have seemed like a deliberate provocation in Powell's reference to Dickens's talent being limited to writing about 'Cockneys', the implication being that was his natural milieu, rather than the experience of a gentleman.

The dispute with Powell and that jibe about 'Cockneys' is mentioned in an interesting article in the *Dickensian*, published in 1994, by Stanley Friedman, in which he poses the theory that Powell was aiming deliberately at a matter he knew to be of no little sensitivity to Charles Dickens: it was, he said:

> the kind of remark that could perhaps arouse Dickens's fear about whether this purported biographer might be aware of the skeleton in the blacking warehouse; similarly, when Micawber meets Uriah, David is apprehensive that his prior employment at Murdstone and Grinby's will be disclosed … and Heep does obtain this information, for he later gibes at Copperfield for trying "to buy" Micawber, "who is the very slum of society, – as you yourself were before anyone had charity on you." Uriah gloats, "I was never on the streets either, as you were, according to Micawber …"[6]

When Powell had been in England, he had been flattered into silence by the patronage of Charles Dickens and associations with his family – once he had fled to America, he was beyond the reach of containment and a danger to be suppressed – although that ended in costing Dickens rather more dearly than he might have expected, settling out of court. His real revenge, in the end, was a literary one, in creating the odious character of Uriah Heep – and sending him to prison.

Chapter Twenty-three

A dishonourable act

Now we must return to the story of Augustus Newnham Dickens, whose wife Harriett was the subject of the marriage settlement whose trustees also signed off the Ravensfield loan.

There are references in some sources to 'a dishonourable act' committed by Augustus, which may have caused him to feel his family would never forgive him and persuaded him to leave for America.[1] This may have been interpreted by most as relating to his seduction of Bertha and the heartless abandonment of Harriett, but shameful though his behaviour may have been – and no doubt it was a large part of his reason for leaving – it was not the only shameful act in which he had been involved.

Records in the National Archives show that in 1855, Augustus Dickens, Henry Warren, the partner mentioned in *The Times* advertisement, and two others, Harley Goodall and Harrison Chilton, were involved as defendants in a case in the Court of Chancery, that place of interminable legal argument so grimly detailed by his brother in *Bleak House*. In this case, the proceedings were not regarding an inheritance, as in the story of Jarndyce v Jarndyce – but something that really was rather 'dishonourable' – an accusation of fraud.

According to the summary in papers filed on 1 December 1855, a man called Alexander Gray had bought a cargo of brimstone from the firm of Lewis Reis & Co. for delivery in the Tyne.[2] The cargo arrived in July 1854, a debt for the reimbursement of charges to Mr Gray was accrued, and a bill to the sum of £205 given to him, which Reis & Co. said had been cancelled, when – it was alleged – it had not. This debt was passed on to Goodall and Chilton, who passed it over in turn to Dickens and Warren. Payment to the latter two was refused by Reis & Co., and the merchant company itself then ceased trading. Dickens and Warren then tried to serve a notice of 'dishonour' on Alexander Gray in respect of the bill.

The plaintiff claimed that Dickens and Warren knew 'that it was a fraudulent transaction on the part of Lewis Reis & Co. or at all events under circumstances of suspicion and without due enquiry and the said defendants are not bona-fide endorsees thereof …'

The Chancery papers include a list of questions to be asked of the defendants. Augustus and Henry Warren responded to theirs on 31 January 1856. They state that they had been in business together for nearly three years, based at the Gracechurch Street address, and had been acquainted with Harrison Chilton 'for many years'. They protested their innocence of any wrongdoing.

According to them, in November 1854 Chilton told them that due to certain financial difficulties that had befallen a Mr Oliver of Liverpool, Chilton was in turn exposed to 'an unexpected pressure in money matters' and became 'obliged to have recourse to his friends'. He asked them for £500 on the back of one of Mr Oliver's 'acceptances' for £1,000, expecting 10 shillings in the pound for the debt owed from his estate. The estate did not pay up, unfortunately, but 'from time to time' similar transactions occurred. By 4 December, however, when payment was due to Dickens and Warren, Chilton had gone the way of Reis & Co. and 'stopped payment'.

The response from Augustus and Henry now addresses something that had clearly come to light in regard to other dealings with Harrison Chilton: they admit that there had been a number of other arrangements in regard to bills from him, foreign bills, twelve in number, but 'we are advised and insist that such a discovery is utterly immaterial to the Plaintiff's case'. They considered that what might be seen as 'accommodation transactions' had only been included in the accusations against them 'for the purposes of annoyance'. They asserted that there had been no fraud or 'impropriety'.

A previous venture in which they had been jointly involved had failed too, listed in *Perry's Bankrupt Gazette* in May and July 1853 with a mention of their debts. It would seem Augustus Dickens and Henry Warren had been ill advised to place their trust in their co-defendants. Goodall had left the country with his family by June 1857, bound for Australia.

The indexes of 'Decrees and Orders' in the National Archives show that on 6 May 1856, 'Time to plead' was noted regarding this case. Two days later, Augustus Newnham Dickens applied for his second passport: where he went is not known, but it is likely he did not return to court. The first of his two passport applications was made on 1 June 1855: the second, however, may have been related to an intended flight from England with Bertha Phillips.

Henry Warren also appears to have applied for passports during the period of the Crimean War (some sources have claimed Augustus was involved in trade with the Crimea at this period too): at least there are records of a Henry E. Warren doing so, who is most likely to be his partner: applications in March 1854, July 1854 and September 1855.

Many Chancery cases were settled out of court, anyway, but it would seem that Augustus did not want to stay around to see what happened. The consequences of Augustus Dickens's failed career in the City did not end with his flight to America. Apart from the distress caused by the desertion of his wife Harriet, now afflicted with blindness, he would appear to have left behind a legacy of debt.

In his absence, according to a notice in the *London Gazette* on 6 February 1857, Augustus was obliged to assign all his personal estate and effects to a man named Miles Beale, a navy agent of 15 Surrey Street, Strand, who was acting as a trustee 'for the benefit of all the separate creditors of Augustus Newnham Dickens'. There was to be a meeting of creditors four days later, 'at twelve o'clock precisely', at No. 11 Bucklersbury, in the City of London.

This new information casts a new light on his reasons for leaving for America. It may well be the case, after all, that Bertha was not pregnant at the time of their departure from England, but the accusation of fraud, the case in Chancery, as well as what would seem to be a significant amount of debt, meant that he was obliged to leave to avoid his creditors and a failing business and decided to start a new life with the young woman with whom he had fallen in love, an ocean apart from the wife whose dependence on him meant little more to him now than a problem to be left behind and forgotten.

This explains why Dickens's younger brother felt obliged to flee England for a new life in America but it also exposes another circumstance that has previously escaped attention, and which is truly extraordinary.

Augustus had been in business with a partner who was a member of the same Warren family that had once employed his brother Charles as a child labourer in the blacking factory.

Henry Edward Warren was the son of Benjamin Warren, the blacking manufacturer. As Michael Allen reveals in his detailed study of the Warren blacking families, Benjamin and Robert Warren were active rivals of their uncle Jonathan Warren's business, situated at Hungerford Stairs, where the young Charles Dickens was employed, pasting labels onto bottles, removed from school and living apart from his family. By the time Charles was taken on, Jonathan had just sold the right to the use of his name to a man named William Woodd, and Woodd had taken on Dickens's relative, George Lamert, as a clerk. Lamert was to secure the position for the boy when his family circumstances made it necessary, or so his parents decided, for him to be put to work.[3]

According to some sources, it is possible that Robert Warren bought the company back from Woodd in the 1830s. New information suggests this may well have been the case – Robert Warren is still described as a blacking manufacturer at the time of the baptism of some of his children born in that decade. His continuing interest in the company is demonstrated by fire insurance records held by the London Archives that show that as late as 1838, Robert Warren is one of the names listed on the payment register for '30 Strand': a combined dwelling house and warehouse: he still owned the freehold. The fact that the two sides of the feuding Warren family were still able to cooperate in matters of business in this period is significant as it implies an intimacy that the much-publicised litigation between them might have been thought to have destroyed.

And here is another very curious thing: Robert Warren, his wife Sarah, and their large brood of children (at least fifteen children were born to the couple) are now revealed to have spent much of their time, from the mid-1820s onwards, at a rented house in the parish of Hendon, only 2 miles from Ravensfield House.

Hendon was a parish with several small settlements, and the Warrens lived at what was originally known as the 'Clock House' (the name was later changed to the Priory), on the Ridgeway, in the hamlet of Mill Hill. Robert and Sarah's first two children, Robert and Ann, were baptised at the parish church of Hendon St Mary's, in 1826 and 1827, by the Reverend Williams's curate. Warren describes himself as a 'gentleman'. But consequent to this elevation, his later children, even when born in Hendon parish, were baptised at St Martin in the Fields, near to the Strand. There he is described as a blacking manufacturer. Perhaps, like so many other parishioners of Theodore Williams, Robert Warren fell out of favour – or dared to argue with him. Williams, being an incorrigible snob, would certainly not have approved of his claim to the rank of gentleman.

Dickens mentions Robert Warren in the autobiographical 'Fragment' that he gave to John Forster to be published after his death, and which, in his biography of Dickens, for the first time disclosed the financial difficulties of his friend's early family life and the time spent labouring in Warren's warehouse: a traumatic period that still, as an adult and a successful writer, had the power to cause him such pain. That Dickens was aware of the Warrens' continuing business success – or at least the success of Robert Warren – is evidenced by Forster. He observes that Mr Woodd, the proprietor who became George Lamert's partner during the period of his friend's employment in the manufactory, sold it ultimately to Robert Warren: 'It continued to be his at the time Dickens and myself last spoke of it together, and he had made an excellent bargain of it.'

Throughout this period, and into the early 1840s, it is quite possible, perhaps even likely, that Patrick Rouse may have had dealings with some members of the Warren family, if not yet in Hendon, through his own business activities in town. The various blacking establishments run by the different and various members of the Warren family were within a short distance of his lodgings in Soho and then his shop in Pall Mall, and it is hard to believe he was not aware of them, or their background. Clearly, as a bootmaker, he would have been familiar with their product and no doubt had regular dealings with their salesmen or he may well have been acquainted with the Warren businesses. Robert Warren died in 1849, before Rouse came to Hendon – but perhaps this was how Rouse became interested in the area, as one where someone from a trade background could re-invent themselves as a gentleman.

It is possible, even if Rouse was not aware of Dickens's 'nightly wanderings' in the Haymarket area, that he knew of the connection between Dickens and the Warren blacking manufactory, knew the story of his childhood misery – and used the information to good purpose. It is very difficult to understand, therefore, why Dickens would willingly tolerate a close connection between any member of his family and the Warren family when at the height of his fame – and when he had become such a popular and respected household name. Such an association would have posed the highest possible risk to his reputation. Unless, of course, he was taking steps to mitigate that risk.

It is interesting, now that we know about the Warren connection, to look again at the previously quoted letter to Helen Dickens in 1859, and consider the emphasis he puts on explaining why he did not see the unnamed partner with whom Augustus was entering into business, referring first to his brother:

> I observed him then to be so stupid in a singular combination of vanity and over-reaching, that I felt it would be a positive act of treachery in me to see the partner, and imply, however distantly, that I believed it possible for him to succeed with such a young man as my brother. I never did see him, though Augustus strongly pressed it upon me, and the same considerations that were irresistible with me at that time, are – as you may easily suppose – greatly intensified at this.

The vituperative words expressed in reaction to the trouble caused by Augustus are stronger than one might expect and the effort with which he underlines his refusal to have had anything to do with Henry Warren, 'I never did see him'

1. Phiz's illustration from *Bleak House* of the Dedlocks receiving a guest includes a 'Mercury', or liveried footman: Dickens's grandfather William held a similar position in the Crewe family's household, before his promotion to butler. (From the British Library Collection, P 283, Bleak House, 1853, Shelfmark VW1/0034)

Above left: **2.** John Dickens. (Public domain)

Above right: **3.** Elizabeth Dickens, née Barrow. (Public domain)

4. A rather enigmatic engraving, from 1809, of a drawing of the staircase at Crewe Hall, by Charles Parr Burney, nephew of Fanny Burney: this family were close friends of the Crewes. The drawing would have been made in the period when Dickens's grandmother was housekeeper for the Crewes. (Author's Collection)

Above left: **5.** Frances Anne Crewe. One of the outstanding beauties of her time, a political hostess, and employer of Dickens's grandparents. From an engraving by Thomas Watson, after Daniel Gardner, published 1780. (Author's Collection)

Above right: **6.** Richard Brinsley Sheridan. Playwright, politician and lover of Frances Anne Crewe. (Author's Collection)

7. Ravensfield House. A postcard image probably dating from the early twentieth century, when the now demolished property was used as a nursing home. (Reproduced with permission of the London Borough of Barnet Archives)

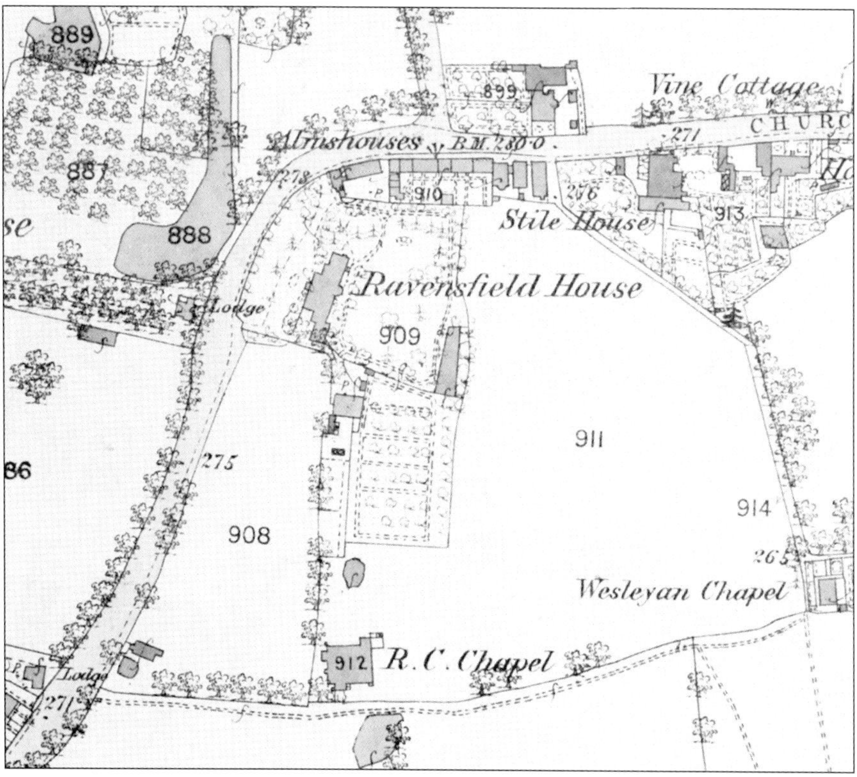

8. A mid-Victorian map of the Church End area of Hendon, showing the location of Ravensfield House. (Reproduced with permission of the London Borough of Barnet Archives)

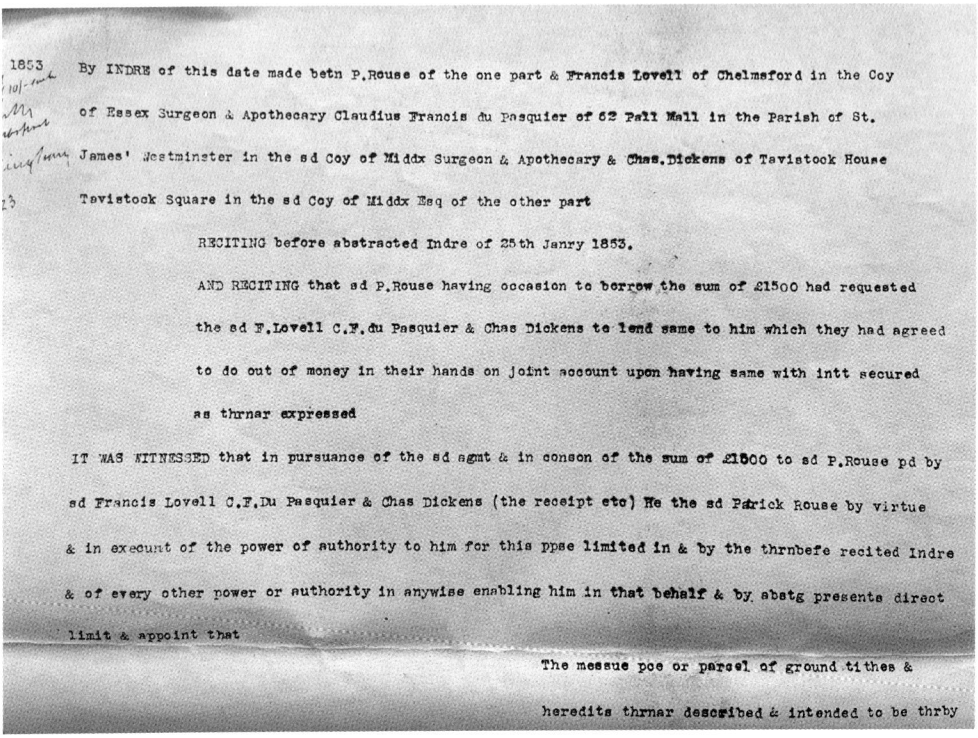

1853 By INDRE of this date made betn P.Rouse of the one part & Francis Lovell of Chelmsford in the Coy of Essex Surgeon & Apothecary Claudius Francis du Pasquier of 62 Pall Mall in the Parish of St. James' Westminster in the sd Coy of Middx Surgeon & Apothecary & Chas.Dickens of Tavistock House Tavistock Square in the sd Coy of Middx Esq of the other part

RECITING before abstracted Indre of 25th Janry 1853.

AND RECITING that sd P.Rouse having occasion to borrow the sum of £1500 had requested the sd F.Lovell C.F.du Pasquier & Chas Dickens to lend same to him which they had agreed to do out of money in their hands on joint account upon having same with intt secured as thrnar expressed

IT WAS WITNESSED that in pursuance of the sd agmt & in conson of the sum of £1500 to sd P.Rouse pd by sd Francis Lovell C.F.Du Pasquier & Chas Dickens (the receipt etc) He the sd Patrick Rouse by virtue & in execunt of the power of authority to him for this ppse limited in & by the thrnbefe recited Indre & of every other power or authority in anywise enabling him in that behalf & by abstg presents direct limit & appoint that

The messue poe or parcel of ground tithes & heredits thrnar described & intended to be thrby

9. One of the pages of the Ravensfield transcript, produced circa 1923. (Author's Collection)

Above left: **10.** Charles Dickens. (Author's Collection)

Above right: **11.** The Royal Opera Arcade, Pall Mall. The premises used by Patrick Rouse for his bootmaker's business, circa 2019. (Author's Collection)

Above left: **12.** The only known image of the notorious cleric Theodore Williams, Rector of Hendon, a possible source of inspiration for Dickens's Reverend Chadband. (Reproduced with permission of the London Borough of Barnet Archives)

Above right: **13.** A view of the Burroughs, Hendon, with the old Workhouse. A postcard showing the pond, and behind it the Burroughs. The low white building is the old Workhouse. (Author's Collection)

Above left: **14.** Augustus Newnham Dickens. The only known photograph of Dickens's youngest brother. (Augustus Newnham Dickens and Bertha Phillips, on the back details of the provenance are: 'Gift of Alexander Greene, October 20, 1924. Bookshop at 816 Cass St.' Reproduced with permission of the Chicago History Museum.)

Above right: **15.** Bertha Phillips. Augustus Dickens's mistress, who lived with him as his wife in America, but was exposed by the revelation in the American press that Augustus's wife Harriett was still alive in England. (Augustus Newnham Dickens and Bertha Phillips, on the back details of the provenance are: 'Gift of Alexander Greene, October 20, 1924. Bookshop at 816 Cass St.' Reproduced with permission of the Chicago History Museum.)

16. Colston's School. An engraving of the Bristol boys' school founded by Edward Colston, a merchant whose philanthropy was funded by the profits of enslavement. Several members of Dickens's Barrow family attended this school. (Author's Collection)

17. A view of Cotham Hill, on the outskirts of Bristol, circa 1819, showing what is believed to be Cotham Lodge, the former residence of Dickens's wealthy and influential great uncle, the merchant John Barrow, before his financial failure. (A View of Mother Pugsley's Field, Cotham, by Lieutenant Colonel William Booth. Reproduced with the permission of Bristol Museums, Galleries and Archives.)

18. Paul Dombey's downfall. New evidence strongly suggests that the story of Dickens's Paul Dombey reflects elements of the spectacular career – and ultimate failure – of his great uncle John Barrow. (Public domain)

19. An illustration of Miss Havisham by Charles Green from the 1899 Gadshill edition of *Great Expectations*. Was the creation of Miss Havisham and her disordered mind influenced by Dickens's view of his mother, aunt and great aunt's struggle with dementia? (From the British Library Collection, P 96, Great Expectations, Gadshill Edition 1898, Shelfmark Dex.311. (7.)

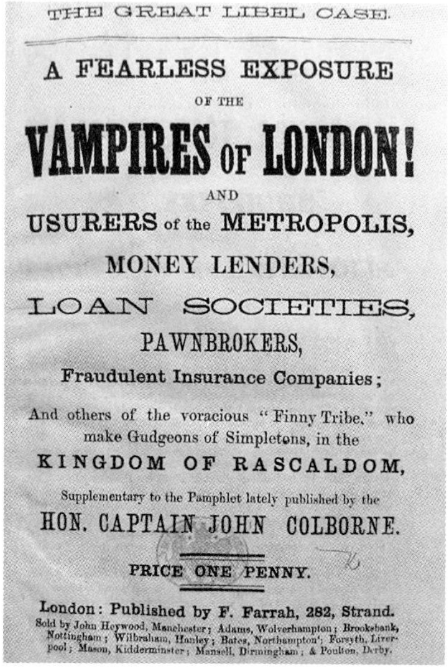

THE GREAT LIBEL CASE.

A FEARLESS EXPOSURE

OF THE

VAMPIRES OF LONDON!

AND

USURERS of the METROPOLIS,

MONEY LENDERS,

LOAN SOCIETIES,

PAWNBROKERS,

Fraudulent Insurance Companies;

And others of the voracious "Finny Tribe," who make Gudgeons of Simpletons, in the

KINGDOM OF RASCALDOM,

Supplementary to the Pamphlet lately published by the

HON. CAPTAIN JOHN COLBORNE.

PRICE ONE PENNY.

London: Published by F. Farrah, 282, Strand.

Sold by John Heywood, Manchester; Adams, Wolverhampton; Brooksbank, Nottingham; Wilbraham, Hanley; Bates, Northampton; Forsyth, Liverpool; Mason, Kidderminster; Mansell, Birmingham; & Poulton, Derby.

Above left: **20.** Believed to be a photograph of Eliza Davis, the middle-aged Jewish woman who took Dickens to task for his antisemitism. (Eliza Davis, date unknown, reproduced with the permission of University of Southampton, Archives & Special Collections, catalogue reference ref MS 116/41/AJ127)

Above right: **21.** The 'Vampires' pamphlet. The cover of a second edition of the virulently antisemitic pamphlet published in 1865 by the Hon Captain Colborne and which became the subject of legal action by Mrs Davis's husband, solicitor James Phineas Davis. (From the British Library Collection, 'The Great Libel Case, A Fearless Exposure of the Vampires of London', by 'Aperitimos', 1865, shelf mark 822J.aaa.6)

22. Redland Church. In 1742 Dickens's ancestor Lewis Casteel was paid by the merchant John Cossins to gild the cupola of Redland Chapel, Bristol. (Author's Collection)

– supposedly for his own good – might well appear to be a conscious act of disassociation from the latter. And then what did he mean by the last remark: saying 'the same considerations that were irresistible with me at that time, are – as you may easily suppose – greatly intensified at this …'?

Charles Dickens simply cannot have been unaware of the identity of Augustus's new partner. If he refused to meet him, the reason seems more likely to be not out of concern for the best interests of Henry Warren, but for his own benefit.

Did Augustus need his brother's approval for his partnership? Did he need financial support? Very probably. Was Dickens approached to set them up in business? It would seem likely. And that would make the choice of partner even more significant. Did Dickens really refuse to see Warren, because of the risks posed by his brother's unreliability? Or did his brother play upon the Warren connection in order to secure support from Charles? Alternatively, Henry Warren may have approached Dickens for support, knowing perfectly well that he had the means to cause him huge embarrassment – and offering a way of ensuring his discretion.

Yet again, in any case, we see how Dickens used money and influence to pre-empt the risk of the emergence of any form of embarrassment, or scandal, that would compromise his hard-won position and success.

PART THREE

The Barrows

"What is money after all!" said Mr Dombey, backing his chair a little, that he might the better gaze in sheer amazement at the presumptuous atom that propounded such an inquiry.

"I mean, Papa, what can it do?" returned Paul, folding his arms (they were hardly long enough to fold), and looking at the fire, and up at him, and at the fire, and up at him again.

Dombey and Son

Chapter Twenty-four

Bristol

It was Dickens's mother's family, the Barrows, who must have represented for him, at least in early childhood, the route to something better, to a place where success and good fortune beyond the experience of his immediate family really were possible – if only for a while.

Charles Dickens may well have entertained the hope, at one point, that he was related to Sir John Barrow, former Second Secretary to the Admiralty and a keen geographer who had a deep interest in Arctic exploration. This included the doomed Franklin expedition, which was the source of inspiration for *The Frozen Deep*, the play created by Wilkie Collins and Dickens, and which was to lead to his meeting and falling in love with Ellen Ternan. Dickens's library included several publications by Sir John Barrow but there was no family connection: Sir John Barrow's family were from Cumbria and Elizabeth Barrow's family were from Bristol.

Dickens's maternal grandfather, Charles Barrow, was baptised on 17 June 1759 at St Leonard's church, in the heart of the medieval city, one of three sons of William and Ann Barrow. His sister, Ann, was baptised there too in 1760, followed by his brothers John in 1762 and William in 1763. About five years after the youngest child was born, a decision was taken to demolish St Leonard's, considered to be a 'nuisance' in the congested lanes of the centre of the city. No further births, burials or marriages took place there after 1768, and the church appears to have gone by 1771.

Little is known about Charles's sister Ann, although she may be the Ann Barrow who married a Thomas Nash at St Stephen's church in 1785. There is a fair amount of information about his brothers, however, some of which was known to William J. Carlton but left unpursued, whether this was due to lack of available sources, or a lack of interest in what appeared to be distinctly working-class origins.

Carlton appears to have looked at the modest circumstances of William Barrow, the father of Charles, William and John, and looked no further. Perhaps he found no trace: not so surprising as the surviving parish records from the central Bristol parishes, even now they have been filmed and in some cases transcribed, are not always easy to read.[1]

The father of William Barrow, the surgeon-barber of Bristol, was a Mathew Barrow, who married Jane Goodman in Temple Church on 24 September 1727. Mathew Barrow, the great-great grandfather of Charles Dickens, we now know from records that relate to his sons' apprenticeships, was, rather fittingly, a schoolmaster or writing master.

Searches of Bristol parish records have now confirmed that William was baptised in St Stephen's church on 8 June 1735, the son of Mathew and Jane Barrow. A Mathew Barrow is listed as an inhabitant of the parish of St Thomas, Bristol, in 1696, apparently in the Redcliffe area, with the family of a Francis and Sarah Philips and their daughter, Isabella. It would appear possible, from the entry in the records, that he was a 'servant' in their household – often meaning, in this context, apprentice. If this is the same Mathew who married in 1727, it would mean that marriage was a late or perhaps second one – which might explain why he died while his children were so young. Or, of course, it may be another Mathew, perhaps another relation.[3]

Francis Philips, or Phillips, is mentioned in a couple of documents held at Bristol Record Office: the first, dated 1679, regarding properties in St Thomas Street and Redcliffe Street, Redcliffe Hill.[4]

It is interesting to see the rise and fall of fortunes in the Barrow family; Mathew an educated, literate man who appears to have died young, or certainly to have left young children, three of whom, William, his elder brother Thomas and his younger brother John, as soon as they were old enough, were entered into apprenticeships: William, as we know, to a barber-surgeon, Thomas to Edward Linford, an engraver and case maker, and John to a joiner named John Roach.

Evidence of the baptismal records of Thomas and John Barrow has not yet been identified, but their approximate ages can be assessed by the date of these apprenticeships, when they would have been no older than fourteen: Thomas in 1747 and John in 1753. In addition, we know that this John Barrow was admitted to Colston's Hospital, the school founded by the slave trader Edward Colston, in 1746. Two of William's sons would also attend this school after his death.

Thomas Barrow may have been the same individual of that name listed in polling records for 1754 as an engraver resident in the parish of St Mary Redcliffe. It is just possible that he could be the Thomas Barrow who died in New York in 1825, just short of his ninetieth birthday: he had a shop that sold prints and artists' materials: he was a vestryman and collector for Trinity Church, which was the subject of some watercolour studies by him, and the subject of an engraving by 'J Evers': Barrow Street in Manhattan is named after him.

According to one source, this Thomas Barrow was an Englishman, 'originally a coach painter, who had remained in New York during the Revolutionary War, and was the only dealer in good prints' … he was said to be 'a large importer of engravings' … That he was formerly a coach painter might be significant, as the Barrow family in Bristol and the family of William Barrow's wife would appear to have business connections with one or two local tradesman working in this line, as we shall see. William's brother Thomas was originally apprenticed as an engraver and case maker, but as other members of the family were obliged to diversify in their chosen occupation, the same may have applied to him. There is no evidence to suggest he continued to work in Bristol after 1754 in any case.[4]

Parish records suggest that Mathew and Jane Barrow, Dickens's great-great grandparents, were also the parents of Sarah, baptised at St John the Baptist church only a couple of months after their marriage, on 3 December 1727 – and of Matthew, baptised on 23 February 1728. If this is the same family, two baptisms in so short a time would presumably mean that Sarah was illegitimate, and that Jane was in mid-pregnancy with Matthew when she married: this might explain the variation in locations of baptism and wedding in order to maximise the chance of hiding any irregularities in their relationship or the illegitimacy of children. Once young Matthew was born, they seem to have settled in St Stephen's parish, where their sons Thomas, William and John were all baptised.

As a schoolmaster or writing master in Bristol during this period, Matthew would have had a fair chance of steady employment: despite a generally poor level of literacy, there were several charity schools in the city.

William Barrow had married Ann Cassteels at St Leonard's parish church in Bristol, in 1758. William was then about twenty-two years of age and had only the year before been admitted as a Freeman of the City, having served an apprenticeship – a term of seven years – to Thomas Newman, one of the many barber-surgeons in Bristol at that time. It was a period of widening division between the traditional function of primitive medical practice and the emerging profession of physician – a phenomenon that was causing the less-qualified practitioners to fear for the future of their occupation.

As Latimer's *Annals of Bristol* tell us in 1739, a group of peruke makers and barbers, freemen of the Barbers' Company, presented a petition to the Council regarding alleged 'diverse impositions and grievances' imposed by their 'surgical brethren'.

That the role of barber-surgeon was in decline was perhaps the reason that William Barrow might have had to focus less on the provision of 'surgery' and take on more work as barber and hairdresser. In the records that list at least some of the apprentices he took on, from 1759 to 1765, he is described variously as a barber-surgeon and peruke maker. In Sketchley's directory of 1775, probably a few years after his death, one of his former apprentices, James Cooling, is listed as a peruke maker at 22 Tower Lane.[5]

There is some evidence relating to his work as a peruke maker and hairdresser in the record of a debt of 15 shillings owing to him for 'shaving and changing a wig' of a deceased coach painter by the name of Edward Crane, in a listing of probate inventories for 1764.[6]

In 1766 William joined a Masonic Lodge – remaining only one year – and it is noteworthy that here he is described in the records as a 'peruke maker' rather than barber-surgeon. The Bristol Masonic tradition was known for its particularly elaborate rituals; perhaps that was part of the appeal of joining: but William's interest in the Union Lodge, No. 372, that used to meet on the second and fourth Wednesdays of every month at the Union Punch House in Princes Street, opposite the Merchant Venturers' hall, was no doubt a sign of wishing to 'network' and further his interests with the right sort of people in Bristol. Were they the right sort of people? This new Lodge's registers show a membership of nearly fifty men, nearly all of whom were tradesmen of some sort, although the largest group was a number of mariners; otherwise an assortment of hoopers, cordwainers, a couple of distillers, a cyder maker, a vinegar maker, a fishmonger, and so on: one attorney at law, five accountants, and only two describing themselves merely as gentlemen. This Lodge, however, was destined to be short lived, and William Barrow's membership even shorter.

Around the time that Barrow 'declined' his short-lived membership of the Masonic Lodge, an address was given to the members by Brother Alexander Shedden, an 'accomptant' who was the Right Worshipful Master of the Lodge. He urged his fellow members to be cautious in their behaviour, making the following observation as his final point:[7]

> … let me advise you to be very circumspect, and well guarded against the base attempts of *pretenders*, always setting a watch before your mouth. And with respect to ay who may *call* themselves masons, but (possessing

> refractory spirits) are at the same time enemies to all order, decency and decorum, speaking and acting as *rebels* to the *constitution* of masons in this kingdom, let me exhort you to have no connection with them …

It may be that Barrow was one of those who possessed 'refractory spirits' and felt unwelcome. It is interesting that the registers show that both he and another peruke maker, James Wareham, the entry before his, left on the same day, 6 April 1767.

Perhaps William Barrow was not the right sort of person for the Union Lodge, or as a Freemason: or it may be he was facing some sort of financial failure, or ill health: he appears to have died young, probably in 1768. If so, Charles Barrow was eight or nine years old when his father died – long enough to have memories of his father: one might wonder to what extent he passed on any stories about him to his children and what might have passed from Elizabeth Barrow to Charles Dickens.

It is interesting to note that one of Dickens's first works was a piece about 'a very odd old barber out of Dean Street, Soho', as Forster put it, who used to shave his uncle Thomas Culliford Barrow; years later he wrote a Mrs Gamp sketch for a benefit performance, with its comic barber Mr Wilson busying over his collection of wigs and talking of powdered balls. And, as we shall see, there is a curious reference to a barber whose premises look down on the office of Paul Dombey, which might indicate some knowledge of his Bristol Barrow family's history.

It seems very likely that the death of Charles Barrow's father is recorded as the burial of a William Barrow noted in the registers of St Augustine the Less for 20 July 1768. Likely not only because it follows the 'declined' Lodge membership of the year before, but because of evidence from a notice published the same week in a local paper – *Felix Farley's Bristol Journal* – advertising the sale of the household goods of a Mr William Barrow at his dwelling place in Frog Lane known as 'Crabbs-well'.[8] These goods included 'useful furniture' and linen but also brewing utensils and 'a very good billiard table'. The 'Crabbs-well' was a tavern: one of several in Frog Lane, and this location, as we shall see, had proven association with another side, previously unknown, of Dickens's Bristol family.

William had been a barber-surgeon and a peruke maker: perhaps he felt the need to diversify – or he may have continued in his barber business as well as invest in a new role as an inn keeper – or 'victualler'. The burial entry notes William Barrow as being of the 'Key': that is the area fronting the harbour, then a short walk from Frog Lane – but it is possible he still had a barber's business in this area, as well as run some sort of beer house in Frog Lane. As Sketchley's directory of Bristol for 1775 demonstrates, it was not unknown for victuallers to have another trade as well as keeping a tavern of some sort at this time. It is also clear that the old title of barber-surgeon had effectively disappeared: apart from a handful of hairdressers, there were more than fifty peruke makers. With the trade to which he had been apprenticed now redefined, and competition so fierce, William Barrow may well have decided to try his hand at another way of making a living.

As the sale of goods took place so near to the funeral at St Augustine's, it seems likely these two events related to the same individual – and it seems likely that the William Barrow buried in 1768 was Dicken's great-grandfather. If so, it means he was only thirty-five years old at the time of his death, his young family left without a father and now facing an uncertain future.

Two of William's sons would benefit from the charitable educational resources and well-organised system of apprenticeship of this uniquely prosperous city, which gave the opportunity of education and access to a skilled trade for many young sons of Bristol: the younger William and John Barrow were also admitted to Colston's Hospital, the charity school only a few steps away from Frog Lane: a route to a future for two fatherless boys rather more promising than might have been otherwise the case.

The younger William Barrow, Dickens's great uncle, began at the school in 1770, leaving in 1777, and being then placed as an apprentice to a wine merchant called Griffith Maskelyn. Maskelyn was an interesting character: his business partner and close friend was a man named Roger Watts, a sometime actor and founder of the new theatre, the Theatre Royal, now the Bristol Old Vic, in King Street, built to the design of James Paty. When William became a freeman in 1784, he is still listed as a scrivener – and after this we do not know what became of him.

It is impossible to write about Charles Dickens's origins in Bristol and not consider the extent to which his family benefited, indirectly or otherwise, from the trade that delivered a sustained period of prosperity for the port city: the trade in human cargo. This tainted history has for two hundred years continued to exert its influence on the life of the city's oldest institutions and foundations: nothing represents this legacy better than the story of the hugely wealthy merchant Edward Colston.

Born in 1636 to a Bristol family, Colston's fortune was founded on his role in the Royal African Company and its involvement in the ignominious trade in enslaved people from West Africa, transported to the West Indies or the Americas. After his retirement in 1708, Colston began to invest in charitable enterprise that would benefit the city of his birth, funding almshouses, schools, hospitals and churches. Colston's Hospital school, which was so important in the lives of Dickens's family, was to be managed by the Society of Merchant Venturers, the elite group that effectively controlled the city, and to offer places to one hundred poor boys.

For this profiteer in human suffering, and late career philanthropist, his need to control the management of his legacy reached no boundary: a guarantee of eternal gratitude from his beneficiaries and a sense of power was as important for him as business or profit, or even salvation. Fittingly, one of the charitable societies founded in his memory is named 'The Grateful Society'. To be forgotten, and powerless, was a fate worse than death: reputation, and dependence of others on his charity and institutionalised benevolence, he calculated, would ensure his memory would continue forever.

Edward Colston died in 1721: his will exposes his character better than anything else – the burial instructions insist that he shuns any gratuitous signs of 'any manner of pomp or ostentation' but then dictate, at great length and in great detail, clear instructions as to how the solemn occasion should be marked. No pomp or ostentation – but a compulsory public display of civic gratitude on the streets of Bristol:

> … my Corps shall be met at Lawford's Gate by the poor Men and Women of my allmshouses on St Michael's Hill and also by the poor Boys of my Hospitall on St Augustines Back together with the six old Seamen maintained by me in the Merchants Almshouses in the Marsh as likewise by all the Boys of the Charity School in Temple Street Cloathed and taught by me and from there accompanied by the to the aforesaid Church directly …

As a lifelong bachelor, with no children, he looked for ways for his surname to continue not just as adopted by the schools and charities founded by him, but also by members of his family: in the case of his great niece and her descendants, her inheritance was dependent on her future husband agreeing to take the name of Colston. The Hospital school was also to offer places to any boy with the surname of Colston – and was commanded to display, in the school room, the portrait of their benefactor that had hung in his dining room at his home in Mortlake – and a portrait of his father.

Edward Colston, of course, would never have foreseen the extent of hostility of future generations appalled by the human cost of the source of his prosperity. Two hundred years after his death, his statue in Bristol was torn down by protestors inspired by the 'Black Lives Matter' movement, and thrown in the river: the Mayor, Marvin Rees, who grew up in Bristol of black African heritage, commented that he felt 'no sense of loss'.[9]

The impact of Colston's influence, and the institutions he endowed, helped to create what has been, until now, a uniquely Bristolian civic culture of deference to wealth and meritocratic privilege, overseen by the Merchant Venturers and the city's Corporation. It is also true to say that without the provision this made for education, apprenticeship and other opportunities for self-advancement, access to a degree of social mobility lacking in other parts of England, the story of the Barrow family would have been far less interesting.

Before we consider the career of Dickens's grandfather Charles, we will first look more closely at Charles's brother John Barrow, Dickens's great uncle.

Chapter Twenty-five

John Barrow: The Mayor of Mudfog

John Barrow left Colston's Hospital in 1773 and was apprenticed with another pupil, Robert Vizer, to the merchant Jeremiah Hill. Vizer was made a member of the Society of Merchant Venturers on the same day as John Barrow in 1803, but died in 1814, leaving his partner as a trustee of his estate: from then on it would be his son, Robert Willis Vizer, who carried on in business with John Barrow.

The profitability of Barrow, Vizer and Co. was largely dependent on the trade in Spanish wool: this was both the secret of their success and ultimately a major factor in their downfall.

As his business grew, John Barrow's civic career also advanced: active in the Society of Merchant Venturers and becoming Mayor in 1823, by then a wealthy, well-respected and powerful member of the city elite, with an influential role in the various charitable bodies – some of which still exist – that undertook much of the welfare needs of the city and offered opportunity for advance for social and political advancement.

The degree to which the Corporation that governed the city used every opportunity to impress its authority upon the citizens of Bristol can be traced in the reports of many public events in the local press. These accounts describe often absurdly elaborate ceremonies involving the Mayor, various aldermen, councillors and members of the Society of Merchant Venturers: a good example is the way in which the demise in 1820 of George III and the proclamation of his son as the new King was marked in the city.

For the Corporation of Bristol, it was paramount that the passing of the King and the announcement of his successor be demonstrated through the expression of its own power and status in the city: after a meeting was held to discuss the best way of commemorating the occasion, it was agreed that they should organise a procession in which the order of rank was followed and impressed upon the 'grateful' ordinary citizens looking on. This would be an event that Dickens would have found highly amusing, and as we will see shows close parallels with details in the stories of his Mayor of Mudfog.

As the *Bristol Mercury* of 7 February 1820 reported:

> The Corporation, after assembling at the Council-House, habited in their black robes, walked round the spot where formerly stood the High Cross, and made proclamation of the demise of the late King. They then returned to the Council-House, and changing their black robes for their scarlet gowns, proceeded in the following order to the ceremony of proclaiming:
>
> Constables of Temple Ward.
> Exchange-Keeper.
> Constable. City Marshal. Constable.
> Constables of St. Nicholas Ward, three abreast.
> Band of Music.
> Troop of Lancers, on foot.
> City-officers.
> Gownsmen.
> Under-Sheriff.
> Chamberlain.
> Town Clerk's Clerk.
> Town Clerk.
> Three Officers of the Bristol Staff.
> Herald.
> A ROSTRUM, borne by 24 Men in which the Mayor and Sheriffs read the Proclamation.
> Sword-Bearer.
> The Right Worshipful the Aldermen.
> Common Council.
> Clergymen.
> Master, Wardens, and Society of Merchants.
> Three Officers of the Bristol Staff.
> Principal Inhabitants.
> Constables of All Saints' and Ewen's Ward, with staves.
> Troop of Lancers, mounted.

Clearly this order puts the members and officers of the Corporation, a cohort of clergymen, and the Society of Merchant Venturers at the centre of the event, with 'Principal Inhabitants' tacked on at the end as an afterthought. The Mayor and Sheriffs making the proclamation on a rostrum 'borne by 24 men' was not enough in itself, it seems, and required a repetition of the act at seven different locations in the city – each time 'preceded by a flourish of trumpets and terminating with a loyal or national air from the band of music'. Up and down they went, from the Council House and back again: the principal gentlemen of the Corporation who assisted in the ceremony listed as the Mayor, William Fripp, six Aldermen – and ten representatives of the Common Council, including Dickens's great uncle John Barrow. Volleys of cannon fire were launched, and hogsheads of wine and porter were distributed to the 'multitude assembled'. In the evening favoured guests of the Corporation gathered in Merchants' Hall to offer loyal toasts to the new King, but with the Mayor of Bristol featuring immediately after the King and the Constitution, and before such eminent figures as the Duke of Beaufort and Lord Grenville.

As the report concludes, the company dispersed at around eleven o'clock, 'gratified with the opportunity this publicly afforded them of expressing their loyalty and attachment to their new Sovereign, as with the urbanity and attention of our Chief Magistrate' – the Chief Magistrate being the Mayor of Bristol, a post that John Barrow would have coveted for many years before his turn came along, on 29 September 1823. This was formally decided at the annual Charter Day on 15 September at a meeting of the Court of Common Council, and the swearing in of John Barrow, as reported in the *Bristol Mirror* of 4 October, took place in the city's Guildhall, with the usual Bristol Corporation pomp, and a semi-regal ceremony of 'handing over, by salutation, the sword of state, cap of maintenance, charters, and strong box'.

Some idea of the degree of Barrow's status at this point is evident in the dedications that preface a history of Bristol, published the year after his Mayoral term, compiled by one John Evans. The list begins with 'The Right Worshipful John Barrow, Esquire, Mayor' firmly placed above all others, including, just below him, the Master of the Rolls.

John Barrow had worked hard to reach this position. Perhaps only in Bristol, in this era, could the impoverished son of a barber reach such a level of success, largely on his own merits – and by deploying his skill at using the network of corporate power to climb his way to the top. He would not have foreseen that this ascendancy would ultimately end in failure, that the era of unparalleled prosperity for Bristol had reached its highest point, that his business would collapse – and that he would see the loss of everything he had achieved.

In 1787, the same year in which he was admitted as a Freeman of the city of Bristol, John Barrow had married Joyce Jane Withington. Baptismal and other records show that John and his wife Joyce were parents to a dozen children, born over a period of around twenty-five years. The first six were girls, followed by a number of boys, and last of all one more, short-lived daughter. Of those children, the first cousins of Dickens's mother, only half survived to adulthood: three daughters, Ann, Elizabeth and Helen – and his sons Robert, James and George. James died only two years after his father, at the early age of thirty-four, and two of his sisters did not live beyond their teens, including Christiana, around eighteen, and Jane, nineteen. His eldest son, John Henry Barrow, died aged fifteen, in 1814, and a notice in the *Bristol Mirror* in 1825 tells us that his second eldest son, Charles, 'deservedly beloved and esteemed by his family and friends', had died in Segovia, Spain, in his twenty-fourth year, three weeks earlier.[1] Presumably he had been there in relation to the family business and its trade in Spanish wool. A terrible blow for a man like John Barrow to lose his two first-born sons and a curious pattern of premature death and largely not, as was more common, in early infancy, but in the teenage years and young adulthood.

Dickens's great uncle and his wife lived in the early part of their married life in a house on College Green, a genteel and historic area of Bristol surrounding the Cathedral which also includes the Mayor's Chapel, a mark of the importance of corporate power in Bristol and its partnership with the city's ecclesiastical authorities.

As his business continued to prosper, John Barrow moved his family to Portland Square, an area in the St Paul's district, then a very smart address, and now a Grade I listed Georgian square rescued from decline. He would seem to have been in residence there by 1808 as his son George Neale Barrow was baptised at St Paul's in June that year – and the parish records record the 'churching' of a Mrs Barrow, to give thanks for the birth of a child, in the next month. But residence in Portland Square, elegant though it was, was not enough for the ever-ambitious merchant, now moving swiftly towards the height of his career not only in business, but in terms of his range of influence and position of civic power.

On 24 June 1815, perhaps encouraged by news of the victory at Waterloo that had reached London three days earlier and might have seemed to point to resumption of easy trading, John Barrow signed an agreement for the lease of a magnificent property, at a rent of £225 per annum, in Westbury on Trym on the outskirts of Bristol, looking down on the city. This was Cotham Lodge, described in several advertisements as a 'mansion house'; it is believed to have been built at the end of the seventeenth century, or the beginning of the next, and stood in splendid acreage with gardens, pleasure grounds, stabling, glasshouses: it was everything, in short, that the man that Barrow now imagined himself to be should want.

This property was let to him by Charles Anthony Partridge, whose wealthy family, like so many other Bristolian associates of John Barrow, had interests in plantations in the West Indies. Charles Partridge's sister Maria was married to Jeremiah Hill, the younger, to whose family firm Barrow had been apprenticed some thirty-five years earlier – interestingly, Maria's family had connections with Barrows in Barbados, who were also related to some of the Alleynes. This is a surname that also has significance in Barbados and Bristol but has a link to another part of the Barrow family, as we shall see. Another surname associated with the Bristol Barrows is 'Gay', which is a name that is also linked to the Barbados Alleynes. Whether or not Dickens's great uncle was related to these Barrows, Alleynes, and the wider family network, it may be that they thought he was – or perhaps more likely, he allowed them to think so – and that they therefore felt he was a suitable leaseholder of Cotham Lodge.

Another local property supported by the profits of slavery was the neighbouring estate Redland Court, which, as will be revealed, was a place of some importance in the story of the Barrow family, previously unnoticed by Dickensian researchers. Barrow's move to Cotham Lodge was therefore a deliberate and significant choice.

That his new residence represented the pinnacle of success for Dickens's great uncle is evidenced by the pride with which his new address is appended to every notice of a family event, such as the wedding, the year after moving in, of his eldest daughter Ann to a member of a local ship-owning family, the Lunells – or even the notice of the death of his eldest son seven years later.

John Barrow of Cotham Lodge needed no other description: the charity schoolboy he once had been was left far behind in the past, as he relished the privilege and power of his hard-won success. That his new life was fated to end and return him to a state of dependency once more on the charitable support of others was unlikely to have occurred to him at this point: but disaster was looming in the future.

Chapter Twenty-six

What's money after all?

In 1834, Dickens's great uncle John Barrow was declared bankrupt. This was a personal failure on a scale that must have been felt acutely by the former Mayor, in a city where success was rooted in business and civic status. His failure was spectacular, but not unique, as Bristol adjusted too slowly to the reality of a changing world.

Some estimates claim that in the 1780s, forty per cent of the income of Bristol's residents came, one way or another, from the trade in slaves, sugar, tobacco, or related exports. It is unclear if John Barrow had direct trading links with the West Indies, but the general economy of Bristol depended on the practice, and the move towards the abolishment of slavery clearly had a massive impact on the city.

Several more immediate factors contributed to John Barrow's failure in business, however: most notably, of course, that the Spanish wool trade in which he and his business partner had engaged for so long had been affected directly by the Napoleonic wars – and his trading activities had also been increasingly eclipsed by the rise of importation of wool from German states, via London.

Barrow's move to Cotham Lodge in the days after the victory at Waterloo must at the time have been made in the expectation of renewal in the wool trade and a resumption of business as it had been in the best years before the war: in the event such hope proved to be illusory, and the fall so much more dramatic, when it came. Regular notices in the Bristol press detailing the arrival of ships bearing stock for Barrow and Vizer tell their own story: the listings of bags of wool from Spain or Portugal slowly change to less predictable ports of origin and eventually show a divergence in type of goods. By 1819, there were some arrivals from Hamburg – still wool, but also deliveries of oranges and lemons from Lisbon, or olive oil, and honey from Gallipoli, cork and almonds from Faro.

In the early 1830s, in order to adapt to the changes in the wool trade and the move of business from Bristol, John Barrow and his partner Robert Willis Vizer had opened an office in the City of London, at 15 Basinghall Street.

This was a location of double significance: on the one hand an area long associated with the wool trade, and the home to the oldest livery company, the ancient Weavers' Company, known as Weavers' Hall, was located at number 22 – but in the same street, rather ominously, as things turned out – at number 82, was the Court of Bankrupts, where, over a prolonged process lasting around four years, the partnership of Barrow and Vizer was to come to an inglorious end.

After his business failure, Dickens's great uncle John Barrow continued to live in Bristol, but his partner Robert Willis Vizer seems to have based himself in London and appears to have lived there for some time. And here is an extraordinary thing: his address, at one period in the 1830s, was that of his mother Ann, the widow of the first Robert Vizer, who had been at Colston's with John Barrow, and apprenticed with him to the same Bristol merchant. Ann Vizer's address is one that immediately draws the attention: it is in Doughty Street – and just two doors away from the house that was shortly to become home to Charles Dickens and his family, in March 1837.

It seems likely that Barrow and Vizer had established an office in London due to the move of the Spanish wool trade away from Bristol. Perhaps that is why the Vizers were established in Doughty Street at least as early as 1826, when Ann Vizer is listed in local rates records. It seems unlikely to be a coincidence, however, that Dickens's great uncle's partner in business was living in the house two doors away from the house that would be his own family's residence, apparently within months of the Vizers moving elsewhere, and after John Barrow and Robert Willis Vizer had been listed in a series of bankruptcy hearings at the Court in Basinghall Street.

Robert Willis Vizer, who appears never to have married, stayed in London, and can be traced through census entries in the next few decades, living with his brother Charles, at several addresses. A rather poignant note is struck by the fact that the name they gave to their last residence, a modest house in Green Lanes, Tottenham, was one that harked back to a rather happier and more prosperous time in their lives: Cotham Lodge, after the mansion that had once been the home of John Barrow.

At the time of the winding up of the Barrow Vizer partnership, from 1834 onwards, and the Vizers' residence in Doughty Street, it is possible that John Barrow stayed with them or at least visited them there. Were his niece and her family also visitors to Doughty Street, and did this play a part in encouraging Charles to move there, within a short time of their departure?

There appears to have been some effort made to avoid the total failure that was to end in bankruptcy in 1834, but by 1829 Dickens's great uncle had to face what must have been the total humiliation of advertisements in the local press detailing a sale of 'the valuable effects of John Barrow Esquire': a list in the *Bristol Mirror* details brewing and dairy utensils, garden tools and a pair of 'useful' cart horses.

An item in the collection of Bristol Museums can now be identified as telling its own part in the story of John Barrow: an undated card of invitation to some sort of evening event from Mrs Barrow to a Mr and Mrs H. Sanders: the card has been printed with Cotham Lodge as the venue, but this has been crossed out and Portland Square written in its place. It is likely, therefore, that this was sent after the Barrows had been obliged to return to their Portland Square property in town – but clearly John Barrow found it hard to let go of his association with the palatial house on the hill overlooking the city, the symbol of his once stellar civic career and substantial wealth.

In 1835, according to records of the Society of Merchant Venturers, the hugely powerful body of which at one time he had been Master, John Barrow was granted the privilege of a pension of £60 a year: such a grant, no doubt, in his circumstances, proving to be a welcome relief – but equally serving, we can be sure, as a source of deep humiliation for one who had been so proud of his civic status and his position of influence.

Two years after the grant of a pension, in January 1837, Joyce Jane Barrow died: her death, according to the registration, took place at the house of a Martha Bonbonous, at 54 Park Street. The Barrows had been forced to leave their own home and were now reliant on the generosity of friends for accommodation.

The Bonbonous family's wealth was, like so many of the Bristol elite, enlarged by the profits of enslaved labour. James Bonbonous, the merchant father of Martha, former Master of the Society of Merchant Venturers, had had a business interest in several ships – including the *James* and the *Jane* – which were known to have carried slaves in the 1760s, one journey recorded as travelling from the Gambia to South Carolina with seventy-five captives, of whom eleven died before reaching America.

John Barrow's financial losses occurred shortly after the abolition of slavery campaign had succeeded, with the subsequent impact on the sugar trade and other areas of business so important to Bristol. It is true that the Spanish wool trade in which Barrow's company had largely dealt was also in decline, but one might wonder if he had had investments in the West Indies that were affected at this point. John Barrow does not appear in the University College database of plantation owners given compensation for their financial loss after abolition – but there are many Barrows, and some John Barrows: their identity is difficult to confirm. Of interest might be a John Henry Barrow, with interests in Barbados. This Barbados-based family of Barrows includes another listed on the database, a Christian Alleyne Barrow, who was almost certainly the mother of the slave owner John Henry. Members of the Alleyne family settled in Bristol after returning from Barbados: Charles Thomas Alleyne, for example, received compensation for his holding of hundreds of slaves while resident in Clifton in the 1830s, but other, earlier Alleynes had had connections too, with Bristol, in the mid-eighteenth century.

It is at least an interesting possibility that there was some previously unknown link of the Barrows to the West Indies – and slavery. Apart from the fact that Dickens's uncle John Henry Barrow was born within months of his namesake in Barbados, and that his great uncle John Barrow in Bristol had a son named John Henry Barrow three years later, another uncle – Frederick, who was born in 1792 – married a woman with family links to Barbados, and the Alleyne family. This was Rebecca Lemarchand, whose mother was a Rebecca Alleyne, the name of a family deeply rooted in the history of Barbados, being early settlers who owned many plantations and intermarried with many of the other notable families on the island – including some by the name of Barrow. We will return to the Lemarchand family's connections with Charles Dickens a little later.

John Barrow's last years, spent with Martha Bonbonous in Park Street, must have been a difficult adjustment for him to make for so many reasons. This house was one of a row of small but elegant properties designed by Paty on a road with a sharp climb out of the city towards Clifton. The row survives but is now fronted by shops. It was just a short walk up from College Green, where Barrow had once lived, and the Mayor's Chapel, his chapel, when he undertook the role in 1823: to be living as a guest in the home of a family friend, only doors away from the Green, in such circumstances was a constant reminder to him of his spectacular fall in fortune. Furthermore, just a step away from the Green, at the bottom of Park Street, was Frog Lane, where John Barrow's father had run his public house – and where new evidence will show that his grandmother's family, previously unknown, had run another inn not far away. A short distance away was Colston's Hospital, the charity school that he and other family members had attended. It must have seemed that his life had come full circle: yet another example, in the family history of Charles Dickens, of the instability of status and good fortune.

Across the road in Park Street, at number 31, was the home of the 'Bristol Institution for the Advancement of Science, Literature and the Arts', opened in 1823. The *Bristol Mercury* of 1 March 1824 carries a report of a dinner held at the Merchants' Hall, chaired by 'the Right Worshipful the Mayor, John Barrow Esquire', to commemorate the anniversary of the laying of the foundation stone for the Institution. This was a centre of cultural and scientific life in the city for many years, boasting a choice of reading rooms, a museum, a magnificent collection of books, historical artefacts, fossils and natural curiosities. The Institution building had been financed by the issue of shares costing £25 each; the records of ownership show that Martha Bonbonous, whose house was nearby, had a share between 1829 and 1834 – and John Barrow was in possession of Share No. 21, purchased in 1821 – and then Share No. 462, which he acquired in 1825. This was then passed to his brother Charles Barrow, Dickens's grandfather, then in the last year of his life, still in exile on the Isle of Man.[1]

This transfer of the share is interesting, in that it is new evidence of a continuing connection between the Bristol Barrows, the disgraced Charles Barrow, and his family living in London. Further proof of at least some contact between the families is the fact that in 1820, John Barrow had been a subscriber to *The Mona Melodies* collection of Manx songs published by his nephew, John Henry Barrow, who would later be mentor to Dickens as he started his career as a reporter, and when the same nephew had begun his career as the proprietor of a parliamentary newspaper, his uncle was listed as one of the subscribers. This was the *Mirror of Parliament*, first published in 1828, two years after the death of Charles Barrow: such an endorsement suggests at the very least that some forty years after Charles had left Bristol there remained a degree of communication between the Barrows in that city and their relatives in London. The later business move to London shortly afterwards would almost certainly have continued some sort of relationship.

It is unlikely, in short, that the London Barrows were unaware of John Barrow's declining fortunes – and indeed there may have been continued contact in the years of entanglement with the dissolution of the company.

There is little doubt that Dickens must have felt strong resentment, during his time of trial in the blacking factory, and his great uncle's term as Mayor of Bristol, at the very existence of relations who could help end his misery but did not. It may well have coloured his view of the family members in the city, as we shall see.

With what wry amusement, perhaps, was the eventual downfall of John Barrow seen by his niece Elizabeth and her family? And to what extent did this sharp reversal in fortune impress upon the creative influences of his newly successful great nephew the idea of a narrative of rise and fall, of the vagaries of fate, and always, at the back of every successful figure, the shadow of failure?

Chapter Twenty-seven

Dickens and Bristol

By 1834, the year in which John Barrow became had been declared bankrupt, Charles Dickens was working as a journalist: as part of his duties in the next year, he visited Bristol and wrote reports, published in the *Morning Chronicle* on 11 and 12 November, of a speech given by Lord John Russell (with whom Dickens would later be friends) to a room of more than 400 people at the Gloucester Hotel, Clifton. We know from Forster that Dickens stayed at the Bush Tavern, an old coaching inn in Corn Street, not such a long walk from Frog Lane, and Park Street – and even closer to the church of St Stephens, attended by many of his forebears – and where his great grandfather, the surgeon barber William Barrow, was baptised, almost exactly one hundred years earlier. And the Bush Tavern, if he had but known it, had been the place where, according to the records of the Society of Merchant Venturers, a committee met that approved the nominations of his great uncles William and John for places at Colston's school in August 1770 and November 1772.[1]

Bristol itself was in a period of change: the mercantile class that had held the governance of the city so tightly within its own closed circle became increasingly challenged by those dissatisfied by the lack of accountability to the citizens whose lives were subject to their rule. Criticism and even ridicule of the self-aggrandisement and self-indulgence of the members of the Corporation began to build – and the groundswell for such dissatisfaction was becoming evident around the time of John Barrow's mayoralty in the early 1820s. Matched with an underlying national move towards reform, all the factors were in place by the time of the Bristol Riots of 1831 for exactly the sort of revolutionary eruption that seemed to be taking place.

During his visit to Bristol in 1835, Dickens certainly acquired some idea of the general layout of the city, as shown in *Pickwick Papers*, through the eyes of Mr Jingle:

> Having inspected the docks and shipping, and viewed the cathedral, he inquired his way to Clifton, and being directed thither, took the route which was pointed out to him. But as the pavements of Bristol are not the widest or cleanest upon earth, so its streets are not altogether the straightest or least intricate …

It is unlikely that any of Charles Dickens's Barrow relatives, staunch Tories, attended the Russell dinner, but it is not impossible that he saw them on this trip. Did he visit John Barrow in Park Street? It would certainly have been en route, while Dickens was going to or from Clifton: and Dickens clearly had gone to and forth from Clifton, as Sam Weller discovers: 'away he walked, up one street and down another—we were going to say, up one hill and down another, only it's all uphill at Clifton …'

We know that years later, in 1851, Dickens did meet at least one of his Bristol relatives, Robert Gay Barrow, son of John, while visiting the city to give a performance with his theatrical company. In a letter to Catherine from Clifton he wrote: 'I find the Barrow who lives here (to my great astonishment) a gentleman of condition and a very agreeable man …'[2]

By then his great uncle was dead and the fortunes of Dickens's family and the Bristol Barrows had undergone a complete reversal, as indicated by the somewhat patronising tone of his comment. In fact John Barrow's sons, despite their father's spectacular fall, had retained a respectable lifestyle and were active in the city's civic, cultural and charitable institutions – and the Church. By this time, of course, Dickens was used to viewing his relatives as likely dependents or a potential source of embarrassment, so clearly he was relieved to find that in Bristol at least this was not the case.

With this new evidence in mind, it is now possible to interpret certain themes and characters in the work of Charles Dickens in a completely new way, or with a greater depth of significance. Turning to, for example, *Pickwick Papers*, one can hardly ignore the description of Muggleton:

> Muggleton is a corporate town, with a mayor, burgesses, and freemen; and anybody who has consulted the addresses of the mayor to the freemen, or the freemen to the mayor, or both to the corporation, or all three to Parliament, will learn from thence what they ought to have known before, that Muggleton is an ancient and loyal borough, mingling a zealous advocacy of Christian principles with a devoted attachment to commercial rights …

Not so far from Muggleton in spirit, we find an expansion on the theme in the *Mudfog Papers* and some sketches written in early 1837, in particular the first story: *The Public Life of Mr Tulrumble, Once Mayor of Mudfog* ...

Mudfog has always been assumed to have been inspired by the place of Dickens's boyhood – Chatham and Rochester. It might be, however, that the description of the location, 'a charming hollow by the side of a river', might equally, or arguably better, apply to Bristol, on a larger scale, as would the disclosure that Mudfog had more public houses than Ratcliffe Highway and Limehouse put together, and with 'very imposing' public buildings.

The Mayor, Nicholas Tulrumble, would now seem highly likely to be based on John Barrow: a man of humble origin who succeeded in business, and then became increasingly involved in 'the Corporation' – the term used for the ruling system of governance in Bristol – who grew 'vain and haughty', lives 'on something he attempted to delude himself was a hill', is elected Mayor by the members of the Corporation, while he is in London: and whose pomposity leads him to devise a 'gorgeous procession' with the Corporation in glass coaches, to mark his appointment, that includes men dressed in striped shirts and black velvet caps, running footmen, banners, men playing wind instruments, the blast of a trumpet – and a sword bearer. All of this is suspiciously reminiscent of the report of the Proclamation attended by John Barrow in February 1820. 'To be a King was all very well; but what was the King to the Lord Mayor?'

Further stories from Mudfog feature 'the Mudfog Association for the Advancement of Everything': an enterprise that sounds remarkably like the Bristol institute across the road from John Barrow's lodgings in Park Street with Martha Bonbonous. Another member associated with the family was a Samuel Lunell – John's daughter Ann had married a George Lunell in 1816 – who according to Latimer was 'an energetic promoter of the institute', and preoccupied with such questions as 'what keeps the moon up in the sky' – perhaps another sign of an early precedent of the interests of the Pickwick Club, as well as the Mudfog Association. The *Bristol Mercury* of 1 March 1824 carries a report of a dinner held at the Merchants' Hall, chaired by 'the Right Worshipful the Mayor, John Barrow Esquire', to commemorate the anniversary of the laying of the foundation stone for the Institution.

Park Street was on a sharp incline, leading up the hill towards Clifton, where the better class of people in Bristol, by then, aspired to live. In his later years, did John Barrow pretend he was 'at the top of the hill', in the more fashionable and exclusive area of Clifton, rather than halfway up Park Street? In fact it is more likely that if this is a dig at his great uncle's pretentiousness, the reference is meant not to the days of Park Street, but a time in the life of John Barrow when his aspirations had reached their height and he must have thought himself to have achieved success far beyond the dreams of most charity school boys and of the son of a barber-surgeon: when he lived at Cotham Lodge, looking down on the city of Bristol.

Another Mayor who features in Dickens's later work at the very end of his life is Mr Sapsea, the Mayor of Cloisterham, in *Edwin Drood*, another corporate figure of unutterable pomposity – and with an unending degree of reverence for his own position. Mr Sapsea is a man who, perhaps like the merchant John Barrow, has never travelled abroad, but has an expert knowledge of foreign goods; he has lost his wife, as did John Barrow in 1837. Was Joyce Jane Barrow as grateful for having been the wife of such an estimable man as Mrs Sapsea is held to be by Mr Sapsea?

One early example, in terms of the idea of a wealthy relative, an uncle who refuses to support his brother's family in their time of need, is to be found in Ralph Nickleby: published at the beginning of his career, Dickens could well have sought to work out a sense of grievance against the great uncle who had not only refused to help the family of his own brother, Dickens's grandfather Charles, when his embezzlement was exposed but was at the height of his success in Bristol, and enjoying a hugely privileged lifestyle while Dickens's parents were living in the Marshalsea – and he was sent to work at Warren's. John Barrow was still alive when *Nicholas Nickleby* was published, although he would die three years later. One must wonder what he made of this story, and if he saw any parallels with his own life.

In 1854, the publication of *Hard Times* introduced the character of Josiah Bounderby – another JB – a self-made man, mill owner and manufacturer, whose hard-headed eschewal of sentimentality appears to be founded on his much-vaunted 'humble' origins (which are not quite as humble as he asserts). The cycle of events yet again presents a cautionary tale of the cycle of rise and fall, with three parts, titled 'Sowing', Reaping', and 'Garnering'. That Dickens may have had his great uncle in mind, and even his background in Bristol, might well be suggested by a curious echo of the legacy of Edward Colston: as we know from Colston's will, not only did he decree that his portrait be moved from the dining room of his home at Mortlake 'to be Sett up in the School Room of my hospitall' – in his charitable school – his memory was to be perpetuated in various ways, bearing his name.

In this light, it is interesting to consider the following passage in Chapter Nine of Part Three, 'Garnering', where, as events move to a conclusion, he stands in front of the fire, 'projecting himself after his old explosive manner into his portrait', the symbol of his own vanity and self-approval, kept in his dining room (and 'habitually addressed' by Mrs Sparsit as 'the picture of a Noodle'):

> Did he see any faint reflection of his own image making a vain-glorious will, whereby five-and-twenty Humbugs, past five-and-fifty years of age, each taking upon himself the name, Josiah Bounderby of Coketown, should for ever dine in Bounderby Hall, for ever lodge in Bounderby buildings, for ever attend a Bounderby chapel, for ever go to sleep under a Bounderby chaplain, for ever be supported out of a Bounderby estate, and for ever nauseate all healthy stomachs, with a vast amount of Bounderby balderdash and bluster?

In the context of the new evidence, and what we know now about Barrow's life, however, perhaps one novel above all others suggests that the tale of his great uncle's life and fortunes wielded a significant influence on Dickens's work: the story of *Dombey and Son*, published six years before *Hard Times*, in 1854.

Chapter Twenty-eight

Rivers and seas were formed to float their ships: John Barrow and Paul Dombey

The merchant Paul Dombey, and the account of the downfall of his House, the extent of his ambition and sense of pride in his status; his fixation with the idea of his son's succession as part of his own sense of achievement, his failure to foresee the dangers of his firm's collapse, and then his bankruptcy, with all his possessions put up for sale, and his dependence on the support of family and friends – all of this might be argued to reflect elements of the life of John Barrow.

Dickens's great uncle was a wealthy merchant venturer whose position in society must have seemed unassailable: whose mastery of the world of business and trading with the world reached as far as that of *Dombey and Son*, which, as we learn in the opening chapter, is virtually limitless:

> The earth was made for Dombey and Son to trade in, and the sun and moon were made to give them light. Rivers and seas were formed to float their ships; rainbows gave them promise of fair weather; winds blew for or against their enterprises; stars and planets circled in their orbits, to preserve inviolate a system of which they were the centre.

With six daughters born to John Barrow before the appearance of his own first son, and then the later loss of his eldest two sons, it might not be so hard to see a parallel with Paul Dombey, whose determination to have a son to follow him in business was so much a part of his sense of self-importance.

Like Barrow, Dombey's dynastic ambitions are thwarted, his firm fails and he becomes bankrupt. Like Dombey, the sons-in-law of John Barrow, rather than any son of his own, will be the ones to achieve lasting success in business.

Barrow's apprenticeship to Jeremiah Hill and his son might have impressed upon him the idea of a model of a family-run firm, whose name was repeated in three generations: he must have expected that his son Robert Gay Barrow would expand the company he had created and exceed his own level of success. Fate was to decide otherwise, as it does for Mr Dombey. Robert Gay Barrow's own career, and that of his brother, after his father's failure, as we know from advertisements in the Bristol press, was obliged to divert its course from the heady life of a Bristol merchant, trading around the world, to the safer but rather lesser position of the Bristol agent of the Sun Fire Office.[1] In *Dombey and Son*, after the failure of the House, a position in the Fire Office is the fate of the messenger Mr Perch: it is hard to escape the thought that Dickens was perfectly aware of his own relatives' employment in a similar venture after their father's failure.

The pomposity of Dombey, the unshakeable sense of self-importance; the deference he demanded from his family and staff; the theme of pride – all of this runs parallel to what we may now understand as the narrative of the life of Dickens's great uncle, and at least must have provided a starting point for a novel that is placed in the world of business, overseas trade, and the power of money. The curious exchange, in Chapter Eight, between the young Paul Dombey and his father on this point – 'Papa! what's money?' – leads Mr Dombey to instruct his son that 'money caused us to be honoured, feared, respected, courted, and admired, and made us powerful and glorious in the eyes of all men …' It mattered little that money, as little Paul observes, had not the power to keep his mother alive: for Dombey, as no doubt for John Barrow, the status that money could provide was an honourable end in itself: the only true purpose.

Even in the naming of characters, it is hard to ignore the associations between the Bristol merchant and Dickens's fictional protagonist. Paul Dombey, his daughter Florence and his son Paul live in a house 'between Portland Place and Bryanston Square' – the Barrows lived for some years in Portland Square, St Paul's parish, Bristol.

Walter Gay, who eventually marries Florence Dombey, bears a surname that is a very interesting choice by Dickens: two of John's children were given the middle name of Gay: his youngest child Mary and his eldest surviving son, Robert Gay Barrow – always known by his full name – whom Dickens is recorded as seeing in Bristol during his visit in November 1851. Gay is also a name associated with West Indian plantation owners, and Bristol.

In Chapter Five of *Dombey and Son*, Mr Dombey arranges for poor Biler, the son of his baby's wet nurse, Richards, to be placed in a school run by the 'Charitable Grinders'. The uniform of this charity school is quite definitely a replication of the costume worn by the boys of Colston's Hospital at the time his great uncle would have been a pupil, based on that of Christ's Hospital, believed to have been attended by Edward Colston: a long blue coat, with red stockings and an old-fashioned cap, all of which marked the boy out as a recipient, grateful or not, of the founder's charity.

Chapter Thirty-eight of *Dombey and Son* ends with a diversion by Dickens to a subject clearly of some significance to him – a less than charitable view of the role of charity schools:

> But they never taught honour at the Grinders' School, where the system that prevailed was particularly strong in the engendering of hypocrisy. Insomuch, that many of the friends and masters of past Grinders said, if this were what came of education for the common people, let us have none.

In Chapter Thirteen: 'Shipping Intelligence and Office Business', we follow the obsequious ceremony of greeting that Dombey's staff repeat on his arrival every morning, and his instalment in his own office, where the company employee Perch leaves him, and he sits:

> to be stared at, through a dome-shaped window in the leads, by ugly chimney pots and backs of houses, and especially by the bold window of a hair-cutting saloon on a first floor, where a waxen effigy, bald as a Musselman in the morning, and covered, after eleven o'clock in the day, with luxuriant hair and whiskers in the latest Christian fashion, showed him the wrong side of his head for ever.

One might be forgiven for wondering if Dickens here, in his placement of the hairdresser's bewigged effigy, 'Perched' above Dombey's head, in resolute defiance of the merchant's demand for continual acts of deference from all around him, is insinuating a sly reference to William Barrow, his great grandfather, and the barber and peruke maker father of John and Charles Barrow, whose family origins clearly were rather less exalted than the merchant might have wished others to think.

None of John's sons was given the name William, and that most of his children seem to be named after his wife's Withington family – with the accompaniment of middle names borrowed from suitable candidates of impeccable respectability – is an indication, perhaps, that he did not wish to acknowledge his own father. It is, of course, possible that he did not remember his father, who may have died when he was only five or so – and what memories he might have had would no doubt have been suppressed by the ambition that drove him to success in business, and as a member of the city's ruling bodies.

Charles Dickens's views on slavery are straightforward in their condemnation of the misery and cruelty of the trade in human lives: in Chapter Seventeen of his *American Notes*, published in 1842, shortly after the death of his merchant great uncle in Bristol, he makes clear his loathing of the idea and practice of slavery.

In *Dombey and Son*, however, we find a clue to his own views in a room in the family house of Dombey's bride, where there are 'two exhausted negroes holding up two withered branches of candelabra on the sideboard' which are undoubtedly meant to remind us of the privileged but decaying ruling class whose wealth derives from the labour of enslaved people.

The uncomfortable truth, of course, is that Dickens's family in Bristol demonstrably benefited from the slave trade indirectly in terms of the Colston legacy, and the wider prosperity of the city. We cannot be sure of the extent to which his great uncle's wealth was linked to the profits of slavery, but one might also question exactly what Charles Barrow was doing in his time as a mariner, working out of the port of Bristol. At one time he was supposedly shipwrecked off the island of Madagascar: he may have been heading for India, but it is possible this might have been connected to trade with Africa. Although most slave trading ships went to the western coast, some did venture to the eastern side of the continent, and Madagascar played a part in the trade in human cargo in this region, some of it, until around 1770, overseen by the East India Company.

By the time Charles Barrow was at sea, however, this trade was decreasing in terms of profitability for Bristol: perhaps this development, either directly or indirectly, was one of the factors encouraging his move to London, and the adoption of a new career, which we will now follow.

Chapter Twenty-nine

The London Barrows and one overwhelming calamity

Why Charles Barrow did not attend Colston's Hospital is not clear. It may be that the younger brothers were only accepted by the school due to the ill health or decease of their father William after Charles' education was already in hand. He must have been reasonably well educated elsewhere, however, to have later sustained employment as a musical instrument manufacturer, a senior position in the Navy Pay office, and a music teacher.

Charles Barrow's departure from Bristol is a matter that has puzzled Dickensian researchers in the past: looking closer at his family connections now may provide some explanation for his change of career.

We know that on 27 January 1788 at St Mary at Lambeth church, on the Surrey side of the river Thames, the twenty-nine-year-old Charles Barrow had married Mary Culliford, a minor of only seventeen years of age. Mary was the daughter of Thomas Culliford, a musical instrument maker, with whom Charles would shortly join in a business partnership – along with William Rolfe, who was a witness at their wedding, and John Goldsworth, who was a relative of Thomas Culliford's wife, Mary Goldsworth: she was most probably John's sister.

Some biographers and researchers believe that Mary Culliford's father was from Penzance in Cornwall, but with a better knowledge of the history of the Barrow family it would seem possible that the association with the Cullifords may have begun in Bristol, where the name occurs in records and directories of the period. This idea was also touched on in the *Dickensian* articles on Dickens's ancestry published in 1949 but not fully explored.

Thomas Culliford had married Mary Goldsworth in St Marylebone parish church in 1770. Some mid-twentieth-century Dickensian researchers were very interested in the Goldsworths and made concerted attempts to try to prove his descent from the Cavalier poet Richard Lovelace, via this family. Looking at this now, it is clear they were barking up the wrong family tree, but it is another amusing example of the way Dickensian research has so often been misdirected due to the desperate efforts of an earlier age to 'retrofit' their man with some sort of more suitable distant pedigree, especially one with a notable literary figure whose legacy might better explain the genius of the man whose more immediate ancestry was, by their terms, so deeply disappointing.

Dickens had little fondness for his grandmother, the former Mary Culliford, daughter of Mary Goldsworth, and may not have been inclined to show any interest in her background, although his family were close to her other two children, that is to say Aunt Charlton, the former Elizabeth Culliford, born in 1783, and his great uncle Thomas John Culliford, who was born in 1781.

The history of the Culliford business partnerships would now seem to suggest that the involvement of Dicken's grandfather Charles Barrow may well have been due to connections with Bristol, the city of his birth.

Thomas Culliford's company, between the years of 1786 to 1795, made keyboard instruments – harpsichords, spinets and pianos – in an exclusive agreement for Longman & Broderip, a firm that specialised in the sale of such goods, as well as printed music. It is unlikely to be a coincidence that both Longman & Broderip had connections to Bristol.

Why Charles Barrow gave up his life at sea and moved to London, or why, when he was around thirty years old, a year after he married Mary Culliford, he entered into partnership with her father's company, has never been explained, until now.

Apart from possible connections from Bristol with the Cullifords, and others involved with their business, the key to a potential explanation for Charles Barrow's association with Culliford and Rolfe may lie in the account of the company's story, recounted at great length by Geoffrey Lancaster in his highly detailed study of the business in *A Tale of Nine Pianos*.[1] The amount of information about the company that has been documented gives an entirely new perspective to the life of Dickens's grandfather in his London years. Lancaster reveals, for example, that Charles Barrow was brought into the partnership to replace Thomas Bradford, who left the partnership in May 1789: a man known to have been based in Kingston, Jamaica. It is also known that Longman & Broderip, who had exclusive rights to sell the pianofortes and other instruments that Culliford's firm produced, were, during this period, selling such goods in Jamaica.

But what exactly was Charles Barrow's role in the firm of Culliford & Co.? There is now a possible explanation that might explain what would otherwise have been an unfathomable departure, from the life of a sailor to that of a musical instrument maker, or at least a partnership in a firm that produced such goods.

The timber necessary for the manufacture of the instruments, particularly mahogany, was at the time largely exported from Jamaica. Such timber might arrive at a number of ports in England that had a regular trade with the West Indies, but Bristol clearly was a major port for imports of this nature, as the regular sales advertisements in the local press remind us. Charles's brother John was a merchant trader with many close associates who dealt with timber imports – such as James Bonbonous – and his wife's father and brother Charles and Robert Withington had a cooperage business, Robert later trading as a timber merchant.

It might be significant that Culliford & Co. moved to a new timber yard in 1784, in Pelican Court, Little Britain, in the same year that Thomas Bradford joined the firm.[2] Kingston, Jamaica, was where the mahogany factors were to be found: it would seem likely that he was in some way responsible for supplying the company with this material – or perhaps that he was their agent there, selling the musical instruments under their name.

If Bradford had been a link in the chain of trade with Jamaica, either in acquiring timber or selling instruments, then it is possible that Charles Barrow, who replaced him, brought with him similar connections. Certainly he was not an instrument maker, although his later career suggests he was musically gifted, and indeed, after leaving the firm, was listed in directories for a while as a 'music master', as well as working as a music teacher and organist in exile on the Isle of Man.

Charles Barrow's partnership with Thomas Culliford and William Rolfe was formalised the year after his marriage to Culliford's daughter Mary, just two months after the couple's first child was baptised. This took place on 26 March 1789, at St Mary Lambeth: the baby was a daughter also named Mary. Dickens's mother Elizabeth Barrow was baptised at the same church just a year later, on 20 January 1790. A further eight children would follow over the next fifteen years or so – altogether Charles and Mary Barrow were to have five surviving daughters and five sons. The next three children – Sarah, Frederick Charles, and Thomas Culliford Barrow – were also baptised at Lambeth: then in 1796 we find the baptismal record of John Henry Barrow, who was to play an important role in the early career of his nephew, Charles Dickens.

This ceremony took place across the river at St Mary le Bow, in the City of London, a location chosen no doubt because, as Carlton observed, the church was opposite to the Cheapside location of the business run by Culliford, Rolfe and Barrow.

A fourth son, Edward, had been born in September 1798, but he remained unbaptised for two years, until the arrival of another daughter, Jane Emily Barrow: the baptism of both these children then took place on the same day in 1800, on 22 December; again at Lambeth. Next came Maria Caroline, whose details may be found, in 1803, at St George the Martyr, in Southwark – and finally the baptism of Robert Irving Barrow is recorded in the registers of St Mary le Strand, in September 1805: a last baptism whose venue tells part of the final stage in the story of Charles Barrow's life in London.

When Charles was involved in the partnership, Culliford, Rolfe and Barrow was based in Fountain Court, Cheapside, then a fashionable shopping area: a retail shop was opened in 1795, after the company had decided not to honour its contract to sell instruments only through Longman & Broderip, who had shops at 26 Cheapside, and 13 Haymarket. The new shop sold pianos, harpsichords and chamber organs, and in 1795 the company also began to publish music, registering various songs and arrangements at the Stationers' Company.

The reason for the failure to baptise Edward in 1798 was that his parents were by then in a state of real difficulty as a result of the failed partnership of Thomas Culliford and Charles Barrow: failure provoked by a schism between the business and Longman & Broderip. Rolfe had parted company, and Charles and his father-in-law had tried to continue, but this venture was to end in disaster and bankruptcy: worse was to come when at the end of October 1798, Charles Barrow and Culliford were arrested for debt and then committed to the Fleet Prison[3] – the place of detention for Pickwick, of course, when he refuses to pay the costs of the case against him brought by Mrs Bardell.

Here was the beginning of the association of Charles Dickens's London-based family with a legacy of debt, bankruptcy and imprisonment. Long before his own father was sent to live in the Marshalsea, or his great uncle's business ended in catastrophic failure, Dickens's grandfather and great grandfather had already followed the route of financial failure to its ultimate end. Dickens's grandmother Mary was left with a month-old baby, three small children to look after – and no money. Dickens's mother was then eight years old: old enough to understand the implications of her father's arrest.

Both Charles Barrow and Thomas Culliford were discharged on 17 November after making payments: in Barrow's case this amounted to a sum of £71 9s 2d. Where did he find the money in a matter of days? Was that just long enough to get a message to his brother John, in Bristol, and ask him to bail him out? If he did so on this occasion, he was to show rather less sympathy a few years later, when Charles was in even worse trouble.

The Barrows were now obliged to find some other means of supporting their family, and Charles Barrow changed direction and found work as a music master. He was living at 27 Walcot Place, Lambeth, by 1799, when Dickens's mother Elizabeth would have been around nine years old. A distant echo of this time in her life is perhaps reflected in a reference, by her son, in *Bleak House*, to Walcot Square, where Esther's suitor Mr Guppy says he has acquired a property: 'a six roomer, exclusive of kitchens …'

Carlton noted that a directory of 1802 still listed Barrow as a music master, by then living at 27 Park Place, Kennington; perhaps this was simply information that was out of date, because by then he had changed career once more.

In 1801, Charles Barrow's career had followed yet another abrupt change in direction: he had taken a post as a clerk in the Navy Pay Office, with an income of £18 5s, and then, in a somewhat inexplicable stroke of good fortune, within a year he had been given a promotion – appointed to the position of 'Chief Conductor of Monies in Town', with a handsome salary of £330 per annum – and a suite of rooms in the former palatial grandeur of Somerset House.

From mariner to musical instrument maker, then music teacher to clerk – and now fast tracked to a lucrative senior position: a curious sequence, and one that was to end in folly and disgrace. Such a well-placed appointment, it has been suggested, may have been as a result of an act of patronage by an unknown benefactor. It was certainly a most surprising promotion for a humble clerk. Whatever the reason for this spectacular promotion, it offered the prospect of a much more comfortable life for Charles and Mary, and their many children. This period in the life of Dickens's mother must have been one in which she felt comfortable, happy and secure. Within a few years, however, the fortunes of the Barrow family were once more set to take a very different turn: Charles Barrow had succumbed to the temptation of misusing his position in order to supplement his income by defrauding the Navy Pay Office of a substantial amount of money.

In the early part of 1810, an investigation into the Honourable George Villiers' inept administration of his post as Paymaster of Marines had also led to the discovery of what was delicately described, in various press reports, as a 'deficiency' in the accounts of the Conductor, Charles Barrow. This represented a shortfall of £5,689, an astonishingly large sum, stolen over a period of seven years.

Only £500 of this amount was deemed recoverable: prosecution was then considered. Barrow claimed that his misdeeds were caused by the burden of his large family, and illness, and he tried buying time by suggesting that a wealthy brother might repay the missing money. This was a reference to John Barrow, of course, by then a very successful merchant and a man of considerable means – but who appears to have been unable, or unwilling, to bail his brother out of trouble. Charles Barrow had no choice then but to resign, making a last plea for mercy, as first revealed by Gladys Storey:

> I most earnestly entreat the forbearance of the Navy Board in not demanding instant settlement of the balance. The demand might drive me into gaol, strip my family of what little furniture, clothes or other resources they may possess for their immediate subsistence. They are now unprovided for and severer steps, by preventing my exertions for their future maintenance, would indeed confound us all in one overwhelming calamity.

No criminal prosecution ensued, but the family's furniture was seized and Charles Barrow fled London.

Dickens's mother Elizabeth had married John Dickens in June of the previous year, no doubt with little idea of the looming disaster about to change the course of her family's fortunes, or that this would be a forewarning of the life she would have with her new husband: a lack of steady employment, a cycle of loss of home, money and possessions; the worry and humiliation of debt, and dependence on the charity of family and friends.

After his escape from London, Charles Barrow is said to have taken temporary shelter with a Mrs Roylance, a family friend who was then living in Brighton, and who would accommodate the Dickens family at another time of need some years later. Mrs Pipchin, in *Dombey and Son*, with whom little Paul Dombey lodges in Brighton and who later becomes housekeeper to his father, was said by Forster to be based on Mrs Roylance. Dickens, as a child, was initially sent to live with her, in Little College Street, Camden Town, during the period in which his family was in the Marshalsea and he was put to work in the blacking factory. The family also relied on her for accommodation for a time after his father was released from prison. The irony of being dependent, as a child, as his own grandfather had been, on the support of Mrs Roylance, cannot have passed unnoticed by Dickens.

Chapter Thirty

I am utterly indifferent to the fact of her existence: the forgotten Barrows

In the aftermath of Charles Barrow's exposure as a fraudster and his flight to the Isle of Man, the impact on his family was, of course, substantial; the change in their financial circumstances was immediate, and lasting, demanding that his children find ways of supporting themselves – and each other. His wife presumably joined him in the Isle of Man once it became apparent that he would have to remain there.

Most of the Barrow sons were able to find steady enough employment; Thomas had his post at the Admiralty, Edward and John eventually became journalists, Robert, the youngest son, was only five years old at the time of his father's exile and perhaps had the least opportunity of all of the boys to find a profession: in later census returns he is working as 'an artist in wood', living with other family members.

Dickens's eldest uncle, Frederick Charles Barrow, became a merchant: in 1816 he married, in Hampstead, Rebecca Lemarchand, who came from an interesting family with connections to the Netherlands, to British Guiana – and to Barbados. By the time of the birth of their second child, Charles, the couple had moved to Maastricht, where three more children were born, two of them dying in infancy, soon followed by the death of their father in 1829. Rebecca had returned to London by 1844, as her death is registered there in that year. The Lemarchands were originally from Utrecht but had relatives in Maastricht: Rebecca's aunt Judith Rigano died there in 1832.

Dickens's aunt Jane Barrow married an architect, Frederick Long, who was responsible for the design of buildings such as the Royal Institution of South Wales, now Swansea Museum, and a Wesleyan chapel in Prescot, Lancashire. In 1841, they were living in Walton on the Hill, West Derby, 3 miles from Liverpool, with four sons and a servant; but this family too met with misfortune – by 1851 Jane was widowed and had returned to London to live in somewhat straitened circumstances, at number 3, Tiger Cottages, John Street, now Wedmore Street, in Upper Holloway.

Another aunt, Maria Barrow, had found work as a teacher of music: she was also in Walton on the Hill in 1841, in lodgings with her mother, Charles Barrow's widow Mary, Charles Dickens's grandmother, now elderly and listed as being of independent means, but clearly very modestly accommodated.

Ten years later, however, things were far worse: the very limited space of 3 Tiger Cottages was home not only to the widowed Jane Long and her five sons; home as well to grandmother Mary Barrow, now eighty: and to two other Barrow siblings: Jane's brother Robert, and her sister Maria. Most of the nine family members were working, but the listing of their modest occupations tells its own story – eldest son Charles Long was twenty and working as a merchant's clerk, but younger Robert was, like his namesake uncle, an 'artist in wood', and fourteen-year-old Alfred engaged in manual work as a tin foil maker. Maria was a schoolmistress, while Jane and her mother were dependent on annuities. The Barrows' neighbours in Tiger Cottages, on one side, were the family of a hay salesman, the house on the other side occupied by a number of working-class tenants: an iron rail maker, a printer, a needlewoman, a carpenter and his family – all in one cottage.

In this year of 1851, Charles Dickens was at the height of his fame, a household name, and increasingly prosperous. His family would soon leave Devonshire House and move to Tavistock House: at this point in his life he was living in very comfortable circumstances, only 3 miles or so from his grandmother, two aunts, an uncle and several Barrow cousins. Did they exchange visits? Did he help support his aunt and grandmother?

A letter he had written to his sister Fanny some ten years earlier, in December 1841, is an indication of the nature of the relationship with his mother's mother: in this he exhibits a real and rather shocking hostility to her, albeit qualified by a commitment to visiting her when in Liverpool on the way to America at the beginning of the new year.[1]

> In the matter of our worthy Grandmother (who as you very well know never cared twopence about us until I grew famous and then sent me a request for Five Pounds or so) I cannot but say that I am utterly indifferent to the fact of her existence; and am only terrified into remembering it by the apprehension that she is attended by a duplicate Sarah. At the same time I would not willingly hurt her by keeping away and therefore I will go and see her before I embark.

The reference to Sarah, the Pilgrim editors note, is to his aunt Sarah Barrow, to whom we will return shortly. What he meant by 'a duplicate Sarah' is unclear, but perhaps refers to her sister, his aunt Maria, who was living with his grandmother Mary Barrow in Walton on the Hill, close to the port of Liverpool: like Sarah, unmarried and middle aged, dependent still to a large degree on the support of family, and in Maria's case useful only in terms of caring for their elderly mother – while trying to supplement their income by teaching. By 1861, Maria was still dependent on relatives, living with her nephew Alfred Long in Salford. His occupation is listed as 'book canvasser', but the household included one servant, so they may have been at least reasonably financially secure at this point.

Other Barrow references in the collected letters include one in November 1864 from Dickens to Frederick Chapman asking for some work to be given to one of his Long relatives:[2]

> A certain Mr. Robert Long, wood-engraver of No 22 Chancery Lane, has asked me for a recommendation, on the ground that he is (as I believe he is) a kind of cousin of mine. This is not to the purpose, he says, further than as excusing such a demand from one whom I never saw. But he has sent accompanying his letter, some very admirable specimens of his work – beautifully done, with great honesty and vigour – and if, on this ground, you can put any remunerative occupation in his way, I shall be extremely glad to help him to a trial.

'From one whom I never saw' is a deliberate attempt at distancing himself from this poor relation, but Dickens must have known full well that Robert Long was his first cousin, the son of his aunt Jane, and had been living with other Barrow relatives in Holloway, as well as in the household near Liverpool, when he visited their grandmother. His uncle Robert Irving Barrow, who lived in close association with his sisters, was also an 'artist in wood'. In the 1841 census, he is described as an artist and living with an engraver named John Wilkinson, his family and his apprentice, in the Grove, Islington.

The suspicion might be, of course, that Dickens only bothered at all with these family members for fear of what they might otherwise do and the problems they might cause in terms of risk to his reputation, and that he dared not leave their pleas for help unanswered.

The year 1851 was a time of great personal loss for Dickens, with the deaths of both his father and little daughter Dora: the demise of an elderly grandmother, who features so little in anything written about him, and clearly meant so little, is likely to have been the least mourned of all these losses.

Mary Barrow died late in August, and her burial is noted in the registers of St Mary Islington, on the 25th of that month. Dickens was in Broadstairs at the time: did he travel up to London to attend his grandmother's funeral? We don't know, but it seems unlikely.

By this time Charles Dickens was hugely successful, highly popular, and well rewarded: he had completed *David Copperfield* and put in plain sight the secret of his own childhood poverty, while now enjoying the lifestyle of a wealthy man, a respected senior member of the literary establishment. Yet close members of his own family, by this time, were still living in financial difficulty – not so much 'shabby genteel', the quality so well described by Dickens, as simply shabby, all pretensions to gentility markedly out of reach. His apparent indifference is hard to understand.

Chapter Thirty-one

Where we stopped growing: Aunt Sarah, Aunt Charlton and Elizabeth Dickens

Of Dickens's surviving Barrow relatives in London in the early 1850s, perhaps only his uncles Edward and Thomas were doing well. Edward Barrow was employed as a parliamentary reporter, and living comfortably with his wife Janet, a talented miniaturist, their two daughters, and one servant, in a cottage near Regent's Park. Thomas Culliford Barrow, whose friendship with Dickens's father had ceased after lending him money that was never repaid, was living with his wife Harriet and six children in Walpole Street, Chelsea, still employed as a clerk at the Admiralty Office, in Somerset House, where, more than forty years ago, his own father had lost a senior and highly paid post through his own folly. Three of Thomas's sons were also clerks, and the household were able to afford a cook and a housemaid.

The eldest Barrow brother, Frederick, had died long before, in Maastricht, leaving his widow and son in straitened circumstances. Dickens's aunts were less well placed than their brothers Edward and Thomas: all in that small cottage in Holloway.

Only one Barrow aunt is so far unaccounted for: Sarah, who was Charles and Mary Barrow's third child, born in 1791 in Lambeth. It is Sarah who signed as witness to the wedding of Elizabeth to John Dickens: the two sisters were only fifteen months or so apart in age, so no doubt close companions as a result. As it turned out, they would both die in the same year, although one of them in considerably better circumstances than the other.

What became of Sarah in the end will now be revealed for the first time: it is a melancholy story, the sparse details of her earlier life overshadowed by what we learn about her final years and her demise. It is a tale that raises further questions about Dickens's family history, and was a matter that caused him no little anxiety, even as it seems to have helped form one of his most enduring literary creations.

In a letter written in 1949, now held in the Carlton Collection at the Dickens Museum archives, Alice Simpson, a granddaughter of Thomas Culliford

Barrow, described Sarah as 'a rather colourless person' – although three years earlier she had described her in another letter as seeming to have been 'very tiresome'. Alice was born four years after Sarah's death and she would therefore have relied on stories told by her father's family – her depiction of her great aunt in this dismissive way may have been reflective of an attempt by the family to distance themselves from a potentially embarrassing story: or perhaps it simply demonstrates a lack of understanding of Sarah's circumstances and the tragic ending of her life.

Records of Sarah Barrow are minimal before the period of her old age and final illness. The lives of most unmarried women of the age were, of course, generally undocumented and for an ageing woman dependent on family support we will usually only find evidence of their lives as members of a relative's household, at best. And so we find Sarah in 1841, living with a Charles Charlton and his wife Elizabeth, in Warren Street: Elizabeth was Charles Dickens's 'Aunt Charlton' – in fact his great aunt, as she was the sister of his grandmother, Mary Culliford – and was presumably the aunt after whom his mother had been named.

Also in the household is another woman, Sarah Taylor, in her thirties, described, like the two Barrow aunts, as being of independent means. There are three servants. Charles, who was in his sixties, is listed as a Prerogative Office clerk: that would be the office that was part of Doctors' Commons, where the young Dickens once worked as a reporter: later he would go out of his way to give David Copperfield an opportunity to voice his considered criticisms, covering a couple of pages, of Doctors' Commons, and specifically the Prerogative Office, in Copperfield's long complaint to Mr Spenlow. However, Charles Charlton was inordinately proud of his position, and determined that others should understand this.

Aunt Charlton and her husband, as we know from Sun fire insurance records held at the London Metropolitan Archives, had been living in Soho in 1817 – at 40 Gerrard Street, three years or so after their marriage. Although Charles William Charlton describes himself as 'Gent', his wife, perhaps rather surprisingly, is stated to be a 'silverer of pianoforte strings'. By coincidence, as a plaque on the property now explains, in the eighteenth century this address was occupied by the famous silversmith Paul de Lamerie. Perhaps some of his workshop had continued in use in some way.

Another fire insurance document from 1825 shows that the couple were living at 16 Berners Street by then, Elizabeth now described as a 'spinner' of pianoforte strings. This might suggest that the Charltons' standard of living was not so secure, or as comfortable, as one might have expected of a 'gentleman' and his wife: but it is likely that Elizabeth's occupation was in some way connected to her family's involvement in the musical instrument trade, and the business run for many years by her father Thomas Culliford, and for some years, her brother-in-law, Dickens's grandfather Charles Barrow.

It is said that while the Charltons were living in Berners Street, one of their lodgers, and family friend, was one Edward Blackmore, who was so impressed by the conduct of their young relative, Charles Dickens, that he took him into his employment, at Ellis and Blackmore, from May 1827 until November 1828. After a period working for another law firm, Dickens started as a reporter from Doctors' Commons, most probably on the advice of his uncle John Henry Barrow, whose son, born in 1832, was named William Charlton Barrow.

All of these connections would seem to imply an intimacy between Dickens's family and his mother's Culliford relations that was much closer than has generally been understood, notably in the years following his grandfather's death in exile on the Isle of Man, and the return of his grandmother Mary Barrow, Aunt Charlton's sister, to live with her children in England.

Berners Street, where many years later Dickens would find lodgings for Ellen Ternan (and her sister) at the beginning of their relationship, was also reportedly a source of inspiration for one of Dickens's most memorable older female characters: Miss Havisham, in *Great Expectations*. Estella, the ward of Miss Havisham, is sometimes held to be a portrait of Ellen Ternan, her cool disdain perhaps a reflection of the young actress as she was in the early days of their affair, in the aftermath of Dickens's separation from his wife, reluctant to succumb to the sexual advances of her older admirer. Interesting, perhaps, that Berners Street was the place chosen by him to accommodate Ellen at the point when perhaps he first hoped to move their relationship to a more intimate level.

Miss Havisham is said to have been at least in part inspired by the 'White Woman of Berners Street', a semi-mythical figure supposed to frequent the area in the 1820s: Dickens wrote about her in *Household Words*, in 1853, in an article with the title 'Where we stopped growing':

> … dressed entirely in white, with a ghastly white plaiting round her head and face, inside her white bonnet. She even carries (we hope) a white umbrella. With white boots, we know she picks her way through the winter dirt. She is a conceited old creature, cold and formal in manner, and evidently went simpering mad on personal grounds alone – no doubt

> because a wealthy Quaker wouldn't marry her. This is her bridal dress. She is always walking up here, on her way to church to marry the false Quaker. We observe in her mincing step and fishy eye that she intends to lead him a sharp life. We stopped growing when we got at the conclusion that the Quaker had had a happy escape of the White Woman.

Little sympathy here from Dickens for the White Woman of Berners Street, or indeed for the unfortunate 'demented woman' that he depicts in the previous anecdote, 'Rouge et Noire': Dickens sometimes displays not only a notable lack of sympathy, but almost a revulsion for elderly women who have lost their sanity – as he clearly felt about his own mother when she became gripped by dementia in the last years of her life. But she was not the only female relative destined to fall prey to this distressing illness: and at least two of these women lived in Berners Street, a newly investigated detail that makes the association of his own family members with the creation of Miss Havisham all the more credible.

Ten years later, the 1851 census shows the Charltons and Sarah Barrow had moved to 15 Grafton Street, near Tottenham Court Road. (This might appear to be a move to a less than respectable address: according to at least one source, five years earlier, there was a known brothel situated across the road, at number 19.)[1]

Aunt Charlton was now sixty-six, and her husband three years older, keen to share with the census enumerator the full details of his occupation – so keen, indeed, that the description determinedly spills over onto the space for his wife's entry – 'Prerogative Office, Doctors' Commons Examiner'.

In the next few years both Aunt Charlton and her husband Charles died, leaving Sarah in need of a new home. Where Sarah Barrow next appears in records – the census return for 1861 – is something of a surprise: she is in the household – at 33 Ampthill Square, near Mornington Crescent – of a woman named Jane Lespinasse, along with a number of other relatives: her nephew Frederick John Barrow and his family. This was Dickens's cousin, the son of his mother's brother – and, of course, Sarah's brother – his late uncle Frederick Charles Barrow, a merchant who had died relatively young while living in the Netherlands, leaving a widow, the former Rebecca Lemarchand, and their son, who had then returned to London.

Rebecca Barrow died in 1844, her address at the time of her death being 13 Osnaburgh Street, St Pancras. This was then the home of her cousin, Jane Lespinasse, the daughter of John Lespinasse, the absentee owner of a plantation in Barbados and son of a former Dutch Governor of Demerara. Anna Maria

Mc Creagh, with whom the house in Osnaburgh Street had also been shared, was Jane's aunt.

Thomas Wright refers to an aunt of Dickens's 'who had married and settled in Demerara', and who appears to have visited London around 1830: Wright claims Dickens questioned her about possible opportunities for himself in the West Indies – but seems confused as to her identity. This must be Rebecca Barrow, the widow of his uncle Frederick, who had died in Maastricht in 1829. Demerara was in the former Dutch colony that was to become British Guiana: settlers used enslaved labour to work on their sugar cane plantations. Rebecca's family had lived there, and it seems likely that she and Frederick had done so too at some point.

Rebecca's brother Michael lived in India, and it was his son who was the Lieutenant Lemarchand who, with his wife and children, was reported as having fled the terrors of the Mutiny in 1857, an incident that may well have partly fuelled Dickens's diatribe against the 'Hindoo people' at the time.

Now we encounter a huge knot of tangled connections, and addresses. Osnaburgh Street, near to Regent's Park, is an address with several associations with Dickens: in 1842 his children had moved there, under the care of a nurse and Dickens's brother Frederick, while he and Catherine were in America and the family home in Devonshire Terrace let to tenants. The family lodged here, for a short while, in 1843 – Forster refers to a letter written from 9 Osnaburgh 'Terrace' on 28 May 1843 – and they stayed here again during the summer of 1844 before leaving for Italy. Forster does not mention, however, that during much of this period Dickens's relatives, including his widowed aunt, were near neighbours.

This was a street packed with artists, such as William Powell Frith, at Number 11, who knew Dickens and produced pictures of Dolly Varden for him, and number 13 was home to a sculptor by the name of William Behnes. Dickens sat for Behnes, so presumably at this address in this period.

Here is another twisted length of thread, leading back to the same knot. By 1851, Jane Lespinasse had left Osnaburgh Street, moved to Harrington Street, and had given a home to Frederick John Barrow, who was then working as a railway clerk. But rate records show that she was shortly to move to the address in Ampthill Square, where they continued to live together for some years.

Ten years later, Frederick John Barrow is still living there, at 33 Ampthill Square, with his wife Emma and their two children, in the household of fifty-nine-year-old Jane Lespinasse. Also in the household by now is his aunt – and Dickens's aunt – Sarah Barrow.

But there is more: this address is also mentioned in the notes to a letter written to Forster on the day of his father's death, in 1851, as being the house where Dickens subsequently placed his mother: 'After staying with Letitia for six months, she took lodgings in 33 Ampthill Square, Mornington Crescent, Hampstead Road.'[2]

This means that for some considerable time, Dickens's mother Elizabeth and her sister Sarah lived with their nephew Frederick Barrow and Frederick's cousin Jane Lespinasse: a period that would overlap with the residence of Ellen Ternan and her family, only doors away at number 2 Houghton Place, a short turning from Lidlington Place into Ampthill Square – a pretty extraordinary arrangement.

It is unsurprising, therefore, that within a short time of Ellen Ternan taking possession of the Houghton Place house, Dickens was looking for a new home for his mother.

Many years later, the artist Frederick Gore would live in rooms in the now demolished house that had once belonged to the Ternans, and he painted a number of pictures of the view from his window, or balcony: including one looking towards Ampthill Square, which adjoins and opens out from Houghton Place and is clearly visible from this point. It is evident quite how close the two households must have been.

Why on earth Dickens would choose a home for his mistress that was so closely located to members of his own family is a very interesting question, and one with no obvious answer.

But this was an area he knew well: living in nearby Johnson Street at the darkest point of his earlier life, when employed in the blacking warehouse – an association you might think would encourage him to avoid the area. But perhaps this is the point: perhaps the attraction of Ampthill Square was the mark of success it meant for him, to have left the poverty and insecurity of his childhood and become a man of property, removed – or at least his family removed – from Johnson Street to the affluence of Ampthill Square, just as the child he was once aspired, with his father's encouragement, to the acquisition of Gad's Hill. The significance of certain locations, for Dickens, is imbued with such associations: the area around the Strand, for example, but also this part of north London, and this time in his childhood.

In terms of the risk of accommodating the Ternans so near to his own relatives, it was evidently the case that neither his increasingly unwell mother, nor his cousin Frederick, a mere railway clerk, living with his family in the household of an elderly aunt and their even more elderly relative, were in any position to stir up trouble. They were no doubt too dependent on the goodwill of their famous relative to do so: and may have provided an excuse for Dickens to be visiting the area, should he be spotted.

There would soon be plenty of trouble anyway, of a different sort. By 1859, the area of Ampthill Square and Houghton Place was now the home of the Ternans, and Jane Lespinasse's extended household, including the Barrows and Elizabeth Dickens, but Dickens's mother would leave within the next eighteen months or so, and Sarah would only remain for a short while longer. In the previous year, Elizabeth had begun to show signs of decline and dementia, and Dickens clearly found it hard to cope with his mother's deteriorating state.

In March 1860 he wrote to W.H. Wills, his sub editor: 'When I got home last night, I found a note from the lady with whom my mother lives, who is terrified by the responsibility of her charge, and absolutely relinquishes it …'[3]

Presumably the note was from Jane Lespinasse, with whom it seems Elizabeth had been living, along with her sister Sarah, in Ampthill Square.

A solution arose now, through the sad circumstances of the early death of his brother, Alfred Lamert Dickens, in July 1860: Dickens arranged for his widow Helen to live with his mother and look after her. It is believed he had already consulted Dr William Charles Hood about her condition.

In June, in a letter to Wills, he wrote that it seemed that his mother's condition was 'on the whole … rather worse than I had supposed her to be'.[4]

Another letter to Dr Hood is noted in August 1857, soon after an article about his work 'The Star of Bethlehem' had been published that month in *Household Words*, written by Henry Morley.[5]

> The reference to yourself in Mr Morley's article is his own honest tribute to your merit … It will give me real pleasure to improve the interesting beginning of our personal knowledge of one another when the approach of winter shall bring me back to London.

The envelope of a further letter addressed to Dr Hood at Bethlehem Hospital survives, from July 1858. In August 1860, Dickens described his mother's condition in the letter to a friend as being 'in the strangest state of mind from senile decay'.[6]

By January 1862, Dickens was clearly distancing himself not only from the deterioration of his mother's mental capacity, but from the reality of caring for her, as evidenced in the less than successful attempts made by his sister-in-law

Helen to involve him in this responsibility. He wrote to Georgina Hogarth to ask her to ensure Helen communicated with her, or his daughter, rather than directly with him:[7]

> I really can not bear the irritation she causes me, and the strife she gets up in my uneasy mind about the whole business. I was completely disgusted and worn out by her on this last occasion.

The home he found for Helen, her children and his mother was at 4 Grafton Terrace, in Kentish Town. This was a road in an area that was still being developed, not far from Hampstead Heath, large enough to accommodate a family of three generations – and with other children in the street of an age to play with his nieces, Katherine and Augusta, seven and six years old, the youngest members of the household.

Other children included little Eleanor, the youngest daughter of Karl Marx, who, as the next page of the 1861 census return reveals, lived only a few doors away, at number 9, Grafton Terrace (now 46): his occupation stated as 'Doctor of Philosophy, Author'.[8]

As Francis Wheen's biography of Marx explains, he and his family had moved to Grafton Terrace in 1856, enabled to do so by a pair of small legacies – and the continuing financial support of Friedrich Engels – thus escaping at last the squalor of their former lodgings in Soho. Marx toiled away in his study on the first part of *Das Kapital,* while his wife struggled with the more urgent need to keep the household fed, the bills paid, and to bring up their children.[9]

By the time Helen Dickens's family and Elizabeth Dickens had moved into to number 4, Grafton Terrace, Jenny and Laura Marx were in their teens, but Eleanor, known as 'Tussy', was around six years old. When not playing at the feet of her father in his study as he worked, as Francis Wheen tells us, Tussy, as a small child, was in the habit of:

> keeping open house for any children who wanted to drop by. In fine weather she would eat her tea sitting on the front doorstep, gadding off between mouthfuls to join in the street games. Such was her fame that most neighbours referred to the whole Marx family simply as "the Tussies".

It seems quite possible therefore that as such close neighbours, and so close in age, Tussy would have known and played with Dickens's nieces. On visits to his mother, perhaps unknowingly, he came within yards of Karl Marx's home. It is believed that they never met, although Marx was an admirer of Dickens and had made this observation, in 1854, in a leader in the *New York Daily Tribune*:

> The present splendid brotherhood of fiction-writers in England, whose graphic and eloquent pages have issued to the world more political and social truths than have been uttered by all the professional politicians, publicists and moralists put together, have described every section of the middle class from the "highly genteel" annuitant and Fundholder who looks upon all sorts of business as vulgar, to the little shopkeeper and lawyer's clerk. And how have Dickens and Thackeray, Miss Brontë and Mrs. Gaskell painted them? As full of presumption, affectation, petty tyranny and ignorance; and the civilized world has confirmed their verdict with the damning epigram that it has fixed to this class that "they are servile to those above, and tyrannical to those beneath them".

This is exactly the space inhabited by so many characters in Dickens's work – and indeed his own family – in a level of the class system that was continually in flux, never constant: its occupants aspiring to better things, and in fear of falling below, to a state of penury, and hardship; the 'shabby genteel', eking out an existence in the margins of their class, clinging to a sense of self respect that they felt set them apart from the uneducated underclass – whose poverty they otherwise shared.

Those annuitants and Fundholders, shopkeepers and lawyers' clerks, identified by Marx: Dickens's family history – and his fiction – is populated by these people, but it is a history marked most frequently by financial ruin, the loss of hard-won status – and worse, in some cases, a long, slow descent into a state of madness.

Chapter Thirty-two

A strong hereditary taint

Three years or so after Helen Dickens, her children, and her mother-in-law had arrived in Grafton Terrace, nature took its course: on 13 September 1863, aged seventy-three, Elizabeth Dickens died – a matter of evident relief to her son.

On the day of her death, Charles wrote to Emile De La Rue to postpone a meeting, describing his mother's state as having 'long been in a terrible state of decay'. The following day, in a letter to his assistant Wills, he mentioned, as an afterthought, that his 'poor mother died quite suddenly at last. Her condition was frightful.' Three days later he told Macready that his mother 'had been in a fearful state, mental and bodily for two or three years …'[1]

Dickens wasted no time in taking steps to give back the tenancy of the house in Grafton Terrace and wrote to the landlord on the 16th, the day before his mother's funeral, to notify him of his intention to vacate the property.

Back in Ampthill Square, meanwhile, during the previous year, Dickens's Aunt Sarah Barrow, also now in her seventies and living with his cousin Frederick, his wife Emma and their young children, had also been showing signs of dementia. This rapidly reached a point where the other members of the household could no longer – or would no longer – accommodate her erratic behaviour. In the year before her sister Elizabeth Dickens died, therefore, Sarah Barrow was admitted to Bedlam.

This was, of course, the infamous institution that dated back, in its earliest form, to the medieval period, and more latterly, during the eighteenth century, to the hellish place illustrated by Hogarth; a place of entertainment for those wishing to be amused by the antics of those suffering from mental illness. At the time of Sarah's admission, the hospital had been for some years under the management of Dr Hood, whom Dickens knew and respected, and had consulted over the care of his mother, and a much more humane regime was in place. Patients were accommodated in the building in St George's Fields, Southwark, which is now the home of the Imperial War Museum. Ironically,

Sarah had spent her early childhood in this part of Lambeth: now she would end her life there. Perhaps the streets seemed familiar, in her confusion, as she was escorted to the asylum.

An article in Dickens's journal *Household Words* published some five years earlier, 'The Star of Bethlehem', written by Henry Morley, had not hidden the horrors of the previous state of Bedlam, but had emphasised the improvements put in place by Hood: the end of chains and cruel restraint: new windows bringing light into darkness, literally, as well as metaphorically. Morley noted the displays of flowers, pictures on the walls, and the sound of birdsong: he did however also make a point of commenting that the separate women's block, and the place for detaining criminal lunatics (to be moved in 1863 to the new facility at Broadmoor) were not as well appointed. He added that Bedlam was not 'a place for the rich': pauper lunatics would be accommodated elsewhere, but Bethlehem offered the best support for what Morley referred to as 'an educated working class', although talking of the sort of people we would see as rather more middle class, down on their luck, or – again, here we are in Dickens's own natural milieu, the shabby genteel – in distress, and no longer able to struggle on, with money, or rather the lack of it, or the pressure of earning it, being the tipping point that led them into the loss of their senses:[2]

> … curates broken by anxiety; surgeons earning but a livelihood who, when afflicted with insanity, are helpless men; authors checked by sudden failing of the mind when bread is being earned for wife and children; clerks, book-keepers, surveyors, many more; who often battle against trouble till the reason fails, and then must either come upon the rates, or, as far oftener happens, be supported by the toil of a brave wife's fingers, or by a sister who from scanty earnings as a governess pays the small fee that can be afforded to a third-rate private lunatic asylum.

Records from the hospital include the notes of Dickens's Aunt Sarah's case, the details of her swift decline, and death.[3]

The admissions register tells a tragic tale; it shows that on 4 November 1862, Sarah Barrow was taken to Bethlem Hospital, by the authority of her nephew, Frederick. Two doctors' names are given in certification, as was required, and two names given as sureties: a Mrs R. M. Wilson, of Richmond Road, and an F. Carpenter, with an address in Islington.

Sarah is listed as a private patient (by then there were no pauper patients) and one might assume that this sort of placement required financial guarantees of some sort. Mrs Wilson was the former Rebecca Mary Barrow, sister of Frederick, and 'F. Carpenter' was Frederick Carpenter, a railway clerk – and presumably a colleague of Frederick Barrow.

At the time of her admission, Sarah Barrow's 'bodily condition' is described as 'infirm, but otherwise healthy'; under the column headed 'Form of Mental Disorder', it is stated that she is 'weak minded & has delusions'. The next column records 'Supposed cause of insanity': in Sarah's case, this is 'not known'. It is noted that the duration of her present attack has been one month, at the age of seventy-two. Later on, we see an entry for the date of her death: 7 March 1863, four months after her arrival, and just six months before the death of her sister Elizabeth, Charles Dickens's mother.

In the last column of her admission entry, under 'Observations', are the names of her journalist brother, Edward: 'Ed. Barrow, at the Herald Office, Shoe Lane' – and last of all, but most interesting of all: the name of 'Chas Dickens', her nephew. No address given: no address needed, no doubt.

It seems likely that the admission of his aunt to Bedlam was in some way connected to Dickens's acquaintance with Dr Hood, knowing as he did, or at least believing as he did, that the state of the hospital now offered the best accommodation for her needs. His reputation would survive the discreet placement of his aunt Sarah in Bedlam, but certainly not that of his mother, for whom such a dismal end would never have been an option, and whose care – by others – he had arranged in circumstances that were at least comfortable and homely.

In Sarah's case notes, she is described as of sober habits, moderate education, with no previous attacks; her state of health here, however, is assessed as 'bad'. She is 'weak minded', with delusions.

Dr Edward Newton, of 30 Fitzroy Square, states: 'She tells me that she heard people talking about her – she will not eat because she thinks poison is put in her food – she is much emaciated from the want of food.' He continues, with comments made by others to him: 'She is restless, & would run into the street without being properly dressed if the doors and windows were not properly secured.'

Dr Harold Sillipant of 1 Thornhill Square, Islington, says that he has observed the following: 'Absence of mind, speaks of hearing persons whispering in her room, holds imaginary conversations with persons absent, great apparent loss of memory, imagines that attempts have been made to poison her.' Others had told him the following: 'Great restlessness, attempts to get into the streets at unreasonable hours of the night & without proper regard to decency in dress & has been obliged to be brought in with some degree of force.'

At the bottom of the page her death is noted as being due to 'Exhaustion & Decay of old age'.

On the next page there are notes made on 8 December. 'This old lady has become unmanageable at home for the last month though it is thought mental imbecility has been coming on for a much longer time, but still it was not necessary to have any person specially to look after her.'

And here comes a highly significant note: 'There is a strong hereditary taint in her family. And her sister is at present insane.'

That 'insane' sister, of course, was Charles Dickens's mother, Elizabeth.

Sarah's notes continue:

> She is very restless night and day, during the day constantly wandering about and saying she ought not to be here that she is not worthy to be taken care of, that she ought not to take food and there is much difficulty in getting her to take any nourishment; during the night she is very frequently out of bed and knocking at her door. She is very thin and weak. She requires to be dressed or assisted in dressing.
>
> 1863 January 4. She is much weaker and her legs swell very much. She is kept in bed as much as possible.
>
> Feb. 2. She is much weaker and can not now leave her bed.
>
> March 7th She has been gradually sinking since the last report and died today at 12 am.

Poor Sarah. In Dr Hood's reformed hospital, and with the protection offered by the name of important family members written in the margins of her notes, one must hope that she was placed in the best available accommodation in what was undoubtedly an institution whose very name must have struck fear into anyone of that period. She was fortunate enough to be admitted at a time when the hospital was run on the more humanitarian approach created by Hood – who in fact left in the year she was admitted, and after whose departure the hospital was to return to a regime of restraint – and worse. While Sarah Barrow's care would have been more enlightened, and compassionate, to die in Bedlam was undeniably an ignominious end for anyone, and a fate notably not visited on her sister, Dickens's mother.

The administration of Sarah's estate, of under £200 in value, was granted to her brother Edward, rather than the nephew with whom she had lived – but who had had her committed to Bedlam. Under the question in Sarah Barrow's admission notes regarding relatives similarly affected, the response was – yes. And the degrees of relationship? Sister and aunt. The sister we know was Elizabeth Dickens: but – an aunt, as well?

It is possible to identify this relative, to a reasonable level of certainty, by examining the details of the death certificate from April 1855 of Aunt Charlton, the former Elizabeth Culliford, Dickens's great aunt, with whom Sarah lived for periods of her life. Even here, in death, Aunt Charlton is obliged to remind the world of her status as the widow of 'Charles William Charlton, Proctor'. Reading on, according to the details certified, as well as suffering from Phthisis (tuberculosis) for seven years, and convulsions for the previous thirty-three hours, she had had 'chronic disease of the brain'. This is likely to mean she too was suffering from a mental disorder – and most probably dementia.

It is perhaps significant that Charles Charlton's will, written in February 1853 shortly before his death and left in his desk at Doctors' Commons rather than at home, makes careful arrangements for his wife's care, leaving his estate in trust to be managed, at their discretion, by a brother and a friend, in a way 'most conducive to her benefit, advantage or welfare'. This is not so unusual perhaps in an era where marriage settlements and wills were necessarily designed to safeguard the financial security of dependent women, but in the case of a widow not likely to inherit a large sum of money, less likely. Also notable is that Charles Charlton's will made arrangements for the distribution of his estate after the decease and funeral of his wife, who would survive him by only two years.

As Sarah Barrow's case notes tell us, dementia, as a disease affecting the elderly, was seen at this time not as a physical illness but as a form of insanity, and in this case was perceived to be an inherited weakness: inherited madness, a preoccupation of Victorian medical science, and the favoured subject of so many sensation novels of the period. Three women in Dickens's family succumbed to this condition: perhaps he feared it would be passed on through generations of the wider family: or he may have dismissed it as a peculiarly female form of insanity – it was generally believed that women were more likely to inherit madness than men.

Looking at the process of developing the themes explored in *Great Expectations*, it might be fair to wonder if it began with the association of his great aunt, Berners Street, and memories of the White Woman, and even his mother and aunt, somehow coming together eventually in the shape of the character of Miss Havisham. It might be the case that the emphasis on mad women in some subconscious way helped distance the chance, as perhaps he feared, that Dickens himself might be at risk of this particular family legacy; that as well as inheriting relations, he might have inherited a related tendency to insanity.

His book of Memoranda, starting at the beginning of the year in which Aunt Charlton died, includes references to names later used in the book, and a letter written on 6 September 1858 to Wilkie Collins also outlines the tracery of a plot involving a lonely house, and a recluse, which became part of *A House to Let*, later featured in *Household Words*. By December 1860, when Dickens had begun to publish *Great Expectations*, in serial form, in *All the Year Round*, his mother's declining health was reaching its most acute stage, and his aunt Sarah Barrow would have been likely to be showing the earlier signs of the 'mental imbecility' noted by her relatives during the time leading up to her final crisis. It is reasonable, therefore, to speculate that the delusional state of Miss Havisham might, in some way, have been informed by Dickens's own experience of his mother, his aunt and his great aunt's decline in their later years, and attached, however tenuously, to the earlier embodiment of older female madness, in the form of the Berners Street case.

Charles Charlton and his immediate family were at first glance little more than examples of dull respectability, but that was not the case: the family's background – and one that would have intrigued the young Dickens – was rooted in repertory theatre. Charlton's parents were both actors, and his father, also Charles, became assistant manager of the Orchard Street Theatre, soon to become the Theatre Royal, in Bath in 1795. He and his wife, the former Miss Glassington, also appeared regularly in Bristol, at a time when Dickens's great uncle John Barrow was becoming a prosperous merchant and highly influential civic figure in the city, and was likely to have been a keen patron of the theatre. Perhaps the families became acquainted in this way. The Charltons, as well as having had a long tenure at Bath and Bristol, travelled around the country as performers before retirement and settling in London, the father dying aged ninety as late as 1846.[4]

Not only were women at this time considered to be at higher risk of inherited madness than men, but they were also seen as prone to mental illness as a natural consequence of their reproductive systems. Hysteria or mania were the perceived causes of insanity in women: dementia as a condition or disease peculiar to the elderly, at least in the case of the three women in Dickens's immediate family, appears not to have been considered.

Dickens had an interest in the emerging science of psychiatry and the care of patients in the new asylums: he visited St Luke's Hospital in 1851 and wrote about it in an article in *Household Words* in 1852 with the title 'A curious dance around a curious tree'. Curious in itself that it would be followed five years later with Morley's article 'The Star of Bethlehem', the second of two articles about the treatment of the insane with titles alluding to Christmas, that iconographic theme central to the idealisation of home and family now so closely associated with Dickens; the asylum being a total inversion of that ideal, for all the homely touches put in place by more enlightened followers of the 'moral treatment' approach to the care of patients.

The work undertaken by John Forster, who became secretary to the Lunacy Commission from 1855 to 1861, and then served as a commissioner, must have been familiar to Dickens, and he was acquainted with not only Dr Hood but also with Hood's mentor John Conolly, who had been involved in 1858 in the scandalous confinement – and then release after a public outcry – in a private asylum, of the wife of Dickens's friend Edward Bulwer-Lytton. Later developments, such as Conolly's involvement in the Ruck case of 1859, further alerted the general public to the horrors of wrongful confinement in such cases, and doubts about the system of admission to asylums.

Conolly had been caught lying about receiving fees from one establishment, which damaged his reputation and that of the profession in general, and there was debate about the unethical activities of certain 'mad doctors' in an anonymous piece in *All the Year Round* in February 1862. In March of the next year, the magazine began serialising Charles Reade's *Very Hard Cash* – a story of wrongful imprisonment in an asylum. Dickens's close friend and associate Wilkie Collins published another story involving the same theme in *The Woman in White*, published in 1860, and of course Mary Elizabeth Braddon's sensation novel of 1863, *Lady Audley's Secret*, ends with a murderous wife sent to a private asylum, her insanity apparently the legacy of her own mother's madness.

Dickens also appears previously, in 1858, to have toyed with the idea of women's natural predisposition to insanity for the purpose of separating from his wife, if you believe the claim that he tried to persuade doctors, as his friend Bulwer-Lytton had done with his own inconvenient wife, that Catherine was mad and should be placed in a private asylum.[5]

You might feel that the natural reaction of most women, already confined and restrained by the social mores of the Victorian period, would have been to struggle with their enforced roles, often ending in breakdown, depression, and other forms of mental illness. In Catherine's case, it seems often to be forgotten that long before their separation she seems to have had some sort of nervous crisis that required the stay in Malvern, and consultation with Dr Erasmus Wilson. Whether from post-natal depression – or post-natal psychosis – after so many pregnancies a subsequent experience of some form of mental illness would not be so unexpected.

It is striking, when looking closely at Dickens's family, how many relatives were secretly battling with mental health problems and poor physical health, almost always in the context of financial insecurity, or fractured family relationships. This was particularly true of the women in his family – his wife, his mother, aunt, and great aunt. Their characters were far from the idealised model of womanly submission and complacency that he so often presented in his fictional work, and it would seem likely that Dickens felt it impossible to extend to them the sympathy they needed because of it, recoiling from the older women whose life experiences had reduced them to the poor creatures they were, fixing on the vision of innocence and goodness that he thought he saw in the young, childless – arguably childlike – Ellen Ternan.

Arguably too there were other factors that may have contributed to the decline in mental health of Dickens's older female relatives, as well as many of the men in the family – brothers, sons, fathers and uncles – who struggled to reach the standards of achievement expected of them and ended in financial ruin or prone to alcoholism. And this struggle is not only something identified by Marx, in his description of the 'shabby genteel' class, but by Dr Hood himself, as noted in Catherine Arnold's *Bedlam*,[6] in which she writes: 'Hood's rationale was that an entire class of mentally distressed gentlefolk had been created for whom there were no available options: the shabby genteel, driven to madness by financial pressures …'

For the majority of women of this class, whose financial independence was strictly limited and usually linked to the prosperity of husbands, fathers, sons or brothers, the economic pressures, and the fear of ruin through the failure of their male relatives' inability to support them, must have made their vulnerability to mental illness so much higher; even more so for widows and unmarried women facing a lonely old age with little or no income, trying to maintain the outward signs of respectability. For older women succumbing to the ravages of what we now recognise as dementia, there can have been little understanding, or tolerance, whatever their circumstances, as their condition deteriorated. From a vaguely amusing, if grotesque, eccentricity to 'imbecility' and decay, Dickens's mother, and aunt Sarah – and perhaps his great aunt Charlton – would, as time passed, have been considered to be lapsing into a state of insanity, a prefigured destiny, that conjured little more than revulsion in Dickens – and perhaps tugged at underlying anxieties of his own risk of inherited insanity, a loss of self-control, and a loss of identity.

PART FOUR

Divers Straingers: The Casteels

Some of us of a curiositie to visite soe flourishing a nation have been here a short time being well assured by the Embassador of the King of Spaine that they may remaine here without any prosecution for their Religion, nevertheless the Petitioners liveing peaceably under his Majty's Governmt are by Justices of the Peace of Westmr committed Prisoners for their Religion to the Gatehouse where we now are in great want and misery …

Chapter Thirty-three

Her Majesty's frame maker

Let us return briefly to Bristol and turn our attention to the wife of Charles Dickens's great-grandfather, William Barrow, the surgeon-barber of Bristol, who married in the city's parish of St Leonard's in May 1758. Until now, the origins of William's wife and Dickens's great grandmother, Ann Cassteels, have not been traced.

One might have thought that the unusual surname would have suggested to previous researchers a line worth investigating. Perhaps it proved too difficult. Perhaps some were looking in the wrong direction. Others may not have wanted to pursue this line of enquiry.

If so, they were turning away from a point of no little significance, and a rich source of information that presents an entirely new perspective and understanding of Dickens's family background.

The unusual surname 'Cassteels', and its variant forms, is not a name local to Bristol. Sketchley's Directory for Bristol, however, published in 1775, includes a listing of a Lewis Casteel, as a 'victualler', of the Unicorn, at number 14, Frog Lane – the same road where William Barrow appears to have owned another licensed premise, Crabbs' Well, just a few years earlier.

What is the connection of Lewis Casteels to Ann Cassteels, if there is one? That was not immediately obvious. Further research identified a passing reference, spotted on a Bristol history website, to a Lewis Casteel who, further investigation revealed, was paid for work he undertook in 1742 in regard to the construction – or rather the decoration – of what is now Redland parish church, then a newly built private chapel on the outskirts of the city, attached to the estate of a very wealthy merchant named John Cossins.[1]

Records relating to the chapel's payment of workmen show that Lewis Casteel was paid £2 10s for gilding the ball and cross that is at the highest point of the cupola.

In view of the rarity of the name, the area, and the period in which these references occur, it seemed likely that there was a family connection with Ann

Cassteels, Dickens's great grandmother. The evidence that confirms the link was found casually jotted down in the notes left by William J. Carlton in the collection of his papers now in the archives of the Charles Dickens Museum – although apparently overlooked by him as evidence, or discarded as of no interest. Looking through these documents, it would have been very easy to miss the crucial clue, written as it was at the bottom of an insignificant piece of paper apparently torn out of a lined exercise book, stapled together with other rough notes. Here were a few hastily written lines, some of it in shorthand, referring to the wedding of William Barrow and Ann Cassteels, at St Leonard's Church, Bristol, on 22 May 1758: the groom was of that parish, and the bride from St Michael's. And there, in the details, previously unnoticed, it would seem, or of no interest – he had noted the names of two witnesses to the marriage.

One was a 'Rob Collier'. This witness is perhaps most likely to be the Robert Collier who was a merchant and insurance broker: his will of 1807 indicates that although he moved to London, he retained interests and properties in Bristol. One of the executors of his estate was business partner Justininan Casamajor, the wealthy grandson of merchant Luis Casamajor, who arrived in Bristol in the 1690s.

Robert Collier was associated with some of the most prominent families in Bristol and was a very successful businessman: his will includes bequests to two pillars of the city's establishment – Colston's School and the Society of Merchant Venturers. Although it must have been early in his career when he was chosen to be a witness at the wedding of William Barrow and Ann Cassteels, his presence is perhaps an indication that William Barrow had aspirations of his own, at this point, to make his mark in the city.

The really significant piece of evidence, however, is the other witness at their wedding. This was a Lewis Cassteels – clearly the same as the Lewis Casteel who had worked at Redland Chapel. Lewis was most likely to have been Ann's father, but it is possible he was her brother. Sixteen years after the work at Redland Chapel, it could be either: but more likely, perhaps, to be the former: if he was still alive and the proprietor of the Unicorn in 1775, his disappearance from further records may indicate a death soon afterwards or at least would seem to add weight to such a probability.

Here is a curious thing – the Redland estate more or less bordered that of Cotham Lodge, where seventy or so years later, Lewis Casteel's descendant John Barrow would live at the height of his success as a merchant and civic dignitary. Did he deliberately choose Cotham Lodge in some act of self-validation: to mark the triumph of his rise from charity schoolboy, the son of a barber, to the master of a property whose neighbour was Redland Court?

Frog Lane, where the Unicorn was situated, is an interesting location from the point of view of the Barrow family history. This road, often known alternately as Frogmore Street, lies at the bottom of Park Street, a step away from College Green, in an area home to Dickens's great uncle at the beginning and end of his business life. It is a very short distance to the site of Colston's Hospital.

These days Frog Lane lies largely unnoticed, passing under a short viaduct constructed to overcome the formerly steep gradient of the road towards Clifton, up and along Park Street.

Some of the road has disappeared, but what remains is interesting enough, although most tourists passing by, on the way to or from Park Street, pay no attention to anything other than a work by the local artist Banksy, 'The Well Hung Lover', sprayed on the side wall of a sexual health clinic situated in the road below.

If you step down to the more shadowy level of the street, in the area closest to the Hatchet, one of the oldest inns in Bristol, you can grasp an idea of the former character of the area from this and other surviving properties, some of which must have been there in the late eighteenth century, when the Unicorn and Crabbs Well establishments were in business.

The Hatchet was long established when Lewis Cassteels took over the running of the Unicorn, in fact – it dates probably from the sixteenth century and has outlived all other taverns that were once located here, offering the opportunity for refreshment for men and horses before the sharp ascent of the hill to Clifton. In 1775, when Lewis was running the Unicorn, he faced stiff competition in Frog Lane: apart from the Hatchet, run by Samuel Maddock, at number 25, there was the White Hart, at number 6; the Horse and Jockey at number 28 and the Lamb at number 30. No Crabbs Well is then listed in Frog Lane (although there is another inn with that name in another area) but it appears in other, later records until at least the 1840s.

While two of William Barrow's sons, William and John, were scholars at Colston's (and Dickens's grandfather Charles Barrow was at sea), Lewis Casteels was only a short distance away from the school. It is unlikely that the brothers were unaware, therefore, of this relative – most probably their grandfather – and it is interesting to speculate the extent to which John Barrow in particular was familiar with his family origins, Casteel and Barrow – especially as the family had probably lived in Frog Lane, at the Crabbs Well, not so long before, when their father was alive. What happened to their mother Ann, formerly Cassteels, is not clear. Perhaps after the death of her husband she was with Lewis in Frog Lane.

There is one other possible reference to Lewis Casteels – and a connection to the Barrow family. Returning to the inventory of Edward Crane,[2] made in 1764, and the mention of a debt owed to William Barrow for working on one of his wigs (Mr Crane had six wigs, worth a total of 18 shillings), we might also note the following entry regarding a sum of £15 15s: 'Also an Allowance for Moneys paid Mr Castel late Assistant to the decesed for his Time and Trouble in assisting in settling the decesed's affairs …' There is mention too of a sum of £30 15s 5d, that had been paid to a Mrs Phillips 'for the deceased's Lodging and Board, Washing and other necessarys to the Time of his Death'.[3]

Again, in the inventory we see two debts listed that are owed by two coach makers: Mr John Clark, and Mr John Chandler: more than £239 by the former, and more than £327 by the latter. In the Sketchley's Directory of Bristol published in 1775, there is listed a John Chandler, coach and harness-maker, at number 9, Frog Lane. Lewis Casteel, victualler, at the Unicorn, is just a few doors away, at number 14. In the same directory, a John Clark, carver and gilder, is noted as living only round the corner from Frog Lane – in Denmark Street.

In 1764, the Unicorn inn in Frog Lane, which would later be taken over by Lewis Casteel, was then run by a family named Phillips. In that year, Mary Phillips is listed as the proprietor, taking over from 'Widow Phillips'. It is quite possible that the Mrs Phillips with whom Edward Crane lodged was one of these women. Certainly he already had two connections with Frog Lane: with Chandler the coach maker – and with Lewis Casteel. Edward Crane was a coach painter: the inventory of his goods at death includes items listed as his stocks in trade, brushes, paints and pigments, and amongst the debts at the time of his death was a sum of 14 shillings for 'Two hundred broad Leaf Gold'.

It seems likely, therefore, to conclude that as a gilder by trade, Lewis Casteels may be the assistant 'Mr Castel' referred to in Crane's inventory: gilding clearly was part of the necessary decoration of the better class of coach, and it would also seem reasonable to surmise that Casteels, deploying his highly specialised skills as a gilder, worked at least to some extent in the later part of his career with Crane and perhaps other coach makers in Bristol.[4]

Lewis's residence in the city coincided with a flourishing period of prosperity and a large degree of development: new streets, new houses; new public buildings.

As well as his work at Redland, he would have found plenty of opportunities for his trade.

The decoration inside Redland Chapel has work by Flemish-born sculptor Michael Rysbrack, whose statue of William III was placed in Queens Square, to be later overlooked by John Barrow when he was installed in the mayor's official residence: the chapel also displays an adornment of carved fruit and flowers that are attributed to the hand of Thomas Paty, one member of a family of architects, carvers and masons who were associated with Bristol at this period, and indeed throughout the eighteenth century. Their work is evident in many of Bristol's churches, as well as in some of the civic buildings, such as the Royal Exchange, and residential properties. This includes some, probably by James Paty the Elder, around 1740, in the area of College Green, and from 1742 in Unity Street, which runs partly along the back of Frog Lane, where we know Lewis Casteel was based in 1775. It is quite possible he worked on some of these developments and refurbishments along with the older Patys, as he had at Redland. The Paty family were also responsible for the Park Street houses that accommodated John Barrow in his last years.

Members of the Paty family are known also to have provided carved and gilded picture frames, including for the Hogarth triptych *Sealing the Tomb* that was installed in St Mary Redcliffe church in the 1750s: as we shall see, Lewis Casteel and other members of his family were also picture framers – before and after the family lived in Bristol.

Owning an inn, as well as following a trade, was not so unusual at the time. How long it lasted, exactly, is not clear: but the name of the Unicorn – itself a nod to the gilded coat of arms of the city – soon disappears from local directories, although it may have continued under a new one, with a new proprietor.

Searches in the baptismal, marriage and burial records of the many parishes in Bristol produces only a handful of references to what may have been other members of the family of Ann and Lewis Casteel.

On the same autumn day in 1779, 29 October, at the church of St Augustine the Less – damaged during the war and demolished in 1962, but which once stood not far from Frog Lane – the burials of a William and Ann Casteel are recorded: their ages and relation to each other are not revealed, but they are linked in the entry with a bracket, and marked with the comment 'poor'. This parish church, as is evidenced by the details of other burials, served the area of Frog Lane, so it would seem the family had remained in the same area.

If we go back to the 1740s, and the registers of St James's parish, north of the city centre, we can see that two children were recorded as baptised there, born to a Lewis Castle and his wife Hanna: a John Castle in 1742, and Elizabeth Castle in 1744. An Elizabeth Castile is noted as an infant buried twenty-one months later at Christ Church, who might be the same daughter. It is not impossible, and perhaps even likely, that these were the brother and sister of Ann Casteels, the mother of Dickens's grandfather Charles Barrow. She was probably born in 1739. Was the Ann Casteel who died in 1779, her mother, Lewis's wife 'Hanna'?

In the records of St Martin in the Fields, London, there are baptisms of at least some of the children of a Lewis and Hanna Casteels, including Ann, baptised in 1739, whose age and father's name would neatly match the Ann Cassteels who married William Barrow in Bristol in 1758. With such an uncommon combination of first and second names, and with both of them living in the city of Bristol, it would seem highly likely then that this Lewis was the father of Ann Casteel: although it is possible that the later records relate to a brother of the same name baptised in London, date unknown.[5]

But what would bring the Casteels from London to Bristol? It is not difficult to imagine why Lewis Casteel found Bristol a favourable place in which to live as a craftsman: as good, if not better, than London, with perhaps less competition and plenty of opportunities in the period's wealth of new buildings, both residential and civic in form, the outward expression of the city's current prosperity and aspirations. It may be that he initially came as a craftsman working on John Cossins's chapel: Cossins was himself based in London before his retirement to Redland and employed other workers from the capital. At least one other carver and gilder, a William Ellis, who advertised for potential customers in the local newspaper, *Felix Farley's Bristol Journal*, stated that he had come from Great Russell Street, Bloomsbury.

From tracing the Bristol-based Casteel family back to a small number of others with this name in London at this time who seem to be related, one very interesting possibility emerges.

The Casteels appear to have come to England directly from the Netherlands: but they may well have been of Sephardi Jewish origins, at one stage, new Christians, or Conversos who had fled the Inquisition generations earlier, perhaps as early as the sixteenth century.

The earliest evidence for the arrival of Dickens's Casteel ancestors in England comes from two documents held among the records of the House of Lords, in the Parliamentary Archives, the first dated 30 November 1678:

To the Right Honourable the Lords Spirituall and Temporall in Parliament Assembled

The humble petition of Henry Gilmans Gold Beater, Peter Van Melder his Servant, Lewis Casteels her Majs Framemaker Thomas Oubretchsts and Giles Bowels his servant John Sleider Silver Chaser John Leissons Taylor and Giles Malvoe Goldsmith Natives of the Spanish Netherlands Inhabiting in St Martins Legrand, and now prisoners in the Gatehouse Westminster. Humbly sheweth That your Petrs having settled themselves and families in St Martins Le grand a Privileged Place for aliens as your petrs now informed have there for serverall years with all honest Industry followed their respective Callings but because they are not willing to take the Oath of Supremacy have been cast into Prison and are there detained to the utter ruins of them and their distressed families.

Wherefore your poor Petrs most humbly pray your Lordships that your petrs may be sett at liberty to follow their severall Callings as before or else have some reasonable time allowed them to settle their affaires and prepare for their return into their Country.

The petition is signed individually by Henry Gillemans, Pieter de Melder, Lewis Casteels, Thomas Oubrechts, Jan Sleider, Jan Leissons, Gilles Malvoe. (Giles Bowels, being a servant of Thomas Oubretchsts, perhaps was not literate.)

The document identifies Lewis Casteels as being from the Spanish Netherlands, rather than the Dutch Republic. Although at this period Jews were enjoying a rare period of religious tolerance in the north, and the community in Amsterdam was flourishing, those living in the areas under Spanish governance were still at risk of persecution: they would have to live as nominal Catholics, if not genuine converts. They may not have been prepared, once in England, for any hostility towards Catholics being directed at them.

St Martin's Le Grand was a parish in the City of London, but it was a 'Liberty', subject to the control of Westminster, a circumstance that extended certain privileges and protections – and even at one time the right of sanctuary – to its inhabitants, especially 'aliens' like Lewis and his fellow 'artificers'.

The Gatehouse at Westminster could happily accommodate any residents of St Martin's Le Grand who had the misfortune to be detained after being arrested. The prison stood next to Westminster Abbey, and in the course of its history held many prisoners, including, eleven years after Casteels and his fellow aliens, Samuel Pepys.

Only a couple of days later, on 2 December, the prisoners signed and submitted a second petition to the Lords: this time they stressed that they had come to England with certain assurances from the King and the Spanish Ambassador and emphasised the hardship caused by the imprisonment, including the impact on their dependents:

> The Humble Petition of divers straingers whose names are under subscribed now distressed Prisoners in the Gate house.
>
> Sheweth
>
> That the Petitioners being borne in the Dominions of the King of Spaine and induced by the gratious Declaration of his Majy for the encourageing Alliens to come into England, and to setle here, have to the benefit of this nation resided here as artificers And some of us of a curiositie to visite soe flourishing a nation have been here a short time being well assured by the Embassador of the King of Spaine that (they) may remaine here without any prosecution for their Religion, nevertheless the Petitioners liveing peaceably under his Majty's Governmt are by Justices of the Peace of Westmr committed Prisoners for (their) Religion to the Gatehouse where we now are in great want and misery ...

They then refer again to their 'distressed families' and state that they 'humbly pray the Lords in Christian compassion for their suffering of your Petitioners', asking for liberty to 'remain heere peaceably without any prosecution for their Religion' or that they may be allowed, with their families, to leave for 'fforraigne parts'.[6]

The reference to the 'gratious Declaration' and the expectation that religious tolerance would be extended to those 'living Peaceably' was a reminder of Charles's Declaration of Breda, made in 1660 and issued from the Netherlands, promising to respect 'tender consciences' and religious freedom.

Having spent his formative years in exile, Charles's taste in design and decoration inevitably meant a renewal of style and form in English art and architecture: the popularity of ornate gilded frames in the Netherlands and elsewhere in Europe had begun during his father's reign, but the Restoration period offered new opportunities for craftsmen to move to England. It is not impossible that Lewis Casteels really was employed in some capacity by the

Queen – but no evidence of this has been identified in the Royal Archives, or records of the Royal Collection Trust. It might seem a high-risk venture to make this claim in such a petition if it were without any foundation, however – and as we shall see, there may be a reason why he considered himself to be within the reach of royal patronage.

The Spanish ambassador mentioned here might be Don Pedro Ronquillo, who was appointed to this post from 1675. He held masses at the chapel attached to the Spanish embassy, Wild House, which Catholics in London could attend – but is also known to have had links to Sephardi leaders in the Netherlands, so whether or not Casteels was a Catholic or a crypto-Jew, he may have found him useful as an ally, if only by nominal reference. Alternatively, the document may refer to Ronquillo's predecessor, the Marques del Fresno, who was ambassador from about four years earlier, who would clearly also have been a useful name to drop.

The repeated lobbying of the detained aliens was successful: records of the House of Lords show that Gilmans and Lewis Casteels, and their fellow prisoners in the Gatehouse, were then ordered to be discharged.

Chapter Thirty-four

The Casteels in London

The arrest of Lewis Casteels and the other prisoners had taken place during the height of fear and suspicion surrounding the allegations of the Popish Plot, spun by troublemaker Titus Oates, with stories of threats against the life of the King from Catholic conspirators who allegedly wanted to replace him with his Catholic brother James. The Queen was rumoured, nonsensically, to have been party to the conspiracy, amid the hysteria that followed the murder of Sir Edmund Berry Godfrey, a magistrate Oates had approached with details of the apparent conspiracy, and whom he later claimed to have been killed by Catholic plotters.

The arrest of the 'artificers' sent to the Gatehouse came six days after Oates had claimed that the Queen was in league with the King's physician, in an attempt to poison him. It was also at a point when all Catholics were under heightened levels of suspicion.

The alien tradesmen, emigrants from the Spanish Netherlands, were Catholic, or at least nominally so: residing in the disreputable Liberty of St Martin's must have made them an easy target at this time: but their pleas were successful – or it may have been that some sort of intervention on their behalf was made.

Dickens refers to this period in his work *A Child's History of England* and in Chapter Thirty-five includes the name of a hapless silversmith that was a victim of the plot:

> Then, a miserable wretch named Prance, a Catholic silversmith, being accused by Bedloe, was tortured into confessing that he had taken part in Godfrey's murder, and into accusing three other men of having committed it.

Could Dickens have had any idea that his own ancestor, a supposed Catholic gilder, had been a victim of the anti-papist hysteria of the time?

After Lewis Casteel's release he continued in his trade: there is record of at least one bill, dated 1702, of £8 paid to him by a Samuel Tufton, of Middle Temple, for gilt frames.[1]

A business connection with Tufton may hold some deeper significance as it is the family name of the Earls of Thanet, whose property in Aldersgate Street, their London residence, was a short distance directly up the road from Lewis Casteel, in St Martin's Le Grand. Thanet House by 1676 had become the home of the Earl of Shaftesbury, Anthony Ashley Cooper, who only two years later was to take a leading role in the attempt to target suspected Catholics, in the period of the Popish Plot. Perhaps it was due to local suspicion centred in the area around Shaftesbury's residence that Lewis and his fellow foreign prisoners had come to the attention of the authorities.

The name of Lewis Casteel (and variant spellings of this surname) features in various Land Tax listings, for St Martin's Le Grand, or Aldersgate Within, from at least 1692 to 1711. There is also a very useful listing in *London Inhabitants Within the Walls*, compiled in 1695, that shows that at this time he and Mary are living in the city parish of St Leonard, Foster Lane, in the Aldersgate area, with a number of children, their names seemingly given in order of birth: William, Lewis, Mary, Jane and Frances. St Leonard's church had been destroyed in the Great Fire of London, and the parish merged with Christ Church, Newgate Street, where several of the children were baptised. Close to Foster Lane was St Paul's Cathedral, also damaged by the fire, and in the process of being rebuilt according to the plans of Christopher Wren. Perhaps Lewis Casteel's skills as a gilder were employed in this project, or some of the other new or newly renovated buildings that appeared as London recovered from the devastation of 1666 – such as the Wren rebuilding of Christ Church.[2]

There is an adult Lewis Casteel whose burial is noted in the register of St Anne's church in Soho on 6 March 1714, which is possibly the same man as the one previously living in Aldersgate: the younger Lewis was living nearby when married, as at least two of his children with Hannah were baptised in St Martin in the Fields, in 1739 and 1741. Clearly the family did not stay in the City of London, and perhaps as the older Lewis Casteel prospered in the next few years, he had moved his family closer to an area where he was more likely to find commissions for his work.

Casteel and many variations of this name: Castiel, Castile, Castell, and so on, have one thing in common: being usually, in origin, a Sephardi Jewish surname: more obviously Castillo or de Castillo and Castro in Spanish, Castilho in Portuguese. These names can now be found in Jewish communities all over the world, but at that time, notably, in many of the places where there had been a settlement of exiled Jews persecuted by the church and state in Spain or Portugal – or related colonies, and, of course, within the borders of the Spanish Netherlands, as well as in the Dutch Republic.

Wherever the Sephardim lived, in fact, there are references to the name: even as far away as India, where important members of the community in Cochin, from the seventeenth century onwards, included several men with the surname Castiel. Records show further examples, including descendants in Israel, but also, significantly from our point of interest, in the Netherlands: for example, as seen as in the register of burials in the Beth Haim cemetery at Ouderkerk van Amstel, just outside Amsterdam, which dates from the early seventeenth century. Here we will find burials of Eliau Castiel (Eliyahu can be the Hebrew name for Louis), who died in 1763, Hanna in 1774, Judith in 1651, and Branca in 1622.[3]

Most Sephardi Jews living in all these diverse locations were descended from expelled or migrant Conversos – New Christians, those who had been required to undergo conversion to Christianity and to submit to the authority of the Catholic church – or Marranos: crypto-Jews; ostensibly converts, but continuing to practise their religion, or suspected of practising their religion, in secret. It would seem likely that Charles Dickens's Casteel ancestors had lived such lives over a sequence of several generations, probably retaining at least some of their Jewish identity until a point where circumstances made it impossible to continue.

If he was of Converso origin, to what extent and how quickly such a family might have become estranged from their Jewish identity – if indeed they were – is difficult to measure. For many Jews living in the Sephardic Diaspora of this period, including those who settled in England, there was a slow but incremental assimilation into the mainstream culture, pressured by the numerous obstacles and restrictions placed on them and the general hostility to the community.

Charles II was tolerant by nature and supportive of Jews who came to London: while in exile he had negotiated with members of the Amsterdam community and in return for money, arms and ammunition offered them his protection when restored to the throne. It is also the case that the King's marriage to Catherine of Braganza was first suggested by the Sephardi Jewish merchant Augustin Coronel Chacon, who received a knighthood in recognition of his services – and converted to Christianity. Catherine's personal physician was a Dr Fernando Mendes, a crypto-Jew who was granted accommodation at Somerset House, and whose daughter Catherine – later to become known as the miniaturist Catherine da Costa – was said to have been the godchild of the Queen.

Not all those in the Netherlands with the name Casteel were necessarily of Sephardi Jewish origin. It should also be noted that there were one or two families with variant versions of the name Casteel in London, from the Low Countries, whose names occur in the registers of French Protestant churches in London and Canterbury, so clearly not claiming to be Catholics: one prominent example is that of Michael Casteel, a wealthy merchant originally from Antwerp who was of great use to Cromwell, supplying the Parliamentary army in Ireland with wheat, beef and corn, and who was owed money for his supplies for some years afterwards. Whether or not he was originally from a Marrano or Converso family is not known, but it is a possibility.[4]

It is also the case, according to some sources, that some Marrano families in the Low Countries in areas like Antwerp converted to Calvinism, but seemingly as a 'façade' for their crypto-Judaism.[5]

It would seem possible that Antwerp was the place of origin of Lewis Casteel: it was the centre of artistic activity in the Spanish Netherlands – and had been the centre for the wider Low Countries until this role was assumed by Amsterdam – and the city was therefore clearly a desirable location for a framer and gilder to live and work.

A significant number of artists from Antwerp moved to London in the Restoration period, including Jacob Huysmans, also known as James Huysmans, who arrived sometime around 1662 and became the favourite portrait painter of the Queen. Indeed it is said that he called himself 'Her Majesty's Painter', or 'the Queen's painter' – accounts vary. This might appear to be reflective of the self-appointed title assumed by Lewis Casteels in the House of Lords petition, 'Her Majesty's Picture Framer'. Had Lewis framed some of Huysman's pictures?

Among the many artists and craftsmen from Antwerp living in London at this time or shortly afterwards who moved in the same social circles and belonged to the same clubs, such as the Society of St Luke and the Rose and Crown Club, was the painter Pieter Casteels. He was one of several artists from the same family in Antwerp who came to London in 1708 along with his better-known brother-in-law, the artist Pieter Tillemans.

In terms of court connections, there were Flemish or Dutch artists in this period appointed to positions relating to the Royal art collection. In 1662, for example, George Geldorp became 'Mender of Pictures'; in 1676 Gerrit Van

Uylenburgh was 'Surveyor of the Pictures' and, of course, Peter Lely was appointed 'Principal Painter' in 1660.

As yet no immediate member of Lewis Casteel's family has been identified in the surviving early records of the first synagogues in London, such as they are in this period – although there are references to members with variants of the name, such as 'Castello'. There is, however, a very significant piece of evidence in an unexpected place that would appear to help confirm the family's origins.

In the pages of the Irish source of records 'Betham's Genealogical Extracts', and in indexes for Diocesan and Prerogative marriage licence bonds, there is to be found the handwritten transcript of a notice in Dublin, dated 26 March 1674, of a marriage between a Lewis de Casteele, and a woman with the name of Beatrice Mountaseene.[6]

Mountaseene is a most unusual surname; certainly not Irish, nor English. In fact, it would seem most likely to be a local interpretation of a well-known Sephardi surname: Montesinos, or Montezinos. Beatrice, or Beatriz, is a name that occurs quite frequently in Sephardi families of the time with links to Spain or Portugal and the Netherlands; the surname Montesinos and its variants can be found not only in the wider Sephardi diaspora, but significantly in some of the earliest records of the Jewish community in London. Bevis Marks' series of published records include circumcision registers in which we find a reference to one Montezinos described as 'Forasteira', or 'outsider', listed in 1680, and another with this name in 1693.

In a document held in the Ets Haim Library in Amsterdam, a census of the 'Nation' – a list compiled by Abraham Israel Zagache of Spanish and Portuguese Jews resident in London – there is mentioned the family of an Ishac Montesinos, including his wife, children and sister, who arrived in 1680. There were several families and individuals of this name with associations with the Spanish Netherlands, or resident there, with links to the greater Sephardic diaspora, stretching from the Iberian Peninsula to the Low Countries, to the New World and the Caribbean – and beyond.

In the mid-seventeenth century, for example, one of the major Spanish wool dealers trading between Spain, Portugal and the Low Countries was a Converso merchant named Fernando Montesinos, working with his sons Manuel and Bartolome and other partners in the family's commercial business, which was active in Portugal, Castile in Spain and several other countries. He was seized by the Inquisition in 1654, and his assets confiscated.[7]

Fernando Montesinos fled to Antwerp with his wife and his son Enrique, leaving his business in the Peninsula in the hands of two other sons. Although the family continued to prosper after his death, by the end of the seventeenth century the Montesinos' fortunes were in decline. Was Beatrice Mountaseene a member of this family? Fernando certainly was known to have had a sister named Beatriz.

Why Lewis Cassteels and Beatrice Mountaseene were marrying in Dublin is not known. There was a small, covert, early Sephardic community recently established in Dublin, around 1660 – most of the settlers are said to have been Conversos from Amsterdam and London.

One family that had been involved in the earliest stage of this community were the Pereiras: two brothers are thought to have settled in Dublin around 1662. Their father was said to be originally from Portugal, but the family had moved to several locations, such as Rouen, Antwerp and London. We know that there were close links between the early Dublin community and Amsterdam, so it is interesting to note that there are records there in this period of Montezinos marriages with spouses with the surname Pereira.

Were Lewis Cassteels and Beatrice Mountaseene connected in some way to the tiny Dublin settlement? The date of their marriage is also significant, just weeks after the ending of hostilities between England and the Dutch.

Applying for a licence would have meant no notices read in church, and more discretion: or it may be that perhaps they were only in Dublin for a short while; although the marriage details state they are 'of Dublin', that may mean only at the time of the application for the marriage licence. The legality of Jewish marriage, of course, was only recognised by Parliament decades later, in 1753: at this time, marriage in church was not unknown for Jewish couples – especially for those at risk of exposure. In Ireland, being married or 'endizened' as a Protestant would have been a better choice than claiming a Catholic identity.

Whereas the entries before and after Lewis and Beatrice's notice describe the groom as a 'Gentleman', their listing markedly does not, which might add weight to the argument that this Lewis de Casteele is the same individual as the 'artificer' Lewis Casteel imprisoned four years later in London. At the very least the combination of names would suggest they were related, and the marriage taken as indicating the family's origin.

If this is the same man, in Protestant London he was suspected of being a Catholic, but four years earlier in Dublin, in a largely Catholic country, he had applied to marry in a Protestant church. If he had been a Protestant in 1674 and was the same person imprisoned in the Gatehouse four years later, now suspected of being Catholic and refusing to take the Oath of Supremacy, this might seem inconsistent. For someone trying to protect his identity, however, hiding under the cover of a minority group was a wise choice. And we know that the Lewis Casteel in London, despite refusing to take the Oath 1678 – supposedly because of being a Catholic – was happy enough then to baptise his children in Protestant churches, which itself represents a clear inconsistency.

Although Beatrice, or Beatriz, was a Christian name, it was obviously a foreign one, and one associated with Spanish and Portuguese Jews: this may explain why Louis's wife in England is known as Mary. The wife of the prominent Sephardi merchant Carvajal, who had died in 1659, was known as Mary, rather than Esther, for example. Alternatively, Mary could be a wife from a second marriage. Or of course, less likely, there could have been another Lewis Casteel – but the marriage in Dublin at least would seem to support the theory that these families were at some point of Converso or Marrano origin.

As Todd Endelman states in his study of the history of the Jewish community in Britain, 'Most of the Sephardim who settled in England had lived as Catholics, not Jews, for much of their lives.' Once they had arrived, although many chose to re-embrace – or to experience for the first time – the opportunity to live, however discreetly, as Jews, some continued as Christians. Endelman points out that 'the very first conversos to arrive tended not to affiliate with the newly established Jewish community – only one-third of those resident in London before 1659 were buried in the Sephardi cemetery in Mile End'.[8]

Evidence of the earliest children that were born to Lewis and Mary in London begins with a baptism six years after the marriage of Lewis de Casteel in Dublin, and two years after the petitions of Lewis Casteel the gilder and frame maker: the baptism of Ursula, in 1680 at Christ Church, Greyfriars. Another daughter, Dorothy, was baptised in 1684, and then buried on 23 September in the same year – noted in the register as being the daughter of Lewis Casteels, frame maker, and his wife Mary – so confirming that he was the prisoner of the Gatehouse.[9]

On 2 June 1687, Lewis lost another child, his son John: his burial is listed in the register of St James, Clerkenwell, noted as being of Sun Court, Swan Alley. This address – that is to say, Swan Alley, now Great Sutton Street – is on the northern boundary of the Charterhouse estate, running between what is now St John's Street and Goswell Road, which ends in St Martin's Le Grand, near St Paul's, where we know Lewis was a resident nine years earlier. Swan Alley is shown on William Morgan's map of London, published in 1682 – Sun Court is clearly marked with the number '151', identifying it in the list of references for the City and Liberties of London, outlined with a group of buildings in a yard – and Swan Alley is still listed in John Stow's survey of 1753, noted as being part of the Liberty of St John's Street.

We know that the frame maker Lewis Casteel was the father of another Lewis who had been baptised in 1682, also at Christ Church, Greyfriars. But could this son be the Lewis who moved to Bristol – or was there another generation?

By the point at which we know a Lewis Casteel was engaged to gild the cupola of Redland Chapel – the accounts show he was paid by 'Mr Cossins' on 5 May 1742 – he would have been sixty years old. If he was the father of Ann who married William Barrow, he would have been in his late fifties when she was born – if she was, as seems most likely, the Ann Casteels, daughter of Lewis, baptised in 1739 at St Martin in the Fields. This Ann's mother was recorded as Hanna. The couple had a son, John, who was baptised on 5 May 1741, also at St Martin in the Fields. Here seems to be the time of departure from London: another John – the first presumably died as a baby – was baptised as the son of Lewis Castle and Hanna at St James parish church, Bristol, on 29 December 1742, and Elizabeth – also of Lewis and Hanna, at the same church on 30 October 1744. This daughter may well be the infant buried as Elizabeth Castile according to the registers of Christ Church parish in Bristol, on 28 July 1746.

It could be that all the children with Hannah were from a late or second marriage. Or perhaps there is a missing generation, and Lewis who was baptised in 1682 had a son, also named Lewis, who married Hanna, and had with her the children that included Ann Casteels, Dickens's great grandmother. Any record of marriages of the two known Lewis Casteels in England have proved elusive so far, so we can only guess.

Chapter Thirty-five

The Jewish community in Bristol

Further research may hold the definitive answers to the origins of Dickens's Casteel family, or not. But there is good evidence to suggest that the association with the surname, the repetition of first names, and the trade of carver and gilder, links the generations that connected his family's origins in the Netherlands, the move to London, and their association with Bristol.

London was not the only major centre of Jewish settlement in England, of course. The second most important area of early settlement – and resettlement – was Bristol. And here we meet another point of possible significance in the story of Charles Dickens's family history.

It may be that the Casteels, if they identified as Jews, had in Bristol some sort of contact or connection with the community there: and there is another interesting possibility in terms of the Barrow family's association with Bristol, albeit one that remains unproven – and less likely, but still something that may have some element of truth in it.

Barrow is also a surname used by Sephardi Jewish families, from the seventeenth century onwards; the derivation of the name being from Baruch, the Hebrew word for 'blessed'. One of the first twelve Jewish brokers formally authorised to engage in business at the Royal Exchange in 1697 was a Moses Barrow, also known as Moses Baruh Lousada: presumably the same Moses Baruh Lousada who in 1663 was elected the first treasurer, or 'Gabay', of the new community that met in Creechurch Lane. Moses Baruh Lousada's signature is also on the petition for support that was submitted to Charles II in 1664.

There are several well-known Sephardi Barrow families, not necessarily connected, some of whom who later abandoned their Jewish identity, living and trading in England (largely in London, but some settling in Bath) – and the West Indies, including Barbados – whose original names were Baruch, or Baruch Lousada, or other variants. These families have links to the Netherlands, and many other countries within the Jewish diaspora. Did any settle in Bristol, the second place of resettlement of Sephardi Jews, and the most important trading port of the period?

In the Sketchley's directory of 1775 in which Lewis Casteels appears, there are listed more than thirty surnames that appear to be Jewish in origin: as well as a 'Jew Preacher' by the name of Isaac Collish, there are many traders, craftsmen, victuallers, merchants and bankers with names such as Isaacs, Levi, Lyon, Marks, Moses and Salmon. Judith Samuel's study of the Jewish history of Bristol lists many other names and sets a clear context for the development of this community. A synagogue had been established in Temple parish, Bristol, by the mid-eighteenth century, as well as a burial ground in St Philip and St Jacob parish.[1]

The earlier history of the Jewish community in Bristol is less well documented, but that is not to say nothing is known about it. Todd Endelman observes that:

> several score New Christian merchants settled in London between the 1520s and the end of the century. Most were linked by family and commercial lives to the important New Christian trading colony in Antwerp. (In the 1540s and 1550s, there was also a small Converso community of cloth traders in Bristol).[2]

He notes that many of the settled merchants were 'secret judaizers', including those in Bristol, such as Henrique Nunes and his wife Beatriz.

Henrique Nunes, a physician, and his wife Beatriz are included in a list of Jews known to be living in Bristol in the mid-sixteenth century that was extracted by the Inquisition at Lisbon. This information was originally taken from a Portuguese sailor who denounced a man named Thomas Fernandes, of Evora, accusing him of having lived as an observant Jew in the port city. Fernandes, who was a nephew of Nunes, in turn gave several accounts to the Inquisition that identified communities and individuals in London and Bristol, where there was said to be a secret synagogue. There were communications between the covert settlements in these two locations, largely between family members – another nephew of Henrique was Hector Nunes, a physician living in Mark Lane, in the City of London, whose patients included members of the court, such as William Cecil, Lord Burghley. Hector was said to have informed his uncle regularly of the dates of Jewish festivals.

What happened to this early settlement of Converso Jews in Bristol is not known: it may be that, as David Cesarani suggests, the community 'faded away'

– on the other hand it is possible that some families remained and continued as 'crypto-Jews'.[3]

By the period of expansion and prosperity that arrived in the mid-eighteenth century there is documentation of an established settlement of Jewish residents living and trading in the port city. As Cesarani also points out, however, Bristol was 'decidedly unfriendly to Jews', which may have resulted in the relatively small size of the community in proportion to the scale of economic success and level of population. Trade in the city was effectively controlled by the Society of Merchant Venturers: an indication of the attitude of the city's governing class is that in 1753 this body petitioned Parliament for the repeal of the Act for the Naturalisation of the Jews, which had just been passed. Four years later, Moses Cohen, a trader in gold and silverware, was prosecuted by the city Corporation for trading without being a 'free burgess': a status that, as we have seen, was crucial to the eventual rise in fortune of the Barrow family.

There are Barrows and Berrows aplenty in Bristol records, and elsewhere in England. That said, it is not entirely impossible that Dickens's Bristol Barrow relatives were descended from a family who were, at one point, part of an early Sephardi Jewish community, either settled with other Marranos in Bristol itself, or arriving there from London, and that they had, like many other Jewish settlers, over several generations increasingly distanced themselves from their original faith and culture.

It might be tempting to indulge in speculation in which Mathew Barrow, the schoolmaster from Bristol, was really a Matthias Baruh, and his wife Jane Goodman a Goedman, also with Dutch Sephardic roots. In Bristol records of the late seventeenth and early eighteenth centuries there are not so many Goodmans, and of the references one finds, one or two have interesting first names: such as Valentine Goodman, and his son Orson Goodman, baptised in the 1740s: both names occur in Dutch records – and the former in some Sephardi families. Could the Casteels have become acquainted with the Barrows due to some sort of common background such as this? A remote possibility, perhaps.

It is interesting to recall that the business of Dickens's great uncle John Barrow and his Vizer partners in the later part of the eighteenth century was in trading in Spanish wool. Although seemingly a business model passed on by Jeremiah Hill, the merchant to whom they were apprenticed, many Sephardi families were involved in this trade throughout Europe at one time.

If it is true that the Casteels were of Sephardi Jewish descent, it clearly puts an entirely new perspective on the relationship of Charles Dickens and the Jewish community of his own period, and the continuing criticism of the portrayal of Jewish characters like Fagin in his work in a manner that so easily pandered to the entrenched antisemitism of the era.

That relationship, and the creation of that character, became of greater significance than has largely been understood, in the later life and work of Dickens: a development that emerged from a well-known correspondence between the writer and a woman named Eliza Davis, published shortly after Dickens's death in 1870. New evidence regarding this correspondence, however, can now be presented that will illustrate the full importance of Dickens's acquaintance with the Davis family – not only due to the letters written by Mrs Davis, but from the wider experience of her family and her community.

Chapter Thirty-six

Eliza Davis and the despised Hebrew

After the separation from his wife and the wedding of his daughter Kate, Charles Dickens sold the lease of Tavistock House to a man called James Phineas Davis, who was a West End solicitor. Dickens referred to Davis in letters to friends in casually derogatory terms: writing to Thomas Mitton on 16 August 1860, he explained that the purchaser was a 'Jew Money Lender'; on the 19th he wrote 'if the Jew Money Lender buys (I say "if" because of course I shall never believe in him until he has paid the money.)' In September, in a letter to Arthur Stone, he referred to the new occupants of Tavistock House as 'the Children of Israel' – it is notable, however, that he had already acquired a more favourable opinion of Mrs Davis, commenting that she 'appears to be a very kind and agreeable woman …' and he admitted that the sale had proceeded with unprecedented ease: 'I have never had any money transaction with anyone, more promptly, fairly, and considerately conducted …' Personal experience was evidently overcoming the expectations of his previously untested prejudices.

Three years later, apparently out of the blue, Dickens received a letter from Eliza Davis, who seemed completely unaware that the engagement between them at the time of the transfer of the lease had been based on anything other than one of mutual respect and on this basis felt she might approach him in regard to some fundraising activity in which she was involved: or at least – that was the pretext of her correspondence. Mrs Davis's underlying motives, as we shall see, may well have been supported by her suspicions about Dickens's possible Jewish family connections – albeit for the wrong reasons.

This exchange of letters was published in several newspapers at the time of Dickens's death, in 1870, and in 1918 appeared in *Charles Dickens and His Jewish Characters* by Cumberland Clark, who sought to downplay Mrs Davis's criticism of Dickens as 'misapprehension'.[1]

Mrs Davis wrote from Tavistock House on 22 June 1863.

Dear Sir,

> Emboldened by your Courtesy throughout my correspondence with you, on the transfer of Tavistock House to Mr. Davis I venture to address you on a Subject in which I am greatly interested.
>
> You may perhaps have noticed in the Columns of the "Times" some short time since an announcement that the Jewish people in England are desirous of raising a Memorial to the late Judith, Lady Montefiore, a lady who conjointly with her husband exerted herself at great personal sacrifice to relieve her oppressed people in distant lands …

Rather astonishingly, Mrs Davis, clearly a brave and intelligent woman, having written to Dickens ostensibly in the hope that he might be interested in contributing to her fund, to honour the memory of one who tried to help 'her Hebrew brethren', now changed course, and launched into a full-fronted attack on the anti-Semitism of Charles Dickens's work, specifically the portrayal of Fagin, in *Oliver Twist.*

> In this country where the liberty of the subject is fully recognised, where the law knows no distinction of Creed, the pen of the novelist, the gibe of the pamphleteer is still whetted against the "Sons of Israel". It has been said that Charles Dickens the large hearted, whose works plead so eloquently and so nobly for the oppressed of his country and who may justly claim credit as the fruits of his labour, the many changes for the amelioration of the condition (of the) poor now at work, has encouraged a vile prejudice against the despised Hebrew.

Eliza Davis notes that although the theatrical portrayal of Shylock had been modified over the last fifty years, the character of Fagin stood uncorrected: 'Fagin I fear admits of only one interpretation; but (while) Charles Dickens lives the author can justify himself or atone for a great wrong on a whole though scattered nation.'

Having delivered this admonition, Dickens is then asked to allow his name to be added to the list of donors to the Memorial fund, referring once more not just to Lady Montefiore, but also to her husband, Moses, perhaps the leading figure in the Jewish community at the time and a dedicated philanthropist.

Dickens appears to have been taken by surprise by the accusations in Eliza Davis's letter, and at a loss to know what to say: he did not reply until nearly three weeks later, on 10 July, from Gad's Hill, apologising for the delay – but protesting that he was not guilty of committing 'a great wrong' in regard to the Jewish people, and defending his portrayal of Fagin:

> I must take leave to say that if there be any general feeling on the part of the intelligent Jewish people, that I have done them what you describe as "a great wrong", they are a far less just, and a far less good tempered people than I have always supposed them to be. Fagin in Oliver Twist is a Jew, because it was true of the time to which that story refers, that that class of criminal almost invariably was a Jew.

He claimed no one could fail to notice that the rest of the 'wicked' characters are Christians, and that Fagin is called 'The Jew' because of his race, rather than his religion, and referred Mrs Davis to his *Child's History of England*, in which he says he had 'lost no opportunity of setting forth their cruel persecution in old times'. He then enclosed what he called a 'nominal' subscription for the Montefiore fund.

Four days later, on 14 July, Mrs Davis replied, thanking him for his 'kind letter', and enclosure, but politely correcting his misunderstanding of the issue of race and religion, explaining that these were inseparable and invoking the example of Benjamin Disraeli, asking, perhaps somewhat naively, if anyone still designated him 'the Jew'. She agreed that at the time *Oliver Twist* is set there were some Jewish receivers of stolen goods, but not that there was one 'so base' as to train young thieves in the way practised by Fagin.

Eliza then made a very good point: bad Christian characters are contrasted with good Christians, however: 'If, as you remark "all must observe that the other criminals were Christians" they are at least contrasted with characters of good Christians, this poor wretched Fagin stands alone "The Jew" …'

She continued her reproach, and made sure to address the commonly held belief that Jews who complained of their treatment were somehow doing so out of a misguided sense of grievance, making it clear that while ignoring the usual culture of prejudice, she felt that when it came to a man of Dickens's understanding, such base misrepresentation was unacceptable:

> I hope we shall not forfeit your opinion of our sense and good temper; perhaps we are over sensitive, but are we not ever flayed? Are we not constantly irritated by the small gnats who may fret us, yet are in themselves too insignificant to be annihilated. It is only when a great mind appears to be against us that we plaintively appeal.

Eliza declared herself to be 'astonished' at the extent to which the customs of the Jewish people in her own country were so little known, seeing them as 'an entirely foreign people', and referring to the blood libel that continued to resurface, and was even repeated in popular papers:

> I hazard the opinion that it would well repay an author of reputation to examine more closely into the manners and character of British Jews and to represent them as they really are to "Nothing extenuate nor aught set down in malice".

Enclosing an unidentified example of 'elegant wit' from some unknown 'comic publication' – presumably an extract of anti-Semitic literature – and before promising not to trouble him any more with her correspondence, Eliza Davis explained that she had forwarded something else to Dickens: ' … some tracts which a Society in our Community distribute for the improvement and elevation of our own people. They are chiefly moral and not doctrinal, and I should be gratified by your glancing over them.'

Dickens was forced, perhaps for the first time, to examine his own motivation in the creation of Fagin – and to acknowledge a latent prejudice. Her presentation to him of tracts that might be used to educate the less-informed members of the Jewish community may well have piqued his sense of intellectual pride, at being thought in need of education.

In his *Child's History of England*, as we shall consider later, it is clear he had already begun to reposition his views on the representation of Jews. Certainly he was fairly swift in moving now towards making some sort of restitution and appears to have been anxious to show to Eliza Davis, and the Jewish community, that he was capable of change and willing to make amends.

This fundamental shift in attitude was made evident by a new work, which first appeared in serial form in May 1864 – and which provoked another letter from Eliza Davis, sent despite a pledge not to continue any correspondence, sixteen months after the last one, on 13 November.

This letter was prompted by the appearance, in the serialised novel, of a sympathetically drawn Jewish character: 'your introduction of the Jew Riah in the 17th No of "Our Mutual Friend" impels me to thank you very earnestly for what I am so presumptuous as to think a very great compliment paid to myself and to my people.'

Mrs Davis could not quite leave it at that, as she needed to point out a few anachronistic details that Dickens had included, such as the use of a certain sacred word in reference to God, and mistakes in the descriptions of appearance, seeing Jews as a single group with common practices rather than as part of a diverse range of peoples.

Riah as a character has been described by many as Dickens's apology for Fagin: equally unrealistic, albeit in a benign way, and undoubtedly created with good intent – a form of 'atonement'. But Riah signifies more than just an acknowledgement by Dickens that he had indeed been guilty of a 'great wrong' in his representation of Fagin – an acknowledgement underlined by his re-editing of *Oliver Twist* to remove many of the references to 'the Jew', and changes in his public readings of scenes involving the character. The changes made by Dickens, and the creation of Riah, also demonstrate the powerful personal influence of Eliza Davis.

There is an undeniable echo of the sentiments expressed in Eliza's letter of 14 July 1863 in the words of Riah in Chapter Nineteen of *Our Mutual Friend*. As Eliza wrote: 'If, as you remark "all must observe that the other criminals were Christians" they are at least contrasted with characters of good Christians, this poor wretched Fagin stands alone "The Jew"' …'

And the words of Riah:

> Men say, "This is a bad Greek, but there are good Greeks. This is a bad Turk, but there are good Turks." Not so with the Jews. Men find the bad among us easily enough – among what people are the bad not easily found? – but they take the worst of us as samples of the best; they take the lowest of us as presentations of the highest; and they say "All Jews are alike."

Was it simply vanity, on Dickens's part, in that he could not bear to be seen as anything less than universally admired for his compassion, and sympathy for those oppressed by social injustice? Or was it the mark of true greatness, in that he could acknowledge his own wrongdoing and attempt to put it right?

His response to Eliza came three days later, on 16 November, acknowledging the letter 'with great pleasure', and saying he hoped to be '(as I always have been in my heart) the best of friends with the Jewish people'. Dickens being Dickens, he had to add that the error she had pointed out (which one is not clear) was something that had already occurred to him, when it was too late to change it. 'But it will do no harm', he observed.

There are no further letters in the published collection until more than two years later, on 8 February 1867. One might question, however, for more than one reason, if perhaps there were other letters that have not been included in this collection, and if perhaps there had been some exchange during this gap that had not been published or perhaps had been destroyed.

This letter begins quite abruptly: a copy of the Scriptures intended as a belated New Year 'offering'. If there had been no correspondence in the intervening two years and three months, one might reasonably expect there to be some sort of preamble, or explanation, or reference to the interval in communication:

> My Dear Sir,
>
> You will favour me by accepting for your library the vols: which accompany this, they were intended for a New Year offering, the binder frustrated that intention.
>
> The selection is made, because with regard to the contents of those sacred volumes we both stand on the same ground and have in them an equal inheritance, and I thought it possible you might not possess a copy of the Scriptures in Hebrew.
>
> It is the only complete translation into English that we have, collated with the Hebrew, it may not be all that is desired, but it is the best we possess.
>
> If you do not disapprove of the inscription placed on the first page – I should be gratified by your inserting it – It does but faintly express how highly I appreciate and how profoundly sensible I am of the nobility of character evinced by him who depicted "Riah" in contrast to Fagin – Most gratefully do my people accept the spirit of the work …

The inscription was:

> Presented to
>
> Charles Dickens, Esqre,
>
> In grateful and admiring recognition of his having exercised the noblest quality a man can possess; that of atoning for an injury as soon as conscious of having inflicted it,
>
> By a Jewess

Dickens replied on 1 March, clearly wanting to show his appreciation of her gesture, and understanding the sensitivity of the action, making sure that she knew it was being treated with respect:

> It is safely awaiting me on my own desk in my own quiet room. I cannot thank you for it too cordially, and cannot too earnestly assure you that I shall always prize it highly. The terms in which you send me that mark of your remembrance are more gratifying to me than I can possibly express to you; for they assure me that there is nothing but good will left between me and a People for whom I have a real regard, and to whom I would not wilfully have given an offence or done an injustice for any worldly consideration.

The next letter in the published collection is written by Mrs Davis, to Dickens's daughter, weeks after his death in 1870, in response to a letter prompted by the publication, in various newspapers, of the correspondence with Dickens. Mamie had sent a 'very kind letter' in response to the publication. Mamie had also sent some photographs of her father, which were very warmly received, although she said she already possessed one: she also revealed that though she had had some correspondence with Dickens, she had only seen him at two of his readings. Eliza remarked upon the 'wonderful humanizing effects' of his powerful pen, and that the act of his writing the character of 'Riah' had impressed her thoroughly with the 'nobility of his character'. She would be leaving Tavistock House in a few months' time but would be pleased if Mamie would call on her.

At the time of Dickens's death, the *Jewish Chronicle* had been one of the papers that had published his correspondence with Eliza Davis – although in this case, her name was withheld. In the same edition, on 17 June, a remarkably generous editorial marked his passing: it was a remarkably gracious and moving tribute to the writer – all the more so when considering the condemnation years earlier by the previous editor of the journal about Dickens's creation of Fagin, and certain articles in *Household Words* (not written by him but still tolerated under his editorship) – criticism that appears to have led to a concerted effort to include examples of Jewish persecution in his *A Child's History of England*. The editorial included:

> How shall the wound be healed! Who is there whose hand is so deft in the author's craft that he shall close it or shall hide it, by taking the place of him who has gone? …
>
> For every bright hour he gave us, and in which he made us happy with innocent mirth, or sad with a pleasant sorrow; for every holy thought that sprung from his great mind and, touching some responsive feeble chord in ours, broke it to a pure echo and helped to make us – each of us – wiser and better; for every object of truth, humanity, and social improvement for which he laboured, and laboured not in vain; for every heart he moved; every ambition he aroused; every influence he evoked; every good he wrought – for everyone of these, some element exists which blends in an atmosphere of earthly immortality in which the light of his life still burns, and cannot die for ever.

The difficult subject of Dickens and his portrayal of Jews is not avoided:

> And surely, in a Jewish journal, some recognition of grateful memory is due to the generous spirit of that writer who, because in the very early days of his life and his writings, he had touched the Jewish character with a somewhat rough and undeserved severity in the unreal character of FAGIN, made ample amends in his later, wiser, more chastened days, by the beautiful, even if equally unreal, character of RIAH, and the brief but forcible reference to the Jewish manufacturer and his wife in "Our Mutual Friend".

Directly below the tribute to Charles Dickens, there follows a short article on a subject that would appear to be rather random in choice, with the heading 'The Jews of Holland'.

There would appear to be no particular reason for this in terms of important news, or placement on that page, in that edition. Coincidence, one must assume. There is a fitting mention, however, of the context in which some of Dickens's own Casteel ancestors most probably arrived in the Netherlands:

> Special interest attaches to Holland from the circumstances when the Jews were expelled from Spain, under the fanatic influence of that the (sic) cruel TORQUEMADA, they took refuge in Holland, where the mild regime of tolerant principles prevailed even in that century.

The Bible that Mrs Davis had given to Dickens in 1867 is revealed, in the *Jewish Chronicle*'s publication of her correspondence with Dickens – in the same edition as his obituary – to have been the translation produced by the editor of the journal, Dr Abraham Benisch: whether he wrote the tribute to Dickens is not certain, but seems highly likely. Interestingly, however, it seems a relative of the Davis family worked as a journalist for the *Jewish Chronicle* and had previously worked for Bradbury & Evans: that was David Anderson, formerly known as David Abrahams, who was a cousin of James Phineas Davis: David's mother was aunt to both James and Eliza, also first cousins.

Mrs Davis's connection with Charles Dickens, however, was not the first time that her family had featured as a subject of interest in the *Jewish Chronicle*. No one previously seems to have noticed the significance of another event in the life of the Davises, reported in the same journal some five years before the death of Dickens and the publication of his correspondence with Eliza.

Chapter Thirty-seven

James Phineas Davis, and the 'Vampires of London'

There is a crucial part of the Eliza Davis story, one that has previously gone unnoticed: that is the libel case taken by Eliza's husband, James Phineas Davis, during the period in which Dickens was writing and publishing *Our Mutual Friend*, and in the interval in the published correspondence with Mrs Davis.

Press reports of a hearing at the Guildhall on 25 January 1865, and later in April a short trial at the Old Bailey, reveal that Mr Davis had become aware of a recently published pamphlet, some fifteen pages long, on the subject of *The Vampires of London*, printed on behalf of the Hon. Captain Colborne, youngest son of the late Lord Seaton, a distinguished army officer and former governor of Canada. This publication was a vile composition, steeped in the worst imaginable anti-Semitic slurs, a prolonged accusation of extortion and exploitation by Jewish money lenders, in which it was falsely claimed that James Phineas Davis – 'Finny Davis' – was the 'arch-vampire'. Extracts were read out in court:

> The clubs are full of their prisoners, and we brush against them at every dinner-party. To be convinced of the fact, go to any office of the first Jew solicitor, whose clients' names are generally displayed in a most conspicuous manner on large tin-boxes round the room; go to the office of the notorious arch vampire, Finny Davis, off Bond Street, for instance, who has ruined no less than 300 gentlemen of property, and involved five scores of estates in irretrievable ruin by kindly lending money to carry on law suits, which have ended by both sides being well looted …

As *The Times* reported, further extracts were read out: 'A recent photo of this worthy represents him with horns, sitting in a hot region …' 'Teach the vulture to live on grain, the wolf on roots, but despair of making the fraternity get their living honestly; that hellish fraternity take counsel together …'

According to a police officer, Colborne, using the pseudonym of 'Aperitémos' in his pamphlet, gave another false name to the publisher, and the address of the St James's Hotel in Piccadilly.

The British Library appears not to retain any copy of Colborne's original libellous publication – most of them were probably destroyed – but it does have a digital version of a revised edition of the pamphlet, which was published between the Guildhall hearing and the trial. It would appear to have most of the original text, as well as further 'observations'. In this edition, Colborne is referred to in the third person as the 'Gallant Captain', and the author purports to be someone else – but clearly it is the work of Colborne himself.

The contents of the second edition, even after being revised, are still deeply offensive, rooted in anti-Semitic themes and tropes that have persisted even until the present time, offering the description, for example, of two alleged money lenders: 'The most ill looking of the two wears blue spectacles, which of course is an advantage to him, they hide his reptile-like eyes …'

Apart from the use of reference to reptilian features, or dirty claws, or hideous appearance, Colborne's tract deploys the use of descriptions of Jews as leeches, the Devil, jackals, and even panthers. Judas Iscariot pops up, of course: and then the 'Gallant Captain' throws in a nod to Shylock, and the *Merchant of Venice*, with mention of a pound of flesh and glittering gold; finally, we see the shadow of Fagin, and an attack on pawnbrokers, in the person of 'Mr Two to One Threeballs', and the idea of Jews as receivers of stolen goods, steeped in crime, deceit, and the systematic exploitation of their defenceless victims.

It also emerged in court that the only dealings James Phineas Davis had had with Colborne had been several years previously, in 1856, when he did some private business with him – and then lent him £5, with no interest, or charge.

At the trial Colborne's position was to admit having wrongly identified Davis, but he also argued, in essence, that Davis had no right to expect much sympathy, arguing outrageously that simply by being a Jew Davis must expect to be associated with the nefarious practices of money lenders, and asserting that that all such money lenders were Jewish.

The case lasted no longer than half an hour. That Davis was a well-known West End attorney and wrongly accused of being a back-street money lender counted for nothing. Colborne was convicted of libel, but given a round of applause in court. Davis was condemned for being a Jew, his personal and professional reputation given a value of only £20.

The *Jewish Chronicle* published a short report on the case after the Old Bailey hearing, not naming Davis, but in its next edition reprinted a piece from *Reynold's Newspaper* that did identify him. More importantly, it also produced an editorial emphatically condemning Colborne's pamphlet, and forensically examining the vicious and deep-rooted, historical prejudice that it exemplified. The widespread coverage of the trial in the press elsewhere, however, was of a nature that must have made James Phineas Davis, the victim of the worst sort of smear, wish he had not taken any action at all.

One example of this was published in the *London Evening Standard* on 12 April. The writer of the article now pursues with relish the theme of 'justification' for Colborne's libel, and in a discharge of hate-filled language, gleefully expanding upon, and exceeding, the theme of the alleged 'vampires': 'They fatten fast upon their spoils, they flit from their greasy dens into dashing mansions or suburban villas, and grow daily richer as they ply their villainous trade …'

In Chapter fifty-nine of *Dombey and Son*, written in April 1848, Dickens had used the term 'vampires', when referring to Jewish – and non-Jewish people – who run through Dombey's house, looking at items put up for sale after his bankruptcy:

> … herds of shabby vampires, Jew and Christian, over-run the house, sounding the plate-glass mirrors with their knuckles, striking discordant octaves on the Grand Piano, drawing wet forefingers over the pictures, breathing on the blades of the best dinner-knives, punching the squabs of chairs and sofas with their dirty fists, touzling the feather beds, opening and shutting all the drawers, balancing the silver spoons and forks, looking into the very threads of the drapery and linen, and disparaging everything.

Only two years after she had written to him of her fears of the damage done by his perpetration of the thoughtless stereotyping of Jews, Eliza Davis and her family were living with the direct and very personal consequences of such material, in a way neither she nor Dickens could have predicted.

Clearly this libel case was one of profound significance not just for the family of James Phineas Davis, but for the Anglo-Jewish community at a hugely important point in its history, when apparent progress in terms of status within a rapidly changing society was still underpinned and disabled by pervasive, systematic prejudice – institutional anti-Semitism: a process in which the judicial system was complicit, as clearly demonstrated by the experience of Mr Davis.

It is impossible to believe that Charles Dickens did not know about the widely reported Davis case, and that he did not feel appalled by the plight in which Davis and his wife were placed; officially victims of a libellous publication, but James's reputation effectively betrayed by the judicial system and savaged by the hostile coverage in the press. The libel case underlined with dramatic emphasis the lasting power of anti-Semitic misrepresentation in the figures of Shylock and Fagin: just as Eliza Davis had dared to say to him, only two years earlier: two literary stereotypes that, as described by Anthony Julius in his history of anti-Semitism in England, 'represent a character-prison from which actual Jews still struggle to escape'. In the case of James Phineas Davis, with grim irony, the dark shadow of Fagin fell with full dramatic effect, as if to shame its creator into recognition of his own failings, through the example of injustice caused to the husband of a woman with whom he had formed a bond of mutual respect, and even friendship.[1]

Julius also observes that the publication of *Oliver Twist*, and the creation of the character of Fagin, marks a point after which 'literary anti-Semitism was in retreat'. This may be the case: it is certainly true that Dickens himself retreated from the anti-Semitism in his own work, as a direct result of the intervention of Eliza Davis.

Was there really no correspondence during the months that followed the first court hearing of the libel action? The Guildhall hearing took place only a couple of months after the letter sent to Dickens by Eliza Davis on 16 November 1864. The next letter in the set of published correspondence was one sent by her on 8 February 1867, and as we have noted, begins with no reference to an interval in their communications.

It may be, however, that Dickens chose to communicate not in the form of personal correspondence, but in a more indirect way: a more lasting and significant way – in the work he was then writing and publishing; *Our Mutual Friend*.

As Michael Slater's biography of Dickens explains, during the first five months of 1865, as Dickens wrote in a letter on 22 April, he was working 'like a dragon' at *Our Mutual Friend*, specifically on parts XI to XIV: these include the chapters in which Riah's story really begins to unfold. He had now reverted to a timescale of working only one issue ahead of publication: knowing now about the unfolding drama of the Davis libel case during this period, the argument might be made that the expansion of Riah's role and character at this point was in response to what was happening to the Davis case.[2]

The Guildhall hearing, in January, was followed by attempts by Colborne to delay the trial, which was not heard until April. The character of Riah had been introduced in Chapter Five, of Book the Second, in the seventh part of *Our Mutual Friend*, published in November 1864. Here we meet the 'gentle Jew', who works for the money lender Fascination Fledgeby, described as:

> ... an old Jewish man in an ancient coat, long of skirt, and wide of pocket. A venerable man, bald and shining at the top of his head, and with long grey hair flowing down at its sides and mingling with his beard. A man who with a graceful Eastern action of homage bent his head, and stretched out his hands with the palms downward, as if to deprecate the wrath of a superior.

Apart from a description that sets up his role as some sort of timeless figure, more cypher than rounded character, at this point we learn little more about him: it is not until Chapter Fifteen, in the tenth part, published in February 1865, that we see him again, coming to the aid of Lizzie Wrexham, after her quarrel with her brother, then 'stealing through the streets in his ancient dress, like the ghost of a departed Time'. Again, his almost unworldly quality is stressed – at odds, most noticeably, with the role forced on him by his ties with Fledgeby, bound to him after dependence on his late father, also a money lender.

The next appearance of Riah is in Book the Third, Chapter One, which was published in March 1865, and came only weeks after the widely reported court hearing in January at the Guildhall regarding the libel case brought by James Phineas Davis.

It is hard not to conclude that the development of Riah's character from this point was influenced directly by the revelations of this case, and the foul contents of Captain Colborne's pamphlet. Whatever the original idea of Riah as an agent of the plot had been, he serves now as an example of the mindless anti-Semitism exposed by the libel case, and Colborne's vicious allegations. It is Dickens's full response to Eliza Davis, and the redemption of his own soul: the unworldly character of Riah almost acting, in the process of that redemption, of the visitations in *A Christmas Carol*. Here, rather than Scrooge, it is Dickens who is saved and born again.

Fascination Fledgeby here serves as a mouthpiece for a range of slanderous misrepresentations of Jews: his constant taunting of Riah including references to 'sweating a pound' and the practice of 'lightening sovereigns' – itself reminiscent of the 'Bad Shilling' story once published in *Household Words*.

Fledgeby's sport with Lammle, a debtor, includes the pretence that the money-lending business of Pubsey & Co. is in fact run by Riah: he projects onto Riah all the extortionate practices he imposes on his own clients, in terms here that surely present another echo of Eliza Davis's letters, although turning the accusation of being 'flayed' onto the Jew he claims is pressurising Lammle:

> "Regular flayers and grinders, my dear Lammle," repeated Fledgeby with a peculiar relish, "and they'll skin you by the inch, from the nape of your neck to the sole of your foot, and grind every inch of your skin to tooth-powder. You have seen what Mr Riah is. Never fall into his hands, Lammle, I beg of you as a friend!"

Among the abuse Fledgeby throws at Riah – 'Catch a weasel at it, and catch a Jew'; '... Don't talk Jerusalem palaver'; 'you Pump of Israel'; 'one of the Patriarchs' – is one less obvious but constant insult: calling him, in various ways, 'a dodger': 'a gallivanting dodger', 'a circular old dodger': later in the book he continues on the same theme, referring to 'one of his dodges ... He's made of dodges ...' 'the dodgerest of all the dodgers', and so on.

This continual reference can only serve to mark the prior significance, in the creation of Riah, of *Oliver Twist* and Fagin's assistant in crime, the Artful Dodger: to act as acknowledgement by so doing, of Dickens's need, as Eliza Davis suggested, to 'atone' for the hurt caused by the reinforcement of a perennial misrepresentation of the Jew as criminal, and exploiter of innocence.

Chapter Thirty-eight

Atonement

There is another aspect to the correspondence between Eliza Davis and Charles Dickens that has not been considered previously. It is one that might add another perspective to a clearer interpretation of their dialogue: a question of motive on the part of Mrs Davis, and her first approach to him, three years after the transactions between them over the sale of the lease of Tavistock House.

Eliza Davis wrote to Dickens on the pretext of fundraising in which she was involved for the memorial to the late Judith, Lady Montefiore, but she quickly moved from this initial subject to the question of the 'great wrong' Dickens had perpetrated on the Jewish people by the creation of Fagin. She makes the point of asking that he 'atone' for this, by donating to the fund, but really she is asking more of him: to acknowledge, in some way, the damage he has done. As we know, Dickens did in fact take on board Mrs Davis's criticism and seek to make amends.

But why did Mrs Davis approach Dickens in this way, at this time, three years after their short-lived acquaintance regarding the sale of the lease of Tavistock House? At this point, it is useful to look at the background of the Davis family. Who was Eliza Davis, and what do we know about her family?

At the end of an article in *Dickens Quarterly* on the correspondence between Eliza and Dickens, Murray Baumgarten appends a cursory outline of the family tree of the Davis family.[1]

Baumgarten mentions that she was born in Jamaica in 1816, and that her husband, James Phineas Davis, was a cousin – he was in fact the son of a Phineas Davis, a wine merchant based in Red Lion Square, and at one time officer to the Sherriff of Middlesex. Phineas's brother, David Davis, was the father of Eliza: her mother being a Rebecca Magnus, who had been born in Whitechapel around 1798.

According to Baumgarten, Rebecca's grandfather, Eleazar Magnus, was appointed in 1774 as 'Reader' to the German and English congregation in

Kingston, Jamaica. Other sources, however, list Eleazar as a minister, or one of the Mohelim (responsible for circumcisions) – it may be that he performed all of these duties.[2]

Eliza Davis's census entries show her to have been born in Montego Bay, rather than Kingston, around 1817: there was a small Jewish community there at one time: six households, it was estimated, in the early 1770s. Eliza had moved to London by 1835, however – the year in which she married James Phineas Davis – but members of her Magnus family continued to live in Jamaica.

It should also be noted that there was also an influential Magnus family in Chatham, the place of Dickens's early childhood, appearing to have arrived there from the Netherlands in the 1790s, headed by Lazarus Magnus, who died in 1821, and was a 'slop seller' (dealing in clothes for seamen) and navy agent: it is not clear if they were connected with the family who settled in London, and then the West Indies, but it is likely. Whether or not Eliza was on close terms with the Chatham Magnus family, even if related, is not known, but it is more likely than not that she would have been aware of their importance in the community there.

Peter Magnus, in *Pickwick Papers*, is – like Fagin and Sampson Brass – red haired, and he is prone to wearing green spectacles. If we attempt to decipher the barely coded messages here, we might recall that Dickens had a habit of attributing this colouring to Jews, not just in the most famous case of Fagin, but also in a few instances in *Sketches by Boz*, for example in Chapter Six, 'Holywell Street we despise; the red-headed and red-whiskered Jews who forcibly haul you into their squalid houses, and thrust you into a suit of clothes, whether you will or not, we detest …' As to wearing green spectacles: this is a detail that might escape notice now but is another sly allusion by Dickens to Peter Magnus's identity as a Jew, and a device he employs later in the same novel. A variation on this theme is repeated in the 'Vampires' leaflet that libelled James Phineas Davis, with a reference to blue spectacles worn by a Jewish money lender, supposedly because 'they hide his reptile like eyes' …

James Phineas Davis and Eliza had ten children, the youngest of whom was born the year before they moved to Tavistock House. By the time she had written her first letter to Charles Dickens, three years later, her focus had moved from constant child bearing to social and charitable activities: when she died in 1903, her obituary in the *Jewish Chronicle*, on 29 May, was paired with that of another woman, Mrs H.E. Symons, both of them described as 'highly esteemed ladies, who had much in common in respect to their philanthropy …' She had been at one time on the Committee of the Jewish Convalescent Home and was noted as being 'of a sweet disposition' and, like Mrs Symons, 'extremely generous, not only to public Jewish institutions, but particularly in dispensing private charity, as to the extent of which both ladies were very reticent'.

Eliza was genuinely committed to charitable work, but her involvement in fundraising also gave her entrée into the highest levels of Anglo-Jewish society: in 1861 a notice in the *Jewish Chronicle* of 12 July, for example, lists her as among the donors at a concert held in the previous month to raise funds for the Jewish Emigration Society. As well as four members of the Montefiore family, the forty or so donors included three Rothschilds, two of them titled, and several other prestigious names.

The challenge made by Eliza Davis regarding Dickens's 'great wrong' in the creation of Fagin may have been part of the reasons for proposing that he 'atone' for his sins, by means of this donation: but could there have been another reason for the timing of this approach?

The use of the word 'atone' itself may bear significance – why use that word, with its echo of the most solemn point in the Jewish year: Yom Kippur, the Day of Atonement? Did Eliza use this word unthinkingly, or with intent?

Well, here is a possible explanation, or at least another question. Did Eliza Davis think that perhaps it was possible Dickens was – at least partly – of Jewish ancestry, and might understand the significance of this request?

This is not such a random possibility as might first appear, if we see the matter from Eliza's perspective.

Growing up in Jamaica and being well acquainted, through her family and social connections, with the relatively small number of Jewish congregations, communities and families living there, it would be certain that she would have been aware of the Barrow and Barrow Lousada, or Baruh Lousada, families who were established in Barbados, Jamaica, other parts of the West Indies, and retained links with England. These families also had links with the Montefiores.

Simon Barrow had connections with, and investments in, the West Indies, including Jamaica, but settled in the West Country and became the Mayor of Bath in 1837, while other members of the same network of families retained a close association and prominent status within Anglo-Jewish society.[3]

As someone interested in charitable activities, and a reader of newspaper reports of such activities, Eliza may well have noted the name Barrow in association with Dickens in the period in which she had become associated with him.

Charles Dickens was much in request as an after-dinner speaker and spoke at many charitable fundraising events. In the month before Eliza wrote to him for the first time, he had given a speech, as Chairman, on 6 May 1863 at a dinner attended by two hundred or so guests, to commemorate the thirty-fifth anniversary of the Royal Free Hospital, to raise funds for the purchase of the hospital's freehold, and to raise funds for more beds.

Newspaper reports note that also appearing at this 'festival', as part of the musical entertainment, was a young woman: Miss Grace Barrow – a singer who had been appearing at similar, high-profile fundraising dinners and concerts for the last three years or so. Grace was Dickens's first cousin – daughter of his journalist uncle, Edward Barrow, and his artist wife, the former Janet Ross.

Grace Barrow appears in quite a few newspaper reviews during this period, during which there appears to have been an attempt to launch a professional career – and a campaign in which she does not fall shy of attaching herself to her famous relative, who was supportive of her ambitions. There survives a letter written by Dickens to Grace on 14 October 1863, in which he observed: 'Through the practical steady quiet course that you take lies the road to self-respect and self-made independence ... In every art there would be far less misery and bitterness if many more began as wisely.' Dickens was probably relieved that this at least was one relative who was not likely to need to rely on his own financial support, and it appears he made an effort to help promote her in the early stages of her career.

It would seem likely that Grace's relationship to Dickens had been widely enough known by the end of April 1863 to be hinted at in a review of another event at which she sang, in aid of the 'Royal Asylum of St Ann's Society'. This had taken place on 23 April, in the presence of the Marquis of Bristol, and Lord Gordon, and a report appeared the next day in the *Morning Advertiser* with a coy reference to her identity: 'Miss Grace Barrow, a promising aspirant for public fame, who boasts relationship with more than one of our most celebrated authors and artists ...'

Less than a fortnight later, Grace appeared as a performer at the Royal Free dinner, presided over by her famous cousin, as Chairman.

Among the newspaper reports that mentioned the event was the *Holborn and Bloomsbury Journal* – covering the area in which Eliza Davis lived – which in its edition of 9 May singled out Grace Barrow 'who sang very charmingly, and with great intelligence and sweetness of voice ...'

The Sun newspaper on 18 May reported the contributions made for the Royal Free fund: among the donors listed there were prominent members of the Anglo-Jewish community, for example several members of the Mocatta family, two Ricardos, Messrs Rothschild and Son – and from the report in the *Morning Advertiser* we know that Baron Rothschild had given £100, 'and for indisposition, he would have been present at their festival'.

Eliza Davis, a keen reader of the press, and with her interest in charitable causes, is likely to have known or read about such events and followed the actions of families such as the Mocattas and Rothschilds with close attention. By then it was clearly known that there was a family connection between Grace Barrow and Charles Dickens. And although Mrs Davis is unlikely to have known about the Casteel family, the connection of the name Barrow to that of Dickens, in the context of her knowledge of the Jewish Barrow families, in England and the West Indies, may well have had consequences that led her to speculate about his own family background.

For Eliza Davis, it would seem a logical step to assume – or at least indulge in speculation – that anyone with a connection with the surname Barrow may be Jewish, whether or not that was indeed the case. As we will see in more detail later, there is also a chance that some of Dickens's Jewish family relations by marriage – the Lamerts and Oppenheims – were known to members of the Davis family.

Is it therefore a possibility that might be considered that Eliza had wondered if Dickens had Jewish ancestry? Could that be one of the reasons she felt moved to take him to task, at this point in their lives? Such an idea might give a deeper significance to the moral obligation she felt he had to 'atone' for his 'great wrong', with its implicit reference to the 'Day of Atonement', and the need to make amends for wrongdoing.

If Dickens had any idea of the origins of his Casteel family, at least, he may have had added reason to address the issue of his 'great wrong'. One thing is certain: until now Dickens's own wider family associations with the Jewish community have been underestimated in terms of the potential significance for him, and his work: a closer look will reveal a new perspective on his own progression from the replication of old archetypes in the creation of Fagin to atonement in the character of Riah.

Chapter Thirty-nine

The Annals of Quackery – the Lamert Family and the Barrows

Let us return to the time of Charles Dickens's childhood in Chatham, to the small, terraced house in Ordnance Terrace, and then a new home in St Mary's Place, where he lived with his immediate family, including for some of this time his mother's widowed sister Mary Allen. Mary left the household in December 1821 after meeting and marrying an army surgeon named Matthew Lamert. A notice in the *London Gazette* announced that Matthew would be Surgeon to the 1st Royal Veteran Battalion, after being on half pay for some time. His military record shows a long career, serving in Egypt, Malta and Copenhagen – and he had been injured at least once while in service. Where and when his first wife Sarah had died is not known, but perhaps this was abroad, where some of his children appear to have been born.

That Matthew left a lasting impression on his new wife's nephew is apparent by Dickens's creation of Dr Slammer, in *Pickwick Papers*, the pompous surgeon attached to the 97th Regiment, stationed at Chatham Barracks, whose interrupted courtship of a wealthy widow at a dance leads him to issue a challenge to a duel. Dr Slammer's intention is to win Mrs Budger's favour as 'a most desirable addition to a limited income', which might appear to suggest that the Dickens family may have thought Mary's marriage to a much older man – he was some fifteen years older – was one of mutual convenience rather than romantic attachment. With Mary's removal from the Dickens household went her naval widow's pension, of course, which may have added to the financial difficulties that were about to unfold her brother-in-law and eventually lead to his imprisonment for debt.

When his aunt and her husband left for a new posting in Ireland, one of Matthew's sons is thought to have remained with the Dickens family and certainly was living with them on their return to London and their residence in Bayham Street. There is some confusion over the identity of this Lamert son: Forster refers to him as James, but Michael Allen believes it was George Lamert who joined the household and then procured employment for Charles when his father fell into debt and the family was forced to separate. Although much older than Charles, his Lamert cousin – Dickens himself referred to him as a relative, and Forster calls him 'a sort of cousin, by marriage', who was 'his great patron and friend' – took him at a very young age to the theatre and encouraged the precocious boy's attempts at storytelling and performing comic songs.

Matthew Lamert was from a German Jewish background: he married the former Mary Barrow in St Mary's Church, Chatham, but his first marriage, to Sarah Lamert, his cousin, had taken place in the Great Synagogue in London in 1798. Synagogue records show that Matthew's original name was Moses, or Moshe, and his father Jacob Joseph Lamert. Sarah's father, apparently a brother of Jacob, was an Isaac Lamert, a quack doctor who died in Spitalfields in 1827. Isaac's son Abraham also used the middle name of Lima, which is Spanish or Portuguese, and this may indicate some Sephardi ancestry.[1]

Isaac Lamert was therefore Matthew's uncle, as well as his father-in-law. The full extent of the wider Lamert family connections with Dickens are worth exploring further, as we shall see.

Matthew and Mary moved to Ireland, where his regiment had been stationed. In the year after their marriage, sadly, Mary died in childbirth, giving birth to twins. Matthew and Sarah's son George, who was close to the Dickens family in Chatham and then lived with them in London, later married a Harriet Oppenheim, and they had several children. Although by then this branch of the Lamert family had seemingly dropped any association with the Jewish community, its sense of identity was still pretty strong in the early years of the century – and was maintained even longer by Matthew's uncle and cousin Abraham, as well as some of the other Lamert relatives with whom George retained ties. New evidence now suggests that for George Lamert, the rejection of his Jewish identity happened rather later than has been formerly assumed.

In his study of the Lamert family in *Charles Dickens and the Blacking Factory*, Michael Allen notes the assimilation of the family of George Lamert and Harriet Oppenheim, their marriage in church, and the baptism and later careers of their children. One significant detail has escaped attention, until now, however: the fact that George did not convert to Christianity until just before his marriage, sometime after his lodging with the Dickens family.[2]

George Lamert's baptism as an adult (he was twenty-three) is noted in the records of All Hallows by the Tower church on 16 February 1826. This, of course, is after the period in which Dickens worked at the blacking factory. 'Lamert's' address was given as of New Street, Whitechapel. This late baptism might well explain why George, despite his five years as a cadet at Sandhurst's military academy, had left in June 1820 with no commission. As a Jew, he could not have served as an officer in the army at this time. Why he chose to convert six years later, before marriage to a woman who had also to convert to Christianity, is not clear, other than perhaps due to pressure from his father and siblings. The twice widowed Dr Lamert had by then married for a third time to an Irish woman and settled in Cork: no evidence has come to light of his own formal conversion or adult baptism, but clearly he had chosen to leave behind his former religion and perhaps to disassociate himself from his Lamert cousins.

Harriet too was a late convert, baptised at the same church on 23 April 1826 at the age of twenty-five. Her address was said to be of 17 Mansell Street, Whitechapel. The marriage of George and Harriet, on 8 January 1827, took place at All Hallows, rather than the local parish church for Whitechapel, but they had chosen what was perhaps a more discreet location, a little further away from the attention of their own families. This especially in the case of Harriet and her Oppenheim relatives, who had businesses at both 17 and 27 Mansell Street and were still very much part of the flourishing Jewish community in that area. George Lamert, of course, had his own interests here: in 1827, his blacking business was at number 56, Mansell Street.

George's first experience of the manufacture and sale of blacking began through a family connection: in March 1820, at a ceremony at St Martin in the Fields witnessed by their father Matthew Lamert, his sister Sophia had married William Edward Woodd, and in 1822 Woodd had bought Jonathan Warren's blacking business – although Warren retained an interest in the company and continued to supervise the manufacturing process, as well as agreeing to continue to lend his name to the enterprise for a limited number of years. In 1823, Woodd, who had employed George Lamert as office clerk, moved his base to Hungerford Stairs and then later to the corner of Chandos Street and Bedford Street, just off the Strand. This was the period in which Charles Dickens worked for the business, removed from school and isolated from family, working first by the river, and then in the new premises.

Whatever view he may later have formed of George Lamert's part in placing him at Warren's, a social relationship with the young Charles appears to have continued throughout his time of employment. There is even some teasing evidence that, as Michael Allen suggests, theatre and the blacking warehouse may somehow have been conjured by George into one horrible performance of dramatic resonance for the young Charles Dickens, at a time when the boy was still employed in his menial duties, perhaps newly moved from the rat-infested warehouse by Hungerford Stairs to the new building, where he would sit by the window looking on to the street.

As Allen points out, on 13 January 1824, a notice was published in *The Times* advertising the performance that day and the following day at the Adelphi theatre in the Strand of an adaptation of the *Heart of Midlothian*, to be followed by a Christmas pantomime with the title: *Doctor Faustus and the Black Demon*; or *Harlequin and the Seven Fairies of the Grotto*. One of the settings to be shown was described as 'Interior of Jonathan Warren's Blacking Warehouse, Hungerford Stairs'.

This was, of course, the location of Charles Dickens's employment, just around the corner from the theatre. Bearing in mind the documentation of George Lamert's later appearances, a year or so later, on the stage of the Adelphi, Allen speculates that he may have had a hand in the inclusion of such a setting in this pantomime. Whether or not it was anything to do with George, it is hard to imagine the young Dickens being unaware of the performance – and it must surely have demonstrated to him, for the first time, the possibility of his own life and experience being the subject of fictionalisation, and a process of conversion of personal conflict into farce, or caricature.

Michael Allen has also suggested that Dickens's story 'Gone Astray' is an account of the writer as a boy being taken out for the day by a young man who had come 'as I had myself', from Kent, the pair separating, and the boy ending up in Goodman's Fields after a somewhat circuitous route from Charing Cross, via the Strand, Fleet Street, and the City of London. In the story the lost boy watches a performance in a theatre on Goodman's Fields: Allen poses the interesting possibility that at least part of this tale is a rewritten memory of Dickens being taken by George Lamert to this area of Whitechapel, where George had relatives and to which he would move his blacking business and residence – and where the Oppenheims were also based. He speculates as to whether such an introduction to Lamert's relatives in Whitechapel might have included the Worms family, one member of which, Henry Worms, may have helped inspire the character of Fagin.

We do not know for certain that Dickens did meet any of Lamert's extended family in Whitechapel, or indeed Henry Worms: but it is likely he would at least have heard about them, and this must have given him some experience, if only at second hand, of Jewish family and business life at that time.

There is evidence that Matthew Lamert continued to correspond with the Dickens family long after the death of his wife – and as new material will show, some other members of the Lamert family had significant associations with his family that have previously been unobserved.

Goodman's Fields and Mansell Street were also home at one time or another to members of the Davis family: James Phineas Davis had been born in Goodman's Fields in the 1820s; James and Eliza's cousin, the journalist David Anderson, had lived in Mansell Street, as well as George Lamert and some of his Oppenheim in-laws.

Charles Dickens's relationship with the Lamerts is hard to define – on the one hand, they were at one stage in his early life, at least, part of his family. George's influence on Charles, for example in introducing him to the world of theatre, was considerable. On the other hand, he was also instrumental in placing him in the hated blacking manufactory, and Dickens is likely to have felt deep resentment towards him for doing so. Did that resentment fuel the later-retracted tendency to anti-Semitic characterisation in Dickens's early works? Was Fagin, the Jewish exploiter of young boys, in some part also a personalised projection of his feelings towards the former friend who had arranged for him to work at Warren's?

Abraham Lima Lamert, who was Matthew Lamert's cousin – and also his brother-in-law – was evidently a controversial but fascinating, flamboyant character. He travelled extensively throughout England and Ireland in the course of his occupation, which was, as he claimed when giving evidence in a trial of an alleged thief at the Old Bailey in 1828, that of a 'medical man'. In fact, like his father, he was no more than a quack doctor, peddling cure-all 'medicines' of the type that were commonly advertised in every newspaper, as well as treatment for an astonishing range of conditions, including cancer and blindness. He sold a product called the 'Balm of Gula', which, he advised in one example in the *Bristol Mirror* of 1 February 1823, was from the recipe of a physician to the Turkish emperor and his harem, and once sent by the Sultan to Queen Elizabeth I, who 'prized it exceedingly …'

And here we begin to see the intriguing association of the Lamerts with Bristol, the place of origin of the family they knew from Chatham and London. One early advertisement for the medical attendance of 'Dr' Lamert, from the *Hereford Journal*, published on 31 March 1824, explains how he made himself available to patients:

> Dr Lamert, (Son of Dr I. Lamert, of the Old Medical Establishment, 10, Church-street, Spitalfields, London, where he has resided above sixty years), and conductor of the Medical Establishment 54, Queen-square, Bristol, ... All persons desirous to obtain the Advice, will find it advantageous by making an immediate application, as the Doctor's numerous engagements at his Establishment in Bristol will preclude the possibility of making a longer stay than above specified ...

Abraham Lamert appears to have taken a certain amount of gleeful pleasure in deliberately promoting himself in Bristol around the time of John Barrow's term as Mayor, also the year when the new Mayor's great nephew was labouring for his own nephew George Lamert. A sudden increase in references to his residence there appear from 1823, and of course Queens Square was also where Barrow would reside as Mayor, at the Mansion House.[3]

Lamert also takes the liberty of including in some of his advertisements a sly reference to a previous Mayor of Bristol, Abraham Hilhouse. Among a collection of testimonials from grateful patients there is a statement supposedly 'sworn' in 1822 at the Mansion House from a John Thomas Franklin cured of 'an asthma' by the prescription of the good doctor, with Hilhouse's name placed underneath.

He had taken the house in Queen Square at the end of 1820, according to this announcement in the *Bristol Mirror*, published on Saturday, 16 December, although he had previously used an address here: chosen no doubt to imply some sort of legitimacy for his dubious medical practices.

He must have been delighted when, in the following year, his brother-in-law and cousin Matthew Lamert married the niece of John Barrow, by now not only a wealthy member of the city's merchant establishment but already a hugely important figure in the city's corporation. And at this point, Dr Lamert's presence in Bristol threatened to become a serious irritant for the new Mayor.

There is a caustic appraisal of Abraham Lamert and his father in one edition of a publication of 1824 edited by an Alex Burnett, MD, which includes a series of articles devoted to the 'Annals of Quackery', with one instalment featuring the two 'Dr' Lamerts, Abraham and his father Isaac. The writer, in the face of apparent threats of prosecution from Abraham, clearly relishes the opportunity to attack the reputation of his subject, and to warn the public of the bogus nature of the family's medical treatments. It should also be noted that a fair amount of his animosity appears to be derived from the usual anti-Semitic representation of the time of Jews as vulgar, flashy swindlers – with or without tails.[4]

Isaac Lamert, he reports, made a good living from 'venereal' treatment, and had then 'grown blind in the service of – the undertaker and Lock-Hospital'. He then goes on to describe his son Abraham as 'a truly terrific comet of quackery, sweeping and destroying everything that is attracted within the fulmen of his dangerous tail …'

We are told that 'this true chip of the old block, resides at Bristol, where he has fixed what he calls his magnum bonum of empiricism – his central "Medical Establishment"' … Abraham Lamert is 'powdered from the occiput to the coccygis, – from one shoulder to the other – from the cape of his coat to the buttons of his waist …' And he is as 'Ignorant as the barber who powders him …'

Lamert had a servant in 'gaudy livery' who stands outside the Exchange in Bristol and gives out the doctor's bills advertising his trade – 'however, the mayor and corporation have lately put a stop to the circulation of them …, so he delivers cards himself and attends the theatre almost every night, making sure his servant calls him out several times during performances: "Dr Lamert is wanted in a minute!" is bellowed out, and out jumps the quack, all puff and powder …'

Here we must note Dickens's recycling of this story in *Pickwick Papers*, in Chapter Thirty-seven, when the quack doctor Bob Sawyer is discovered by Mr Jingle, in Bristol, running a business with the name 'Sawyer, late Nockemorf'. Quite clearly Sawyer displays many similarities to Abraham Lamert: 'Nockemorf' sounds like a pastiche version of a German Jewish surname: he uses 'wide lipped crystal vases inscribed with a variety of cabalistic characters': again, in barely coded language meant to indicate Sawyer is Jewish, like Peter Magnus, he is described as wearing 'green spectacles'.

But there is one overt clue to the inspiration behind Sawyer's quack doctor practices: one that reworks Lamert's reported advertising scam in Bristol, only a few years earlier: Sawyer tells Mr Jingle how he goes about encouraging new trade for his new business:

> … my boy always rushes into the church just before the psalms, when the people have got nothing to do but look about 'em, and calls me out, with horror and dismay depicted on his countenance. "Bless my soul," everybody says, "somebody taken suddenly ill! Sawyer, late Nockemorf, sent for. What a business that young man has!"

Dickens's version places this activity in church, rather than in the theatre, but otherwise it is the same trick, in the same city.

Returning to the 'Annals of Quackery', next we see what must surely be a reference to Matthew Lamert, his cousin, former brother-in-law and latterly the husband of Dickens's aunt, the former Mary Allen, recently deceased:

> This fellow (Abraham) has the impudence and audacity to declare openly that he belonged to the army, and that his brother is now surgeon of a regiment. The fact is this: – There is a Mr Lamert in the army; but a very different man from the quack, and no relation whatever; he is a man of high respectability; he has been in one of our crack regiments for many years, and has received the testimonial of respect from his brother officers …

The writer tells us that the early years of 'Lamert the quack, of Bristol', were spent in Whitechapel 'in idleness, and in making an ass of himself of the Royalty Theatre, where he attempted frequently to sing amidst thunders of groans and hisses …'

This ill-fated career apparently included a rendition of 'Black-ey'd Susan' at the same theatre: 'the whole six verses-amidst pelting of oranges and clashing of thunderbolts, even to the last line; and then, waving his hat three times, laughed and snapped his fingers at the hissing audience!'

We read too of an incident, also reported by Michael Allen, in which the unfortunate doctor – 'a more dangerous quack does not exist now in England', claims the writer, who rightly points out the risks for those in serious ill health resorting to such – was given a taste of his own medicine, or rather a taste of a concoction of urine, water and brandy, ginger and snuff, passed off as his Balm of Zura, and which he was induced to drink in order to demonstrate its quality.

From the 'Annals of Quackery's excoriating assessment of Abraham Lamert we learn some interesting facts about the family: that there was a connection with Bristol, that like his cousin George, the companion of Dickens's childhood, he had an interest in theatre – and that his connection with his army surgeon cousin Matthew Lamert was not unknown.

Dr Lamert's association with Bristol was clearly long-standing: in May 1818, according to insolvency notices in the press, he was detained in King's Bench Prison for debt and described as being formerly of High Street, Southwark, and Queens Square, Bristol. His son Samuel also married a woman from Bristol, Sarah Jordan, born in there in 1811 – the Jordans, like this branch of the Lamerts, were well-known quack doctors, also Jewish, and largely based in London.

Perhaps the connections between the Lamerts and the Barrows was older and more complex than has been previously realised and predates any introduction in Chatham: certainly once the former Mary Barrow had married Matthew Lamert, his brother-in-law and cousin appears to have deliberately exploited the link to one particular Barrow family member.

Abraham Lamert took the opportunity during the period in which John Barrow was Mayor to emphasise more than ever his Bristol residency, as we may see from the advertisements of this period. Publication of the volume of the *Medical Adviser* which included the claim that Abraham's leafleting had been stopped by the Mayor was in the year Barrow's term would end: if the Mayor in question was Dickens's great uncle, it is highly likely that he was fully aware of the Lamerts' connection to his family – that his recently deceased niece Mary had been married to Abraham's brother-in-law, and cousin.

That this side of the Lamert family retained their Jewish identity is demonstrated in various family events recorded in synagogue records, including a reference to Abraham, in the course of his travels to Ireland, who can be safely assumed to be the Dr La Mert (using his Hebrew name Judah) listed in Dublin synagogue records as acting as 'sandek', or godfather, to the son of a German Jewish settler in 1831.

According to a notice in the *Dublin Correspondent* of Thursday, 28 August 1823, Abraham Lima Lamert returned to Bristol on the steam packet from Cork, which had a Jewish community at the time but was also the home of his cousin – and former brother-in-law – Matthew Lamert, recently widowed. The timing of this arrival in Bristol, shortly before Barrow's term as Mayor began, was almost certainly deliberate.

The reference in the 'Annals of Quackery' piece on Abraham Lamert to barbers, and powdering, offers up a teasing hint of the occupation of William Barrow, Charles's father. Did any members of the Barrow family continue the family business after his death? Or was it common knowledge that the Mayor's father had pursued this trade? It does appear that Dr Lamert and John Barrow were fully aware of their family connections, and that Lamert exploited this for his own purposes.

A tradition of quackery in the Lamert family did not end with the demise of Abraham in 1836, and it is necessary to follow the story of this family for one generation more in order to explore another Dickens association that poses more questions than it answers.

His son Samuel, who styled his name La Mert, and sometimes La'Mert, had a more conventional medical training and a long career, which was, however, to lead eventually to ruin and an ignominious end partly engineered, it seems, by two men with links to Charles Dickens. This may have been complete coincidence, but it is worth noting.

Samuel, like his grandfather Isaac, appears to have specialised in medicine of a 'venereal' nature, including those most sensitive areas of personal wellbeing – the preservation of virility, and mitigation of the effects of sexually transmitted disease.

Around 1841 he first published in Manchester and then advertised the following guide for men: the text varies slightly, but this one from 3 June 1848, from the *Exeter and Plymouth Gazette*, will give a general idea:

> Self-preservation: A MEDICAL TREATISE on the Physiology of Marriage, on Infelicitous and Unproductive Unions, and on the Secret Infirmities and Disorders of Youth and Maturity, usually acquired at an early period of life, which enervates the physical and mental powers, diminish and enfeeble the natural feelings and exhaust the vital energies of Manhood …

Just to add a certain frisson to an already lurid subject, we are informed the illustrated publication is available in French as well as English. A digital version is available via the British Library website, and its title page makes even clearer that the book gives explicit descriptions of the signs and consequences of venereal diseases, as well as warning, in lubricious detail, of the temptations – and consequences – of 'certain solitary habits' and 'youthful excesses'.

There was a rising tide of concern in the mid-Victorian era about 'quack doctors' and their unsavoury practices. Several medical journals, including the *Lancet*, produced by Dickens's friend Thomas Wakley, took the lead in pushing for the suppression of such charlatans.

Much indignation was expressed in the press of the dangers of not only useless patent medicines, but a tendency by some of those dealing with the so-called cures for impotence, or venereal disease, to threaten blackmail and exposure should any man complain about the ineffectual treatment they sold.

After moving to Bedford Square in London and continuing his work there, Samuel La Mert's treatise remained in print – and widely advertised – for more than twenty years, until misfortune struck and the Lamert family's long history of unregulated medical practice was brought under uncomfortably close scrutiny. For some reason, after the publication had been so widely available for so long and featured openly in the commercial columns of so many newspapers, in the early 1860s the advertisements for the treatise became the pretext for a crackdown on the Lamerts and their particular brand of quack medicine.

Records at the Royal College of Physicians of Edinburgh show that Samuel's son Lima Abraham Lamert – or 'La Mert' as they now styled themselves – had been allowed to become a licentiate of the College in 1859 in a short period during which admission had not required that the individual had a medical degree. A new charter, however, had introduced new professional standards in regard to conduct that the college felt Lima had breached, and they sought legal advice as to whether or not they could remove his licence on the grounds of 'conduct unbecoming', as evidenced by what the submission to lawyers referred to in relation to the treatise as 'of the most disgusting description and contains plates of the most revolting nature ...' They knew that Lima and his father Samuel ensured that the advertisements were 'cunningly framed' so as to imply that both were qualified physicians. Of course, Samuel was only registered as an apothecary, although he claimed to have a medical degree from the University of Erlangen.

Samuel was the subject of a complaint to the General Medical Council of the Royal College of Physicians in London, charged with publishing 'an indecent and unprofessional treatise'. According to newspaper reports, evidence from the College in Edinburgh was used in London to pursue proceedings against the Lamerts.

After a hearing of the Council in May 1863 (to which the case of a member of the Jordan family of quack doctors, related by marriage to the Lamerts, was also brought), Samuel was removed from the medical register: Lima's removal was to follow a few years later. Although this did not immediately end their ability to continue to offer their dubious medical treatments, the reputational damage was substantial: financial ruin was not far behind, and procedures to pay off Samuel's creditors began within two or three years. When he died in 1876, his estate came to a value of less than £50, and at least one of his sons had changed his name, as noted in the probate details. The other appears to have used an alias. The family, in short, was pretty much on its uppers.

One significant detail, however, about Samuel La'Mert's downfall is that the petition for his removal was presented by no less a figure than Frederic Ouvry, the GMC's solicitor, and of course the faithful lawyer and friend of Charles Dickens.

It is interesting too that among the case papers in Edinburgh is evidence of opinion sought in 1863 by the College from Montague Smith, of Farrer,

Ouvry and Farrer. One of those most prominent in calling for action against the notorious quack doctors had been another associate of Dickens: Thomas Wakley, the pioneering coroner and editor of the *Lancet*. Even more curious, perhaps, is the identity of the solicitor who acted on behalf of creditors of La'Mert, following this belated disciplinary action. This was a man called Edmund Francis Davis – and he was none other than the son of Eliza Davis, with whom Dickens had been corresponding since 1863 and who was now living in his former home, at Tavistock House.

The question arises as to whether, directly or indirectly, Dickens played any role in the downfall of the La Merts, or whether all of these associations were entirely coincidental. Dickens may well have been only too pleased to see an end to the potential risk posed by a prominent member of a disreputable family that had connections to him – distant now, but likely to have been in possession of embarrassing personal information about his earlier life.

Chapter Forty

Chatham

Dickens must have been aware of the background of the wider Lamert family, and the link to Bristol, but was the experience of this family a context that was not actually so unfamiliar at least to the older members of his own? To what extent was he aware of the experience of Jews in his childhood?

Those early years were spent in Chatham, which had, and has, a small synagogue located centrally in the middle of the long High Street, a few minutes' walk down from Ordnance Terrace. As a boy, Charles Dickens must have been familiar with the building and walked past it frequently: the synagogue there now is from the late 1860s, but on the same prominent site as the older one.

In his first published novel, Dickens allows Mr Pickwick to give a summary of the 'Four towns' – Stroud, Rochester, Chatham and Brompton – Chatham and Rochester, of course, being conjoined by one long High Street: 'The principal productions of these towns … appear to be soldiers, sailors, Jews, chalk, shrimps, officers, and dockyard men.'[1]

Chatham's formerly bustling, prosperous street is hard to imagine now, as you walk along, in the direction of Rochester, past the long string of empty shops, empty cafes, and tattoo shops. A homeless man lies on the step of the synagogue entrance: until a recent act of desecration of the burial ground you could step to the side and push the already open gate leading to the back of the building, whose windows are carefully protected by metal screens. In the small graveyard, now entirely overlooked, in a rather oppressive way, by buildings taller than the synagogue itself, there is a number of headstones, some now illegible, recording the history of a vanished congregation of Jewish residents of the former naval town: Solomons, Isaacs, Magnus and other families, mostly traders traceable in the old Pigot's directories, with premises on the same High Street.

In 1824, Pigot's Directory for Kent lists a number of Jewish surnames under the heading 'Salesmen etc': the majority of the dozen or so names given in this category, in fact, all in the High Street, or Hammond Place. Important to note, to contradict any stereotypical assumption of this period, that of seven pawnbrokers, offering a service that must have been used by John Dickens on a regular basis at one time, only one appears to have been Jewish.

Before choosing to marry Mary Allen in church, had Matthew Lamert been in any way, formally or otherwise, a member of the Chatham Jewish community? Probably not, but that is not to say the Dickens family, and the doctor's second wife, were unaware of his background: in fact it is quite evident from what we now know about the wider Lamert family that they could not have been.

On the other side of the High Street from the synagogue there is a passageway leading across to the waterfront called Hulkes Alley: the name taken from the family whose brewery still stands here, but perhaps now mistakenly serving as a reminder of the prison hulks that used to be moored at Chatham. Here they sat, in view of the waterfront, for the accommodation of convicts in theory destined for transportation, or simply incarcerated for years offshore, in unimaginably wretched circumstances rife with disease.

The image of the unforgettable Magwitch, escaped prisoner from one of these hulks, rising up in the graveyard of a church in a marshy estuary landscape to reveal himself to the young Pip, is one lasting acknowledgement of the impression these ships and their inmates must have had on the young Dickens in his time in the town.

One of those who endured perhaps up to four years of imprisonment in a Chatham hulk was a figure believed to have inspired the character of Fagin, in *Oliver Twist*: that is to say the notorious 'fence' Isaac 'Ikey' Solomon, whose representation in the press reports of his interesting career helped encourage the repetition of a thousand anti-Semitic caricatures of Jews as criminals and exploiters of children. Solomon may also have had family links to the Chatham area.

Michael Allen believes that Henry Worms was more likely to be the greater influence on Dickens in his creation of this character. It is hard to believe Dickens was not aware of the Solomon story, however, and perhaps the truth is that the character was a conflation of both men – and aspects of other stereotypical perceptions of the time. The influences that came to bear fruit in the shape of his own version of an ancient anti-Semitic archetype, the character of Fagin, perhaps are traceable to the time of his childhood and his own clouded observation of Jews in that period of his life.

The Lamert connection, which led to the young Dickens's time of employment in the blacking manufactory, may have given left him with a lingering sense of resentment against the family. If it is true that he based the character of Fagin on Henry Worms, that might even be seen as a form of belated vengeance on the family.

That Charles Dickens did have some knowledge of the later lives of the Lamerts is suggested by Forster's reference to a letter sent to Dickens's mother in August 1840 by Matthew Lamert, in which he refers to Cork and seems to imply a continued correspondence over all the years that had passed since he had been married to Dickens's aunt.

And then there is the curious incident mentioned in the letter written by Emily Barrow, Dickens's cousin, born in the 1830s, to her relatives, describing, in passing, the time her father had been sent to India as a correspondent by Dickens, in early 1846, and was stopped while at Malta, going along a gangway to a steamer, by a man who asked if he was not John Barrow: it turned out to be someone whom Emily claimed was his cousin by marriage, the father of 'Jane Lamert', whom he had not seen for many years – she claims thirty-five years.

There was a Jane Lamert, born in 1831, who was the daughter of Dickens's childhood companion, and boot blacking manufacturer, George Lamert, the son of Matthew. This incident, if true, does support the idea that, even in the lifetime of Emily Barrow, the family connection to the Lamerts was not forgotten.

Afterword

Let us return to the company of Charles Dickens in one of his night walks described in *The Uncommercial Traveller* as he finds himself wandering across the river and then by Bedlam, the Bethlehem Hospital where his aunt's life would soon end, his name on her admission documents:[1]

> ... I had a night fancy in my head which could be best pursued within sight of its walls and dome. And the fancy was this: Are not the sane and the insane equal at night as the sane lie a dreaming? Are not all of us outside this hospital, who dream, more or less in the condition of those inside it, every night of our lives? Are we not nightly persuaded, as they daily are, that we associate preposterously with kings and queens, emperors and empresses, and notabilities of all sorts? Do we not nightly jumble events and personages and times and places, as these do daily?

This was written around the time when his mother and his aunt were both moving towards the last stages of dementia: by the standards of the age, succumbing to madness. In this piece Dickens seeks to blur the boundaries between the worlds of sanity and insanity: perhaps this is from a need to minimise the impact of witnessing the degeneration of his mother, aunt and probably his great aunt: to render it less frightening – or perhaps it comes from the fear of his own destiny; fear of a risk of breaking down, and a descent into madness.

The lives of many family members had ended in failure and financial ruin, despite an earlier life of great promise and years of success in business. His own father had lived a life punctuated and punished by financial difficulties, debt, and even imprisonment. Dickens's siblings were largely dependent on him and his financial support; one brother a divorced drunk, another had deserted his wife and run away to America with his mistress. His children were problematic, another burden. Perhaps Dickens feared that some of these traits and failings, expressive, to a Victorian mind, of weakness and degeneration, were indications of an underlying, inherited instability. The creative forces that drove his imagination, as a writer, were not so different to the daytime dreaming that troubled the minds of the insane after all.

Here in his 'Night Walks' piece, written as part of a series begun soon after the death of his father and in the period leading up to the loss of his mother, under intolerable strain in the early days of the breakdown in his marriage to Catherine, he embarks on a journey that is not only physical, but also a tracing of routes in the landscape of his subconscious, passing through places of personal significance. Central to his wandering is the river: central to the circumference of his route, but unacknowledged, is the location of his childhood trauma, the pivotal moment of his life: the period of employment in the blacking factory, on the very water's edge, by Hungerford Stairs.

During this period, separated from his family while he worked at Warren's, and lodging in Camden Town, once a week, on Sundays, with his sister Fanny, he would cross over the river to the Marshalsea prison to visit his parents and brothers. Once he moved into lodgings in Southwark, on the south side, he would walk home from the warehouse, crossing over Blackfriars Bridge. The river was a point of demarcation in identity: from the daily exploitation of his value as a child labourer to the worthlessness he felt as a son abandoned by his parents.

As he crosses and re-crosses the river now, he passes through into that other world, one of darkness, imprisonment, madness, and death. Here is the dead woman in the water, floating downstream, pulled out by his grandfather. Here are the Adelphi arches, where a woman lies holding her dead baby: here is the place where in moments of insanity, despair, or perhaps total clarity, a leap from a bridge is the end of all life.

Now he passes an empty theatre, where the power of the spoken word, his voice, is silent and devoid of purpose; then on, not to the Marshalsea but Newgate, with 'that wicked little Debtors' Door', 'Death's door to so many', and then to another jail, King's Bench prison, another destination for debtors; he follows a route taken by his father, and his grandfather, and Little Dorrit's father, and Micawber – and so many others, in life, in fiction, and in his family, past and present. Here is a place that provokes Dickens's reference to the phenomenon of 'Dry Rot' in men: 'a looseness respecting money … a looseness respecting everything …'

Next in the sequence comes Bedlam: from poverty, debt, to madness: the story of the lives of some of his own family, and a fate to be fought against, perhaps within the bounds of his own fears for himself.

It might have occurred to him that his state of mind, while in the grip of his night walking, was itself a lapse into some form of madness: as Matthew Beaumont notes in *Night Walking*: 'Locked in the state between waking and sleeping, Dickens ... really is almost mad.' Here, in his walk across and around the river, a place of so much symbolism in his work, measuring the ebb and flow of life, a point of boundary, and a place of transition, it would seem the process was inverted, as he tried to separate his sense of self from that of his family, and the expectations they had of him: or the influence of his past on his future.[2]

In this walk, Dickens suggests the state of dreaming is a form of insanity, the surrealism of our dream-lives no different to that of the 'reality' of the insane: but he then reminds us of his own connections to royalty, and 'notabilities of all sorts', although he implies these are mere 'night fancies', even as we know that he had already performed before the Queen and moves freely among the most privileged circles. The pretext of demonstrating the similarly surreal quality of his own life fails to disguise the truth: that his own social success is to him some sort of protection against the fate of his poorer, less fortunate relations, and a door to a separate, alternative destiny, in which their narrative of failure, and madness, would play no part; the fat old silver watch in his pocket replaced by a legacy of his own making: his life's work.

Bibliography

Allen, Michael, 'An English Lady in Paris', Oxford Stockley Publications, 2011.

Allen, Michael, 'Charles Dickens and the blacking factory' 2011, Oxford Stockley Publications.

Atkinson, Diane, 'The Criminal Conversation of Mrs Norton', Preface Publishing, 2012.

Beaumont, Matthew, 'Night Walking, a Nocturnal History of London', Verso, London, 2015.

Cesarani, David, and Romain, Gemma, editors 'Jews and Port Cities 1590 – 1990, Commerce, Community and Cosmopolitanism', Vallentine Mitchell, 2006.

Clark, Cumberland, editor, 'Charles Dickens and His Jewish Characters', Chiswick Press, London, 1918.

Endelman, Todd, 'The Jews of Britain, 1656 to 2000', University of California, 2002.

Forster, John, 'The Life of Charles Dickens', Chapman & Hall, 1872-4.

Hartley, Jenny, 'Charles Dickens and the House of Fallen Women', London: Methuen, 2008.

Hinchcliffe, Edward Hinchcliffe, 'Barthomley In Letters from a Former Rector to His Eldest Son', Brown, Green and Longmans (London and Newcastle-under-Lyme, 1856).

Israel, Jonathan I., 'Empires and Entrepots: The Dutch, the Spanish Monarchy and the Jews, 1585-1713', The Hambledon Press, 1990.

James, N. B., 'Story of Hendon Manor and Parish', Warden, 1932.

Julius, Anthony, 'Trials of the Diaspora – A History of Anti-Semitism in England', OUP, 2010.

Kirkpatrick, Robert J., 'Charles Dickens and the Yorkshire Schools, Fact v Fiction', Mosaic (Teesdale) Ltd, Snaisgill, Middleton in Teesdale, 2017.

Lancaster, Geoffrey, 'Culliford, Rolfe and Barrow: A Tale of Nine Pianos', UWA Publishing, 2017.

Moss, Sidney P. and Moss, Carolyn J., 'Charles Dickens and His Chicago Relatives', The Whitson Publishing Company, Troy, New York, 1994.

Nayder, Lillian, 'The Other Dickens: A Life of Catherine Hogarth', Cornell University Press, 2010.

Noake, J., 'Noake's guide to Worcestershire', Longman & Co, 1868, London, P 86.

Orwell, George, 'Charles Dickens', 'Inside the Whale' Victor Gollancz, London, 1940.

O'Toole, Fintan, 'A Traitor's Kiss, The Life of Richard Brinsley Sheridan', Granta Books, 1997.

Patten, Robert L., 'Charles Dickens and 'Boz': the Birth of the Industrial-age', CUP, 2012.

Powell, Thomas, The Living Authors of England Philadelphia: D Appleton & Co, 1949.

Purton, Valerie, 'Dickens and the Sentimental Tradition: Fielding, Richardson, Sterne, Goldsmith, Sheridan, Lamb' Anthem Press, 2014.

Richardson, Ruth, 'Dickens and the Workhouse', OUP, 2012.

Samuel, Judith, 'The History of the Jewish Community in Bristol from the Middle Ages to the Present Day', Redcliffe Press, 1997.

Slater, Michael, 'Charles Dickens', Yale University Press, 2009.

Storey, Gladys, Dickens and Daughter, Frederick Muller Ltd, London, 1939.

Tomalin, Claire, 'Charles Dickens: A Life', Penguin Viking, 2011.

Tomalin, Claire, 'The Invisible Woman', Viking 1990, revised edition Penguin Books, 1991.

Wheen, Francis, 'Karl Marx', Fourth Estate Ltd, London, 1999.

Wilson, Edmund, 'The Wound and the Bow', Houghton Mifflin Company, Cambridge Massachusetts, 1941.

Wise, Sarah, 'The Italian Boy', Jonathan Cape, 2004.

Notes

Foreword

1. John Forster, *The Life of Charles Dickens*, Chapman & Hall, 1872–4.
2. Thomas Powell, *The Living Authors of England Philadelphia*, D. Appleton & Co., 1949.
3. Thomas Powell 'Leaves from my life', *Frank Leslie's Sunday Magazine*, Vol. xxi, February 1887, pp.98–99.
4. George Orwell, 'Charles Dickens', *Inside the Whale*, Victor Gollancz, London, 1940.
5. John Drew, 'A Twist in the Tale', *The Guardian*, 1 November 2003.
6. Edmund Wilson, *The Wound and the Bow*, Houghton Mifflin Company, Cambridge Massachusetts, 1941.

Part One: The Lord No Zoo: Dickens and Dickins

Chapter One: Who was your grandfather?

1. See 'Household of Prince William Augustus Duke of Cumberland, 1731–1765, Compiled by Sarah Deas and R.O. Bucholz, 2019, Loyola University Chicago.
2. *Dickensian*: Vol. 57, Iss. 333 (Jan 1, 1961): 5.
3. J. Noake *Noake's guide to Worcestershire*, Longman & Co., 1868, London, p.86. He makes this point in earlier guides too, e.g. his *Rambler in Worcestershire*, published in 1854.

Chapter Two: Elizabeth Ball

1. 'Some Erroneous Traditions', the Rev. J.E.A. Auden, *Transactions of the Shropshire Archaeological Society*, Volume XLIX, Part I (1937).
2. 'Tong and The Old Curiosity Shop', J.E.A. Auden, *Dickensian*: Vol. 4, Iss. 7 (1 July 1908): 187.
3. *Dickensian*: Vol. 57, Iss. 333 (1 January 1961): 5.
4. Volume 1. 1820–1839: The Pilgrim Edition, ed Madeline House and Graham Storey, 1982, p.447.

Chapter Three: William Dickens, your butler

1. *Dickensian*, Vol. 45 (1 January 1949): 64.
2. 'Informations taken this fourteenth day of October 1779 at the Parish of St. George Hanover Square within the Liberty of Westmr. in the County of Midsex upon an an Inquisition touching the death of a Woman unknown lying dead in the said Parish, Liberty and County': City of Westminster Coroners: Coroners' Inquests into Suspicious Deaths CW/IC 1st January 1779–29th December 1779.

3. Masonic records are available online at Ancestry.co.uk.
4. John Bott prospered in his career and eventually became Secretary to the Keeper of the Privy Purse.
5. See: 'The Shorthand of Robert Willis, Physician-in-Extraordinary to King George III Timothy', Underhill and Timothy Peters BLJ, 2018, Article 2, www.bl.uk/eblj/2018articles/article 2.html

Chapter Four: Praising Amoret: Frances Anne Crewe

1. Edward Hinchcliffe, *Barthomley In Letters from a Former Rector to His Eldest Son*, Brown, Green and Longmans (London and Newcastle-under-Lyme, 1856).
2. Frances Anne Crewe's journal is to be found among the Windham Papers, Vol. LXXXV, in the British Library manuscript's collection: Add MS 37926: 1779–1795.

Chapter Five: Elizabeth Dickens, servant at your town house

1. See again: *Dickensian*, Vol. 45 (1 January 1949): 64.
2. Gladys Storey, *Dickens and Daughter*, Frederick Muller Ltd, London, 1939.
3. Michael Allen, *Dickensian* Vol. 83, Iss. 413, 1987: 131.

Chapter Six: The odd love-child, here and there

1. Unpublished MS 'A History of Crewe Hall', by Roy Gladden, 1988, p.28 – held at Cheshire Record Office. Gladden's family worked for the Crewes.
2. Cynthia Colville, *Crowded Life*, Evan Brothers Limited, London, 1963.
3. Gilian West, 'Family Connections: The Influence of the Crewe Family on Bleak House', *Dickensian*; London Vol. 91, Iss. 435 (Spring 1995):5.

Chapter Seven

1. See Robert J. Kirkpatrick, *Charles Dickens, Nicholas Nickleby and the Yorkshire Schools, Fact v Fiction*, Mosaic (Teesdale) Ltd, Snaisgill, Middleton in Teesdale, 2017.
2. Michael Slater, *Charles Dickens*, Yale University Press, 2009.
3. See extracts from this interview in Kirkpatrick's *Charles Dickens, Nicholas Nickleby and the Yorkshire Schools, Fact v Fiction.*

Chapter Eight: Playing the fool

1. Michael Allen, *An English Lady in Paris*, Oxford Stockley Publications, 2011.
2. From 'Some Unpublished Letters of Mrs Sheridan to Mrs Canning', ed Michael T.H. Sadleir, as Appendix III of Michael Sadleir, *The Political Career of Richard Brinsley Sheridan* Oxford: B.H. Blackwell, 1912 – there seems to be some confusion about the date of this letter but it appears to have been written in January 1790.
3. Claire Tomalin, *Charles Dickens: A Life*, Penguin Viking, 2011.
4. Fintan O'Toole, *A Traitor's Kiss, The Life of Richard Brinsley Sheridan*, Granta Books 1997, Chapter 3, p.26.
5. According to Amanda Foreman in *The Duchess*, Harper Collins, 1998, although no source is given for the description.

Chapter Nine: John Dickens and Thomas Powell

1. Thomas Powell, *Leaves from my life*, 1887.
2. Michael Slater, *Charles Dickens*, 2009.
3. Slater, Chapter One, pp.8.

Chapter Ten: Will and Sally: Uncle William Dickens and Sarah Latham

1. London Archives, Royal Sun and Alliance Group policy, 26 February 1817. CLC/B/192/F/001/MS11936/476/927516
2. See Angus Whitehead, 'The Blakes' French Fellow Inhabitants at 17 South Molton Street, 1805–21', *Blake – An Illustrated Quarterly*, Vol. 43, Iss. 3, Winter 2009–10.
3. As published at www.oldbaileyonline.org.
4. Available online at Ancestry.co.uk

Chapter Eleven: Bleak House revisited

1. *Dickensian*; London Vol. 91 Iss. 435 (Spring 1995):5.

Chapter Twelve: Dickens and the Sheridans

1. See for example Valerie Purton, *Dickens and the Sentimental Tradition: Fielding, Richardson, Sterne, Goldsmith, Sheridan, Lamb*, Anthem Press, 2014.
2. Pilgrim i, p.302 (probably August 1837).
3. Pilgrim ii, p.3.
4. Diane Atkinson, *The Criminal Conversation of Mrs Norton*, Preface Publishing, 2012, pp.300–301.
5. Ibid., p.330.

Part Two: Blacking and Blackmail

Chapter Thirteen: Ravensfield

1. In the author's collection.

Chapter Fourteen: A brilliant scapegrace: Augustus Newnham Dickens

1. The Whitson Publishing Company, Troy, New York.
2. Slater, p.32.
3. Robert L. Patten, *Charles Dickens and 'Boz': the Birth of the Industrial-age*, CUP, 2012.
4. Pilgrim iv, p.346.
5. Available online at Ancestry.com

Chapter Fifteen: The eyes you have trusted in: Harriett and Bertha

1. For example *Bells' Weekly Messenger*, 6 February 1841, regarding the loss of the *Dryad*, Mr James Phillips for the prosecution.
2. 20 March 1869, from Liverpool, to Georgina Hogarth 'My love to Letitia and Harriette'
3. Claire Tomalin, *Charles Dickens, A Life*.

Chapter Sixteen: Amboy and Chicago

1. Pilgrim VII, p.635.
2. Such as the *New York Times*, 7 May 1868.
3. Moss & Moss, p.41.
4. Moss & Moss, p.33, from the account reported by Eli Perkins, *The New York Daily Sun*, 1876.
5. *Chicago Tribune*, 6 October 1866.
6. According to Moss & Moss.
7. *New York Sun*, 19 August 1876.
8. 'Emigrant in Motley', edited by J.M.D. Hardwick, Rockliff Publishing Corporation, London, 1954.
9. Letter to James Grant Wilson Esq, from Augustus Dickens, Augustus Dickens Collection, Archives & Manuscripts Department, Chicago Historical Society.
10. *The Chicago Tribune*, 6 February 1868.

Chapter Seventeen: Other people's money

1. Veronica M. Stokes, 'Charles Dickens: A customer of Coutts & Co', 1 January 1972, *Dickensian* 68:366.
2. Moss & Moss, pp.41–43.

Chapter Eighteen: The Arcade of Melancholy-Mad Bootmakers

1. *London Daily News*, 2 July 1906.
2. See: Arthur A. Adrian, *Mark Lemon: First Editor of 'Punch'*, Oxford U.P., 1966
3. *Punch*, Vol. 6, 1844, p.248.
4. Sarah Wise, *The Italian Boy*, Jonathan Cape, 2004.
5. The Holm story, and the location of Hendon Churchyard, is said to have inspired Bram Stoker when writing Chapter Fifteen of *Dracula* and the beheading of Lucy Westenra. See: Philip Temple, 'The Origins of Dracula', *Times Literary Supplement*, 4 November 1983.
6. See, for example, *The Morning Post*, 'The late atrocious murder ... Confession of Bishop and Williams', 5 December 1831.

Chapter Nineteen: Hendon

1. N.B. James, *Story of Hendon Manor and Parish*, 1932, Warden, p.114.
2. Ruth Richardson, *Dickens and the Workhouse*, OUP, 2012.
3. *The Times*, Wednesday, 16 November 1836.

Chapter Twenty: Arcadia

1. Pilgrim vi, p.655, to Frank Stone.
2. At the time of writing the Arcade is inaccessible as there is a major refurbishment and restoration under way. Until recently one of Rouse's shops was still occupied by a shoe repair business and the shopkeeper showed me inside, including the upper- and lower-floor rooms, all of which are very small.
3. Editor Nicholas Fyfe, *Images of the Street: Planning, Identity and Control in Public Space*, Routledge, 1998.
4. *Household Words*, 'Arcadia', Vol. VII, p.376, 18 June 1853.

Chapter Twenty-one: Nightly wanderings

1. Methuen, 2008.
2. Pilgrim vi, p.83.

Chapter Twenty-two: My bachelor state

1. Lillian Nayder, *The Other Dickens: A Life of Catherine Hogarth*, Cornell University Press, 2010.
2. Tomalin, *Charles Dickens, A Life*, p.124.
3. Ibid., p.316.
4. Claire Tomalin, *The Invisible Woman*, Viking, 1990, revised edition Penguin Books 1991, 2012, p.83.
5. See for example the listings in *The Morning Post*, 30 October 1857, for the Theatre Royal Haymarket, 'Tom Taylor's New Comedy VICTIMS' ... the cast includes Miss Ellen Ternan.
6. *Dickensian* 90.432 (Spring 1994):36.

Chapter Twenty-three: A dishonourable act

1. See for example the *New York Times*, 7 May 1868.
2. National Archives reference: C 15/200/G98.
3. Forster named him as James Lamert, but Michael Allen's research makes it clear that this was an error.

Part Three: The Barrows

Chapter Twenty-four: Bristol

1. Filmed parish records now available at Bristol Archives.
2. See: Bristol Record Society's Publications, Vol. XXV, *The Inhabitants of Bristol in 1696*, 1968, edited by Elizabeth Ralph and Mary E. Williams.
3. Bristol Record Archives reference, 09471/2.
4. See: *The History of the Rise and Progress of the Arts of Design in the United States*, Vol. 2, William Dunlap, George Scott & Co. printers, 1834.
5. Barber surgeons and peruke makers are included in a very useful 'Summary of Medical Practitioners in Bristol, circa 1716–1800', edited by Jonathan Barry. Available online as part of the Bristol Records Society's Occasional Series, No. 9, July 2024.
6. Bristol Probate Inventories: 1690–1804, Bristol Record Society, 2008, p.187.
7. As published in *A Candid Disquisition of the Principles and Practices of the Most Ancient and Honourable Society of Free and Accepted Masons*, Welling Calcott, 1769.
8. See *Felix Farley's Bristol Journal*, Saturday, 16 July 1768, p.3.
9. BBC website news, 8 June 2020.

Chapter Twenty-five

1. *Bristol Mirror*, 8 October 1825.

Chapter Twenty-six: What's money after all?

1. The Institution's records are held by Bristol Archives, reference 32079/BI.

Chapter Twenty-seven: Dickens and Bristol

1. See Colston's school records, SMV 5/1/2/2, now held by Bristol Archives.
2. *The Letters of Charles Dickens*, Vol. 6, Clarendon Press, Oxford, 1988, p.538.

Chapter Twenty-eight: Rivers and seas were formed to float their ships: John Barrow and Paul Dombey

1. See for example the *Bristol Mirror*, 3 October 1835.

Chapter Twenty-nine: The London Barrows and one overwhelming calamity

1. See Geoffrey Lancaster, *Culliford, Rolfe and Barrow: A Tale of Nine Pianos*, UWA Publishing 2017: an extensive and highly detailed study of the company.
2. See Lancaster, *A Tale of Ten Pianos*, p.122.
3. See Fleet Prison discharge records online via Ancestry.co.uk

Chapter Thirty: I am utterly indifferent to the fact of her existence: the forgotten Barrows

1. Pilgrim vii, pp.837–8.
2. Pilgrim x, p.452.

Chapter Thirty-one: Where we stopped growing: Aunt Sarah, Aunt Charlton and Elizabeth Dickens

1. Sarah Wise, *Inconvenient People: Lunacy, Liberty, and the Mad-Doctors in England*, Bodley Head, London, 2012, p.179.
2. Pilgrim vi, p.343.
3. Pilgrim ix, p.227.
4. Pilgrim ix, p.266.
5. Pilgrim viii, p.417.
6. Pilgrim ix, p.287.
7. Pilgrim x, p.22.
8. His name has been wrongly transcribed as 'Mara'.
9. See Frances Wheen, *Karl Marx*, Fourth Estate Ltd, London, 1999.

Chapter Thirty-two: A strong hereditary taint

1. Pilgrim x, p.288.
2. *Household Words*, 15 August 1857, Vol xvi, p.145.
3. London Bethlem Hospital admission registers and casebooks, now available for online public access via the Find My Past subscription website.
4. For more on the Charltons' theatrical background, see 'Dickens, Macready and the Theatrical Charltons', William F. Long, *Dickens Quarterly*, Vol. 30, No. 4 (December 2013) pp.299–309.
5. See Sarah Wise, and the *TLS*, 22 February 2019, p.18, John Bowen – 'Unmutual Friend: How Dickens tried to place his wife in an asylum'.
6. Catherine Arnold, *Bedlam*, Simon & Schuster UK Ltd, 2008, Chapter 9, pp.205–6.

Part Four: The Casteels

Chapter Thirty-three: Her Majesty's frame maker

1. See about-bristol.co.uk
2. J. Charlton & D.M. Milton, *Redland 791–1800*, Arrowsmith, 1951.
3. Bristol Probate Inventories: 1690–1804, Bristol Record Society, 2008, p.187.
4. It is interesting that the Thomas Barrow who settled in America was a dealer in engravings, sold artists materials, and was said to have been a former coach painter.
5. The Ancestry.co.uk entry for Lewis, the son of Lewis and Hanna, gives no further source or reference for parish or date and searches in deposited parish records so far have not identified the source.
6. Petitions – Parliamentary Archives reference HL/PO/JO/10/1/383/36, 30 November 1678.

Chapter Thirty-four: The Casteels in London

1. Held in the archives of Essex Record Office, reference from the *Dictionary of English Furniture Makers, 1660–1840*, ed by Geoffrey Beard & Christopher Gilbert, 1986.
2. 'London Inhabitants Within the Walls' index available online via 'British History Online': originally published by London Record Society, London, 1966.
3. See JewishGen.org, and Sephardicgen.com for links to records connecting this name with the wider diaspora.
4. See various references in the journals of the House of Commons and the House of Lords in the 1640s.
5. See Geoffrey Parker, *The Dutch Revolt*, Allen Lane 1977, p.60, Note 36.
6. Accessible via Find My Past subscription site.
7. See Jonathan I., Israel, *Empires and Entrepots: The Dutch, the Spanish Monarchy and the Jews, 1585–1713*, The Hambledon Press, 1990.
8. Todd Edelman, *The Jews of Britain, 1656 to 2000*, University of California, 2002, pp.32–33.
9. According to Ancestry.co.uk: Christ Church, Southwark, but further research suggests this is probably mistaken for Christ Church, Greyfriars.

Chapter Thirty-five: The Jewish community in Bristol

1. See Judith Samuel, *The History of the Jewish Community in Bristol from the Middle Ages to the Present Day*, Redcliffe Press, 1997.
2. Todd Edelman, *The Jews of Britain*, p.17.
3. David Cesarani, Gemma Romain, Vallentine Mitchell (eds), *Jews and Port Cities 1590–1990, Commerce, Community and Cosmopolitanism*, 2006.

Chapter Thirty-six: Eliza Davis and the Despised Hebrew

1. Cumberland Clark (ed.), *Charles Dickens and His Jewish Characters*, Chiswick Press, London, 1918.

Chapter Thirty-seven: James Phineas Davis, and the 'Vampires of London'

1. Anthony Julius, *Trials of the Diaspora – A History of Anti-Semitism in England*, OUP 2010.
2. Michael Slater, *Charles Dickens*, p.127, 527.

Chapter Thirty-eight: Atonement

1. Murray Baumgarten 'The Other Woman – Eliza Davis and Charles Dickens', University of California, Santa Cruz, in the *Dickens Quarterly*, Vol. 32, No. 1, March 2015.
2. See: Jacob A.P.M. Andrade, *A Record of The Jews in Jamaica, from the English Conquest to the Present Time*, Kingston, 1941, for listings of Mohelim, and Eliza Davis's obituary in the *Jewish Chronicle* in 1903 for the claim her grandfather was 'minister' to this congregation.
3. See the UCL database 'Legacies of Slave Ownership' and www.barrowlousada.org

Chapter Thirty-nine: The Annals of Quackery: the Lamert Family and the Barrows

1. See records available via Synagoguescribes.com
2. See Michael Allen, *Charles Dickens and the Blacking Factory*, Oxford-Stockley Publications, 2011.
3. Pigot's Directory of Bristol for 1822 confirms that an A. Lamert (medical establishment) was located at 54, Queen Square.
4. See *The Medical Adviser and Guide to Health and Long Life*, printed by P. Fanning, 3 Paternoster-Row, 1824.

Chapter Forty

1. See Chapter 2, *Pickwick Papers*.

Afterword

1. See *Night Walking, a Nocturnal History of London*, Matthew Beaumont, Verso, London 2015, Chapter 12, 'The Dead Night: Dickens's Night Walks'.

Index